Money, Finance and Development

By the same author

Financial Development in Malaya and Singapore, Canberra, ANU Press, 1969.

Australian Economic Policy (ed. with J. P. Nieuwenhuysen), Melbourne, MUP, 1977.

Money, Finance and Development

P. J. DRAKE

A HALSTED PRESS BOOK

John Wiley & Sons
New York

© P. J. Drake 1980

First published in 1980 by Martin Robertson, Oxford.

Published in the U.S.A.
by Halsted Press, a division
of John Wiley & Sons, Inc.,
New York.

Library of Congress Cataloging in Publication Data

Drake, Peter Joseph.
 Money, finance, and development.

 "A Halsted Press book."
 Bibliography: p.
 Includes index.
  1. Underdeveloped areas—Finance. 2. Under-
developed areas—Money. 3. Economic development.
 I. Title.
 HG4517.D7   332′.09172′4   80-14964
 ISBN 0-470-26992-8

Set by Santype International Ltd., Salisbury, Wilts.
Printed in Great Britain by Billing & Sons Limited,
Guildford, London, Oxford, Worcester

To my Mother and Father

Contents

List of Tables and Figures

Preface

This book is set in that ill-defined area between the fields of textbook and research monograph. That territory may be a no-man's-land, but it is not in my view waste land; on the contrary, it may well bear more fruitful cultivation by books such as this which seek both to consolidate and, in a modest way, to expand knowledge. My main purpose in writing this book has been to convey a novel and whole view of the subject of money and finance as it pertains to countries that are loosely described as underdeveloped, less developed or developing. I shall be well satisfied if I have succeeded in producing a book that gives a co-ordinated and coherent understanding of the subject to students, teachers, research scholars, officials—and even politicians—who are concerned with the wellbeing and economic advancement of the developing countries. Within what I hope is a tidy and logical framework, the reader may also find some new ideas. But theoretical discussion or refinement has not been my main objective; those who wish to go further into theories may find some guidance in the suggested readings at the end of each chapter and the extensive bibliography.

Many acknowledgements are due, and it is my pleasure to give them. For more years than any of us would care number, and at least since my interest in this subject was first kindled as a graduate student, I have been encouraged by H. W. Arndt, A. I. Bloomfield, E. K. Fisk and W. M. Corden; their writings have also provided a constant source of stimulus and example. So far as the present work is directly concerned, Professors Arndt, Bloomfield and Corden supported me for the award that helped make possible a period of research in the United Kingdom. Professors Arndt and Bloomfield were helpful in discussing the early outline of the book, while Mr Fisk read and commented upon a draft of Chapter 4 and generously gave his permission for me to reproduce his work and diagrams in the appendix to that chapter.

Although I have developed my interest and knowledge in this field over many years, most of the reading and thinking on which the work is built was done in the United Kingdom in 1976. I was then fortunate to enjoy a year of study leave from the University of New England and to hold the Hallsworth Fellowship in Political Economy in the University of Manchester. I am grateful to both universities for supporting me, to Professor Michael Parkin who encouraged me to go to Manchester, and to Professor D. J. Coppock and other staff of the Department of Economics at Manchester for their academic, and other, hospitality. I owe Peter and Rosemary Stubbs a very special debt for their constant kindness: this seems the appropriate place to thank them. The people of Ashley, Cheshire, by adopting my family and me into the life of their village, added greatly to the ease and pleasure of working on this project.

In planning the content and structure of the book, I benefited, while in the United Kingdom, from discussions with P. C. I. Ayre, W. T. Newlyn, Michael Parkin, L. S. Pressnell, A. P. Thirlwall and the late John Knapp. I am grateful for their various opinions and advice which, although not all followed, have contributed greatly to the final design of the work. My colleague M. L. Treadgold read at least one draft of every chapter and once again provided the thorough and enlightening criticism and discussion which I have enjoyed from him for many years; I hope I have never been guilty of taking his invaluable help for granted. In its semi-final form the whole typescript was read by P. C. I. Ayre and W. J. Blackert, for whose helpful comments I gladly record my thanks.

For permission to reproduce my material which originally appeared in the *Journal of Development Studies* (Vol. 13, No. 2, January 1977) I must thank Frank Cass and Company, the publishers of that journal. Messrs Eyre and Spottiswoode kindly gave permission to include substantial quotations from *Primitive Money* by the late Paul Einzig. M. L. Treadgold, E. K. Fisk, Nurali Peera and Anne M. De Bruin allowed me to draw on their unpublished writings.

Finally, my deepest thanks must go to those who have lived with the composition of the book almost as closely as has the author. Jayne Carlon, my secretary, has assisted the work in many ways and produced a fine typescript without detriment to her other duties; she has borne with me in unfailing helpfulness and good humour, though I fear I may at times have been very demanding. Above all, my wife and children have had to suffer some neglect and tolerate the ups and downs to which authors are prone. I can only thank them for their support, assure them that their sacrifices have not gone unnoticed, and express the hope that their satisfaction at the completion of this work is as great as mine, though doubtless for different reasons.

Armidale, N.S.W.   P.J.D.
July 1979

CHAPTER 1

Introduction

In the voluminous literature of economic development, it is remarkable that relatively little attention has been given to financial aspects of the subject. This neglect is especially surprising in view of the key emphasis given to capital formation. When treated at all, money has been regarded chiefly as an aggregative variable among the weapons of government economic policy, while finance has come to mean, narrowly, public finance (i.e. government revenue and expenditure). Not much has been written about the ways that money and finance, or credit, pervade the wider workings of the developing economy.

On financial development generally there are a few broad and theoretical books (notably, McKinnon, 1973; Shaw, 1973), which stand a good distance apart from several detailed studies of the financial systems of individual developing countries (for example, Sowelem, 1967; Drake, 1969a; Rozental, 1970a; Jao, 1974). In this book, I have attempted to cultivate the middle ground while consolidating ideas and evidence drawn from these two extremes. This contribution is intended, therefore, neither as original theory nor as fresh empirical work. It is rather a new and whole view of both money—in all its aspects—and finance, as they together relate to the operations of developing economies in general. I shall have achieved a worthwhile objective if this book provides a framework for viewing the financial aspects of any developing economy and analysing policy alternatives in that field.

It is desirable to begin by saying something about the

1

relationship between *money* and *finance* (or *credit*). Both concepts have domestic and international aspects. A simple plan will help to sort out the various connections and divisions between money and finance, domestically and internationally:

		1 Money	2 Finance (Credit)
A	Domestic	1A	2A
B	International	1B	2B

This plan reflects, horizontally, that money and finance are in some sense a continuum and, vertically, that the domestic aspects of both shade into their international aspects. The first consideration, then, is where to draw the vertical division within the money and finance continuum. Both money (currency or bank deposits) and the financial instruments (or claims) that come into being when credit is given are assets of their holders and obligations (liabilities) of their issuers. This dual asset/obligation character of all forms of money and finance should never be forgotten.

From the point of view of a spender, finance/credit and money both represent purchasing power, but the latter is immediate and the former is not. It is this 'immediacy' that marks out money as a special, and narrow, class among the range of financial assets: its principal distinguishing characteristic is that it is generally and readily accepted in exchange. Finance/credit is no alternative to money in this role. Of course, it is often possible to resort to finance and then settle immediate debts with borrowed money. But in this case it is obviously money that actually satisfies the immediate debt, and the borrower is still left with a new debt to a different lender; obtaining credit to pay a debt is simply the substitution of one obligation for another. So finance/credit never truly competes with money in its role as medium of exchange. By this medium of exchange criterion, economists usually draw the line so as to confine money to currency and current account bank deposits (the so-called M_1 category). There is some professional debate about whether or not to include also fixed deposits in banks (M_2) and, further, savings bank deposits (M_3). However, for this exposition the vertical division will be taken, conventionally, as separating M_1 from all else.

The next issue is where to draw the horizontal division between the domestic and international rows. This may appear to be merely a by-product of drawing the boundaries between nations. But the economic decisions are not so automatic or simple. Should domestic money, and finance denominated in it, be confined to the nation-state? Should a nation permit its currency to be used over a wider area? Might not a small nation find it advantageous to use the money, and the financial facilities, of a larger neighbour? Should the large sovereign states composing the European Economic Community allow a European currency to displace, or serve beside, their national currencies? These general questions are enough to show that issues of currency reserve standards and exchange rate fixity or flexibility are at the heart of the problem of determining the appropriate currency area. It would seem that the more confined is the use of the domestic currency, the lesser is its economic importance and the larger will be the overriding influence of foreign money within the area over which the domestic currency circulates; conversely, the wider the ambit of the domestic currency, the less important within its area will be the rest of the world's money. But the particular truth or otherwise of this statement cannot be determined without regard to the consumption, production and trade patterns of the country concerned. The theory of optimum currency areas must be invoked to some extent for guidance about where to draw the horizontal line.

Let us now indicate some of the subject matter of each of the four areas created by making the vertical and horizontal divisions. Area 1A involves macroeconomic considerations. How is money created? How is it managed? How is the exchange rate of local against international money determined? What is the relationship between the volume of money, the rate of interest and domestic economic activity? Orthodox theory has hitherto taught that a country's money supply is formed and governed chiefly by its central bank, but we shall see that this is often not so in less developed countries; moreover, many theorists now hold that the quantity of money is determined primarily by the demand for it. Inflation must also be entered under this heading; for inflation threatens the value of domestic money, posing problems about nominal versus real money and interest rates.

International money comes into area 1B. What serve internationally as mediums of exchange, stores of value and units of account? Acceptability is again the main criterion, which has historically meant that gold, silver, the so-called 'key' currencies and, since 1970, the Special Drawing Rights (SDR) units of the International Monetary Fund have served as international money. Key currencies are the national monies of major international trading and investing countries—until lately, chiefly Great Britain and the United States. In recent years both the US dollar and the pound sterling have lost appeal as international reserves (stores of value) but they are still most used as 'vehicles' (units of account) to denominate international contracts; correspondingly, gold and strong currencies such as the West German deutschmark and the Japanese yen have been sought as reserves.

The formation of international money is haphazard; it depends on gold mining, on international trade and investment and lending, and on decisions taken by the members of the IMF. There is, of course, no world central bank at the base of the system, creating all primary money and managing the volume of it for defined policy ends. Nevertheless, economic activity in each country may be affected by fluctuations in the volume and distribution of international money, as well as by changes in exchange rates between national currencies. The international reserves, which form each nation's store of value, are affected proximately by exchange rate fluctuations but fundamentally by differing rates of inflation as between individual countries. The individual nation therefore is not immune from the behaviour of money in other countries: areas 1A and 1B are directly connected in that events on the international scene (trade, investment and institutional changes) 1B directly or indirectly affect the domestic volume of money and interest rates 1A. (The creation of extra SDRs in the IMF does not directly affect the volume of money in any country, but it may indirectly make a central bank willing to initiate or countenance domestic money expansion. This is no place to attempt to unravel the complexities of the SDR facility; interested readers may care to refer to Grubel, 1977, Chap. 24.) Hence, domestic monetary policy cannot be properly discussed without having regard to the influence of a country's balance of international payments. And the management of international money—as distinct from the spontaneous international trade and investment that determine each nation's balance of payments—emerges as an important area of policy. In the absence of a world monetary authority, the field is left open for consultation and bargaining between nations and power blocs, and in such negotiations the rich nations inevitably are more influential than the poor.

Column 2 covers finance/credit, going beyond the narrow conception of money to take in assets/obligations not readily acceptable in exchange. (Financial assets and credit instruments will be dealt with in the next chapter.) These items nevertheless serve as stores of value and sometimes even as means of transfer. In the home economy (2A) finance can influence economic activity in the aggregate. Finance also plays a major microeconomic role in the allocation of resources. Later chapters of this book will deal with the connections between financial development, the availability of finance and the level of economic activity, and the operations of finance markets. For government, credit policy generally is much more difficult to formulate and manage than is mere monetary policy. Finance is diffuse, hard to monitor and to measure. Its 'fungibility' means that any stopping-up of some credit lines encourages the emergence and tapping of others. Left unsupervised, the finance markets may generate conflicts between private and public interests; on the other hand, regulatory overkill can inhibit beneficial financial development.

Finally, the world's payments arrangements (area 2B) depend not just on international money (of whatever form) but also on international trade credit, international lending (public and private) and institutional lines of credit. International activities falling notionally into area 2B may exert a good deal of influence on domestic finance markets and credit patterns (2A). For instance, the domestic capital market may be stunted to the extent that—as often happened historically—local savings are channelled into overseas portfolio investment. On the other hand, incoming foreign portfolio investment may give a desirable boost to the domestic capital market in terms of financial initiatives, methods and competition, as well as funds employed. Further, development credit supplied by foreign governments or international agencies may do much to meet important credit needs which have not been supplied by the local market.

This book concentrates on row A, i.e. money and finance within the domestic economy. We do not deal directly with row B, although international influences upon domestic money and credit are touched on in several places. The book is divided implicitly into four unequal parts. The first, consisting of this chapter and the next two, uses theory, social accounting and history to present a perspective on money and finance and their role in economic development.

Any effective financial system performs two distinct functions: it provides an adequate supply of acceptable money, and it transfers resources efficiently between lenders and borrowers. The second part of the book, Chapters 4 and 5, narrows the focus to the first function. In these chapters the evolution of money, the demand for it and arrangements for supplying it are dealt with, and there is also some discussion of monetary policy in the particular sense of regulating the total volume of money as an instrument of economic management. In terms of the areas of our plan these chapters fall into 1A. Chapters 6, 7 and 8, belonging in area 1B and constituting the third part of the work, turn to the second task of a financial system. In this allocative role, the financial institutions and the money and securities markets (formal and informal) come into play.

Finally, Chapter 9 brings the whole work together and welds points made separately in previous chapters into a consistent overall approach to financial policy. The final chapter is intended not so much as the polemical advocacy of a particular set of beliefs but as an argument for consistency and complementarity of macroeconomic and microeconomic financial policies in any situation.

Having outlined a view of money and finance and described the plan of the book, we move now to Chapter 2, which identifies some important concepts and presents a static framework for analysis of money and finance flows from the standpoint of the individual economy. Chapter 3 then takes a more dynamic, long-run approach to the relationship between financial and economic development.

CHAPTER 2

The Framework for Financial Transactions

The object of this chapter is to put money and finance on the same plane, within a framework that embraces real saving and investment as well as financial activity. Economic transactions are either real (involving the production, sale or transfer of goods and services) or financial (involving the creation, sale or transfer of financial assets, including money). Economic theorists are preoccupied with real variables, and applied economists find that real transactions are reasonably readily observed and measured. Most countries nowadays compile national income accounts, in which real transactions are captured and organized for analysis. Financial transactions, however, have not been so well served theoretically or practically. In less developed countries especially, economic analysis and policy discussions are all too commonly conducted as if financial activities are unimportant. It is useful, therefore, to begin with a few words about the nature of financial transactions and the way that they may be observed and co-ordinated with real production, consumption and investment.

In any period of time, the value of a nation's aggregate investment (real capital formation and net addition to stocks) is formally identical to the value of its savings (unconsumed income) plus or minus capital movements from or to the rest of the world. But individual acts of saving and investment are seldom alternate sides of the same coin. In the main, these acts are separated, either because those who save are not those who undertake investment or because those who both save and invest do not do so simultaneously and in identical amounts. It follows that, in any economy where decisions about saving and investment may be made privately and independently, the transfer of resources from savers to investors requires some financing channels. Moreover, these financing channels may also be used to transfer resources from savers to dissaving consumers.

Finance may be direct or indirect in form. *Direct finance* occurs where an actual saver (person, firm or government) lends to the actual spender (for investment or consumption). *Indirect finance*, far more important quantitatively than direct, involves *intermediaries* or middlemen: savers lend to intermediaries who in turn lend to spenders. The intermediaries, who may be individuals or firms, engage simultaneously in borrowing and lending. In advanced economies this middleman role is played predominantly by banks and other financial institutions, but in the developing countries individual traders and moneylenders are very important intermediaries. For completeness, one should also mention *self-finance*, or *internal finance* (in which the spender finances his own spending) as a further category.

Each act of 'external' financing brings into being simultaneously a *financial asset* for the lender and a *financial obligation* for the borrower. In other words, financial assets originate in the process of borrowing and lending. Direct financing creates a single financial asset, namely the lender's claim upon the party who borrows. In indirect finance, at least two financial assets arise: the saver–lender's claim against the intermediary, and the intermediary's claim against the borrower–spender. In any chain of intermediation, each additional link will generate a further financial asset. (In contrast to these external forms of financing, self-finance does not give rise to any financial asset; indeed, it may even involve the extinction of a financial asset as, for example, when a firm's past savings embodied in, say, a bank deposit are drawn down.) 'At any point in time, the *financial stock* of a country consists of the grand total of the various financial assets owned by its population. This financial stock represents the cumulative sum of past financing operations as yet undischarged, that is, all previous borrowing/lending less repayments.

The financial assets generated in borrowing/lending activities may be either negotiable (e.g. bills, bonds, debentures, shares) or non-negotiable (e.g. bank overdrafts or private loans). Negotiable financial assets are embodied in transferable paper form, such as a bill of exchange or a share certificate. These are sometimes referred to as *financial instruments*, or *securities*, or—colloquially—*paper*. Though non-negotiable financial assets are commonly recorded in books of account, they need not have any physical representation or even notation; for example, a private loan, which is a claim for one party and an obligation for the other, may not be evidenced in writing by either person and may exist only in their minds.

Markets exist for all financial assets. The markets for negotiable instruments are obviously like markets for real goods and are characterized by the determination of prices through the interaction of supply and demand, as on the stock exchange. Supply and demand also influence the 'prices' (rates of interest) and quantities of non-negotiable financial assets. Bank overdrafts and trade credit—to take two leading examples—depend at any given level upon the willingness of borrowers to pay the interest rates demanded by banks and wholesalers; otherwise either the relevant rate of interest must fall in order to sustain the volume of credit, or the volume will contract as fewer borrowers are prepared to pay the going rate of interest. In this sense, non-negotiable financial assets are marketable but they are not transferable; their markets resemble the markets for services. A haircut, for example, does not come into being until the customer subjects himself to the attentions of the barber; and the customer cannot transfer the completed service to another person. The price of haircuts is determined broadly by the intersection of customers' demand for the service and hair-dressers' willingness to supply it. Notice too that, also like service transactions, the operations of the financial markets often actually create the financial assets. This applies not only to the creation of non-transferable finance like bank loans but also to the generation of some negotiable instruments; for example, in a new issue of shares when the number of shares actually created depends on subscription demand. But the created shares are then, like any existing securities, amenable to unlimited subsequent transfers through buying and selling, in this instance on the stock exchange.

The role of financial institutions is an intermediary one, borrowing and lending in some cases involving, and in others not, the creation of financial instruments. However, the stock exchange, which is of such very great importance in the marketing of securities, is neither saver, spender, borrower nor lender and, of itself, does not create financial assets. The stock exchange is not an intermediary but an agency, which provides the means of contact between those who buy and those who sell securities. The so-called *new issue market*—so closely linked to the stock exchange that one may regard it as a *de facto*, if not formal, branch of exchange activities—provides a means of direct finance for corporate borrowers from public lenders. The new issue market may also provide an avenue for indirect finance as, for instance, when a hire purchase company makes a public issue of debentures and uses the proceeds to make loans to purchasers of durable consumer goods.

A final point about the finance markets is that each type of financial asset is, from the lender or buyer point of view, competitive with every other type and with real assets such as land, buildings, capital goods, gold, silver, works of art, and so on, as stores of wealth. The influences that determine the choices of asset holders about the composition of their wealth have been examined most rigorously in theories of portfolio choice (for example, Duesenberry, 1963;

Fama, 1978), which fall largely outside the purview of this book. We turn now to *flow-of-funds accounting*, which brings out the size, interrelationships and relativities of financing activities and their connection to the real aggregates of national income, consumption, savings and investment.

Modern social accounting began with the preparation of national income and product accounts, in which data concerning current output of goods and services are arranged to reveal the magnitudes of income, consumption, savings and investment for the whole economy and for its broad constituent groups, or sectors, such as households, government, business enterprises. The national income accounts deal with transactions in goods and services but ignore the money and credit flows that complement them. In the jargon of social accounting, national income accounts embrace 'non-financial' but not 'financial' flows (other than international and inter-sectoral net lending). Flow-of-funds accounts are designed to chart the financial flows—capital and current—of an economy in any given period of time. When the pattern of money and credit flows is discovered, financing problems may be apparent which call for the attention of policy-makers; this is particularly likely to be the case in poor countries where money and credit flows settle of necessity into limited and, as will be seen, often inadequate channels.

It would be possible to embrace all monetized economic transactions in the flow-of-funds accounts but, given the existence of separate national income accounts, it has become conventional to omit all non-financial flows other than gross savings (i.e. including capital consumption allowances), investment and capital transfers. (In other words, flow-of-funds accounts ignore all other payments for goods and services.) As these last mentioned non-financial aggregates appear also in the national income accounts, they provide the means of linking the two systems of social accounting. This emphasis on the capital account items as the link between the two systems must not be allowed to give rise to the mistaken impression that flow-of-funds accounts deal only with the financing of capital goods. On the contrary, they are also concerned with the financing of consumption activities and with transactions in financial assets. For any economic unit or group the balance of its financing activities— whether related to consumption, real investment or transactions in financial assets—must necessarily be equal to the difference between its saving (income minus consumption) and investment in real terms. This comes about because, in the nature of double entry accounting, total sources of funds (income plus borrowing) must be equal to total uses of funds (consumption, investment, lending). Thus, for example, a household's purchase of consumption goods on credit, which would add to its borrowing as recorded in the flow-of-funds accounts, would be reflected as a corresponding dissaving in its non-financial capital account. Conversely, a farmer whose savings exceeds his real capital formation must necessarily have increased his lending, that is, acquired financial assets. Looking at these points from a different angle, we can again perceive the importance of financial assets as the necessary means (other than taxation) of transferring real resources between units, groups and sectors in free enterprise or mixed economies.

Like the income and production accounts, the flow-of-funds system requires the economy to be divided into a number of sectors. The choice of sectors should, in principle, be determined by economic significance, but in practice it is rather arbitrary and is constrained by the limited and imperfect nature of available data. A fully articulated set of flow-of-funds accounts (a *matrix*) would show each sector's surplus or deficit on capital account and the range and magnitudes of its transactions in financial assets/obligations. A sector's capital account surplus/deficit may be extracted from the national income accounts as the difference between its savings and its investment (net of transfers). The resultant figure must conform (in principle exactly but in practice broadly, because of statistical inadequacies) with

the sector's net lending/borrowing as measured by the difference between changes in its financial assets and obligations.
A surplus sector, with savings exceeding its capital formation,
will correspondingly increase its financial assets or decrease
its liabilities; conversely for a deficit sector, which must
finance the excess of its real investment over savings by
increasing its financial liabilities or running down financial
assets accumulated in the past.

From any set of national income accounts, it should be
possible to make up an articulated table showing savings,
capital formation, domestic capital transfers and net borrow-
ing/lending, by any number of chosen sectors, as the hypothetical Table 2.1 shows. Notice that it is necessary for completeness to include a 'Rest of world' sector in order to capture
the economy's international financial transactions (though
not, of course, all financing *in* the rest of the world). The
net borrowing/lending of the 'Rest of world' sector equates
with our economy's balance of payments surplus/deficit on
current account. For all sectors (including 'Rest of world')
taken together, gross savings equals gross capital formation
(including net acquisition of foreign assets, real and financial)
and domestic capital transfers cancel out, as does the net
borrowing/lending item.

The flow-of-funds matrix joins a balancing set of financial
transactions to these aggregates; that is, it identifies the
changes in each sector's financial assets and liabilities which,
when netted, equal the sector's lending or borrowing. Table
2.2 itemizes in rows the various asset forms in which each
sector's financial transactions occur. It has become conventional to order the rows of assets in broadly descending
degree of liquidity, but no analytical significance is attached
to this practice. Financial *uses* equal financial *sources* both
individually and in total; in other words, purchases of each
class of financial asset by some sectors equal sales of that
particular item by other sectors, and in aggregate the acquisition of financial assets equals the incurring of liabilities.
Transactions by foreigners in domestic financial assets are

TABLE 2.1 Hypothetical National Income Aggregates ($ million) Arranged in Flow-of-Funds (Non-financial) Form[a]

	Government		Private sector		Financial institutions		Rest of world		Total	
	S	U	S	U	S	U	S	U	S	U
Gross saving	276		321		10			164	607	164
Gross capital formation										
Fixed		70		280		6				356
Stocks		9		78						87
Capital transfers		50	50						50	50
Net borrowing or lending		147		13		4	164		164	164
Total	276	276	371	371	10	10	164	164	821	821

[a] S = source of funds; U = use of funds.

15

TABLE 2.2 *Hypothetical Flow of Funds (Financial) ($ million)[a]*

Forms of financial assets	Government		Private sector		Financial institutions		Rest of world		Total	
	S	U	S	U	S	U	S	U	S	U
Currency		3		29	32				32	32
Bank deposits		67		147	191		23		214	214
Bank loans and advances			210			210			210	210
Other loans			188	110		78			188	188
Government securities	250	91		100		42		17	250	250
Company securities			50	69	103		30	114	183	183
Foreign assets		236		6			242		242	242
Net increase in financial assets or liabilities = surplus (S) or deficit (U)	147		13		4			164	164	164
Total	397	397	461	461	330	330	295	295	1483	1483

[a] S = source of funds; U = use of funds.

16

attributed, in the relevant asset row, to the 'Rest of world' sector; while the home economy's transactions in overseas financial assets appear, according to relevant sectors, in the 'foreign assets' row.

In principle, the components of Table 2.2 could be calculated directly, so that the final row, 'Net increase in financial assets or liabilities', would reveal for each sector a figure exactly matching the relevant 'Net borrowing/lending' amount in Table 2.1. It is therefore possible to join Tables 2.1 and 2.2 together as 'top' and 'bottom' of a single matrix (in the style of Table 2.3 below), in which the common row appears once only (designated 'Net borrowing/lending', 'Deficit/surplus' or 'Change in financial assets/liabilities', according to taste) and represents simultaneously the net result of changes in the real magnitudes of the 'top' and in the financial magnitudes of the 'bottom'. In practice, however it would be extremely difficult, if not impossible, to calculate all the financial rows directly. For each sector there is therefore usually some residual figure derived as the difference between the identified flows and the net borrowing/lending figure revealed in the top. For example, in Table 2.2 the government must have acquired net financial assets equal to its surplus of $147m: if its non-currency financial movements are all observable and add to $144m, the remaining $3m may be attributed to an increase in its holdings of currency.

It is not our purpose to discuss the conceptual and statistical difficulties involved in the construction of flow-of-funds accounts (for a start, see Bain, 1973) but a few points needed to be emphasized. First, the balance sheet concept is fundamental to the construction of flow-of-funds accounts (Ritter, 1963). Actual flows cannot often be observed and recorded and so must be deduced as the differences between the values of balance sheet items at the beginning and end of the relevant period. This leads to many complications, owing principally to the fact that numerous balance sheet changes do not involve market transactions but may result simply from one enterprise effecting a change in asset valuation within its own books. The revaluation of financial assets (e.g. owing to observed fluctuation in share prices) is the main problem, while depreciation allowances, valuations of stock, land, buildings and equipment and the issue of bonus shares provide further examples.

Of course when there are, as almost always, many enterprises in any sector, many balance sheets will be involved. In the balance sheet of one enterprise an asset item may increase (a *use* of funds), while in the balance sheet of another firm in the same sector the relevant item may decrease (a *source* of funds). The sector's transactions in the particular item will appear differently according to whether the changes in the item are recorded 'gross' or 'net'. Indeed, given the multiplicity of enterprises usually belonging to any sector, and the further possibility of even a single enterprise both buying and selling any particular type of financial asset during an accounting period, it is clear that any number of alternative degrees of 'netness' are possible. The theoretical extremes range from presenting every source (credit transaction) and every use (debit transaction) for every enterprise in the sector, to showing a single net source or use figure for the whole sector. 'While statistical practice varies, it is clear that the optimum degree of netting in the flow-of-funds accounts cannot be settled without reference to the question which the analyst has in mind' (Bain, 1973, p. 1064).

A central problem, in principle and practice, is the selection and delineation of sectors. Flow-of-funds accounts that adopt without variation the sectoring of the national income accounts (which is generally based on homogeneity of production or consumption activities among the constituent units of each sector) will not adequately reveal financial patterns. On the other hand, sectoring determined by financial homogeneity could not be joined readily or clearly to the national income and production accounts. Moreover, there is the practical difficulty of obtaining relevant data to fit any theoretically desirable financial matrix. Therefore, something of an *ad hoc* approach commonly prevails, in which sectoring is carried as near as possible to the desiderata of the financial analyst, consistent with the availability of data and with the broad sectoring of the national income accounts.

The essential sectors for both real and financial social accounting are *government*, *private sector*, *financial institutions* and *rest of world*. Where reasonable data are available, it is probably easy to divide government into *central* and *other government* and the private sector into *companies* and *unincorporated business and persons*, without losing comparability between the national accounts and the flow-of-funds accounts. The financial sector should be divided at least to separate the monetary authority from other financial institutions. And since financial flows are the focus of our interest, it is desirable further to divide the financial institutions. It should not be too difficult to distinguish, as collective groups, commercial banks, insurance companies and perhaps building societies from other financial institutions.

These general problems of sectoring are magnified in underdeveloped countries. The most serious difficulties concern the subdivision of the private sector into companies, unincorporated businesses of a non-agricultural nature, farms, and households. The first three groups cover producer entities, and the last group consumers; but it is always easier to observe the institutional division of the private sector between companies and households-cum-unincorporated firms than the functional division between production and consumption activities. Consequently, it is often necessary to treat households and unincorporated businesses jointly as a 'personal' sector. This practice is far from illuminating in most developing countries, where agriculture is the main economic activity and is conducted chiefly in the 'personal' sector. Further, underdeveloped countries are noted for the important volume of informal (as opposed to institutional) finance (for instance, loans by shopkeepers and pawnbrokers to peasant farmers) which would not be revealed by adopting the conventional personal sector because such finance is internal to it. For economic analysis of developing countries it would therefore be highly desirable to separate the production, consumption and financing activities of the personal sector. This is an improbable outcome but, by cautious estimation based on sample surveys, trade statistics and records of institutions such as co-operative societies, it might be possible to subdivide the personal sector into 'farms and rural households', 'urban households', 'moneylenders and retailers' and 'co-operative societies'. The agricultural picture may be made more complete if corporate agricultural enterprises, such as some plantations, can be separated out of the company sector.

The horizontal rows (categories of financial assets) are also based on analytical relevance and availability of data. In developing countries, where habits about holding and using money are still evolving, it is desirable to subdivide 'money' into coin, notes and the various classes of bank deposits. Trade credit, moneylender loans, and co-operative society deposits and loans may be important enough to be distinguished in separate rows; on the other hand, corporate securities may not merit subdivision.

Putting the desirable sectoral and asset-type divisions together, and having regard to the likely availability of data in a developing economy, we may propose an illustrative model matrix (Table 2.3) which might be feasible to complete and useful for analysis.

The mere charting of financial flows in this articulated form is likely to be a major contribution to economic knowledge in a developing country. Before any monetary and financial policies can be contemplated it is essential to be aware of the aggregate and sectoral savings–investment gaps and the existing financial patterns (and, if a series of period flow-of-funds matrices can be constructed, the course by which the pattern has emerged). Moreover, the flow-of-funds matrix provides a valuable aid to rigorous thought for policy-makers: the matrix brings out interrelationships and financial balance, thus promoting the formation of consistent policies and providing a check against partial analysis. A next step may be to draw on flow-of-funds data in considering the scope and performance of financial markets, as Goldsmith (1965) has done for the United States; and the flow-of-funds pattern provides a convenient framework for the interpretation by a central bank of capital market behaviour.

As flow-of-funds data become fuller and more reliable, they may serve to support more complex forms of analysis such as forecasts of inter-sector financing and of interest rates, under various assumptions about real activity and official monetary policy. These and other possible uses are discussed, and many further references given, by Bain (1973).

Of more immediate relevance for developing countries are the sectoral financing patterns and the period-to-period changes in them. Examination of these changes may reveal autonomous financial impulses and induced responses which may be linked with expansions or contractions of producer and consumer activities. This approach leads to the so-called *liquidity analysis*, which focuses on the financing of sectoral surpluses or deficits.

> The idea is that sectors which are reducing their liquidity—increasing their short-term borrowing or running down holdings of liquid assets—are providing an inflationary stimulus to the economy, whereas the reverse holds for those sectors which are increasing their net liquidity. [Bain, 1973, p. 1069, where qualifications to this approach are also noted]

In principle, the flow-of-funds framework provides a full, systematic and consistent account of an economy's financial transactions. Its articulated, double-entry structure prevents the omission of relevant transactions and provides internal checks on the accuracy of data. Subject only to the availability of sufficient data, the construction of flow-of-funds accounts is the desirable first step in studying money and finance in any developing economy. With the flow-of-funds sector and row concepts in mind, we now go on to describe and discuss *financial development*, that is, the expansion

TABLE 2.3   *Illustrative Flow-of-Funds Matrix*

	Government(s)		Central bank		Commercial banks		Insurance companies		Other financial institutions		Co-operative societies		Companies		Farms & rural households		Urban house-holds & uninc. businesses		Rest of world		Total
	S	U	S	U	S	U	S	U	S	U	S	U	S	U	S	U	S	U	S	U	
Gross saving																					
Gross capital formation																					
Fixed																					
Stocks																					
Capital transfers																					
Net borrowing/lending"																					
Coin																					
Notes																					
Bank deposits—current																					
Bank deposits—time																					

Bank loans and
advances
Trade credit
Other loans
Co-operative subscrip-
tions and deposits
Government securities
Company securities
Insurance and pension
fund contributions
Foreign assets—official
Foreign assets—private

Net increase in financial
assets/liabilities[a]

Total

[a] Sector surplus/deficit; excluded from 'total' row.

and elaboration of financial structure (institutions, instruments and activities) over time. The next chapter deals broadly with the evolution of financial instruments and borrowing/lending patterns (essentially inter-sectoral) in the course of economic development. The succeeding chapters deal, in a sense, with the various financial assets (beginning with money) described by the rows in terms of their origins, uses, the parties who deal in them and the ways in which they are negotiated.

Further Reading

Goldsmith (1965) offers a long, and Wilson (1966) a briefer, discussion of financing concepts and terminology. Bain (1973) provides an excellent survey of flow-of-funds analysis. The seminal work in that field is that of Copeland (1952). Ritter (1963) gives an excellent short exposition of the flow-of-funds system; Powelson's (1960) is fuller and highlights the system's relationship to national income accounting. Davies and Drake (1964) expound the technique simply and discuss some problems encountered in constructing flow-of-funds accounts for a developing country. Rozental (1970b) shows how even broad and rudimentary flow-of-funds estimates can throw light on important questions of economic analysis and policy. The recent study by Bank Negara Malaysia (1979, pp. 78–81), though not organized in the form of a complete matrix, illustrates the relationship between real savings of the private sector and savings held in various classes of financial assets. The pioneering study of the Philippines by Hooley (1963) is very revealing about sectoral savings, capital formation and financing patterns but, lacking the articulated flow-of-funds matrix, does not convey an overall, dovetailed view of the economy's financial transactions.

CHAPTER 3

Financial Development and Economic Growth

The pervasiveness of financing activities in economic life may be indicated by various ratios. One would be the ratio, in any period of time, of the net increase in all classes of financial assets to gross domestic product. Another, which could be derived from the flow-of-funds accounts, would be the ratio of financial transactions to gross capital formation in the given period.

These indicators focus on relationships between current flows of financial and real variables. But flows produce changes in stocks: the stock of financial assets, its division by type and its distribution among sectors are all affected by flows of funds in any period. Analogous to the flow-of-funds matrix, therefore, would be a matrix of financial stocks—a national balance sheet—which would identify the totals of each type of financial asset, classified by issuing and holding sectors. It is not our present purpose, however, to construct a national balance sheet. Rather, having noted that the financial stock must respond, in size and pattern, to financial flows, we may shift our attention to snapshot or point-of-time observations of financial stocks. We can then envisage the *financial structure* of any country at any chosen point in time. This financial structure can be said to consist of the present stock of various financial assets, together with the pattern of financial institutions in existence.

Since the financial structure is a composite of instruments

25

and institutions, it cannot be represented by any single indicator. In attempting to measure the financial structure, we must therefore take notice of several signs, as proposed by Raymond Goldsmith (1969). The principal indicator is the ratio of total financial assets to national wealth (real assets plus net claims against the rest of the world). Goldsmith terms this indicator the *financial interrelations ratio* (FIR). It will be greater in value the higher is a nation's level of financial development. (This indicator, based on observations about stocks, is parallelled by ratios based on flows; for instance the ratio of net new issues of financial assets to gross capital formation.) A second indicator is the composition of financial assets, by types of instrument and by their distribution among holders.

The importance of financial institutions in the financing process may be measured by the ratio of financial assets held by financial institutions to the total of financial assets. This ratio reflects the degree of institutionalization of borrowing and lending and the importance of indirect finance, which is greater the higher is this ratio. The relative importance of different types of financial institutions is indicated by the share that each has in the total assets of all financial institutions. (These points are developed further, and parallels with flow relationships noted, in Goldsmith, 1969, pp. 26–30.)

Goldsmith has observed these and other dimensions of financial structure in different countries over long periods of time and has identified the existence of three fairly distinct types of financial structure under free enterprise conditions. (A fuller typology may be found in Goldsmith, 1969, p. 34.) The first main type of financial structure, Type A, may be recognized by a low financial interrelations ratio (FIR), of value beneath one-half, by a predominance of fixed claims (loans, debentures, etc.) over equity assets, and by a small share of financial assets accounted for by financial institutions (predominantly banks). These features are characteristic of an economy in which bank notes and deposits (*scriptural money*) are gradually superseding coinage, and in which there is little corporate enterprise. The main example given by Goldsmith (1969, p. 33) is Europe from the early eighteenth to the middle of the nineteenth century.

A second type of financial structure, Type B, resembles Type A in having a low FIR, a predominance of fixed claims among financial assets and of banks among institutions; the significant additional feature of Type B is the existence of government financial institutions and activity on a considerable scale. This characterization fits many underdeveloped countries in modern times. Type C is that of the advanced industrialized economy in which both government and corporate enterprises loom large in both production and financing. This type is identified by a high FIR (a ratio of financial assets to national wealth of one or more), a markedly higher ratio of equities to claims, and a higher share of financial institutions in total financial assets than are found in Types A and B, and by diversified and specialized financial institutions (with a corresponding decline in the relative importance of banks).

This identification of different types of financial structure leads to consideration of the process of *financial development*, which may be defined as the expansion and elaboration over time of the financial structure (institutions, instruments and activities). Goldsmith has examined the financial history of many countries over the past 150–200 years and has reached the general conclusion that there is a fairly common path of financial progress marked by uniform behaviour of the FIR, of the share of financial assets owned by financial institutions, and of the importance of the banking system. Thus the financial interrelations ratio rises with economic development as the financing web becomes more intricate in relation to real production and wealth; a rising ratio of the financial assets owned by financial institutions to the total of financial assets reflects the growth of indirect financing and the institutionalization of savings and investment; and the banking system which first leads financial development declines in importance as real growth and financial development continue.

> ... apart from the different path taken since World War I or II by the countries that have a centrally planned economy in which the government owns most of the means of production, the existence of clearly different paths of financial development is doubtful. The evidence now available is more in favour of the hypothesis that there exists only one major path of financial development, a path marked by certain regularities in the course of the financial interrelations ratio, in the share of financial institutions in total financial assets, and in the position of the banking system, deviations being primarily connected with war finance and with inflation; a path on which different countries have started at different dates, in the twofold sense of different calendar dates and of different phases of their nonfinancial economic development; a path along which they have traveled at different speed, again in the sense of both calendar time and of phases of economic development; and a path from which they have deviated only to a minor extent. [Goldsmith, 1969, p. 40]

Perhaps the main reason for this broadly uniform path of financial development is the fact that there seems to have been little spontaneous and indigenous development of financial forms and institutions in countries other than the United Kingdom, France, and perhaps Germany, whose financial structures served as prototypes for modern financial systems in all parts of the world. Goldsmith carefully points out that this does not deny the qualitative importance and ancient form of instruments such as bills of exchange and mortgages, and of institutions such as banks (1969, p. 42). But in the quantitative sense, financial development is a very modern phenomenon, being inhibited before the nineteenth and twentieth centuries by the absence of non-household forms of business enterprise and the consequent limited separation between saving and investment activities.

The striking historical regularities observed in financial development around the world during the last two hundred years have been set out by Goldsmith (1969, pp. 44–8) and need be only summarized here. In the broadest terms:

1. The financial interrelations ratio (financial assets: national wealth) rises with a country's economic growth. In other words, the financial structure grows faster than national wealth (and than national product).

2. Eventually the FIR levels off, at a value of about 1, perhaps up to $1\frac{1}{2}$.

3. At present, the FIR is lower in less developed than in advanced countries.

4. The value of the FIR reflects the degree of specialization in the economy, in both production and finance.

5. The share of financial institutions in the ownership of financial assets increases as economic development proceeds.

6. The ownership of fixed claims is predominantly institutional but the ownership of equities is predominantly by individuals (nevertheless, institutional ownership of equities has increased very greatly in the last decade in many countries).

7. Financial development starts with the banking system and depends especially on the diffusion of scriptural money, which the banking system provides. As a corollary, the ratio of money (and of each of its components, coins, notes, deposits) to national wealth first increases with growth but eventually levels off or declines.

8. As countries become highly developed, the share of the banking system in the assets of the financial sector declines, while that of newer and more specialized institutions—such as building societies, life insurance companies, retirement funds and finance companies—increases. Thus in advanced economies the financial assets of the banking system are of lesser value than the financial assets held by all other financial institutions, whereas the reverse is true in economically underdeveloped countries.

9. Foreign financial links—either providing sources of

funds or serving as avenues for overseas investment of surpluses—have been of substantial importance at some stage in the development of most countries.

10. The transfer of financial techniques from advanced to less developed countries has been observed frequently.

11. The real resource cost of providing finance is distinctly lower in financially developed countries than in those not so developed.

12. Over long periods, there has been in most countries a rough but unmistakable parallel between economic growth and financial development. But the direction of cause and effect in this obvious association is not clearly established.

As economic development proceeds, most countries experience a faster growth of financial assets than of gross national product or of real wealth. This has been borne out by time series observations of, for example, the financial interrelations ratio in a number of countries. In Japan the FIR rose from about 0.1 around 1880 through 0.4 in 1913 to over 1.5 in the 1960s. Great Britain, a leader in economic development, had an estimated FIR of about 0.35 in 1880; by 1913 the ratio was 1.04—well ahead of all other economies at that time—and by 1963 had reached 1.70. In the United States the FIR was less than 0.50 in the 1880s rising through 0.80 around 1913 and reaching 1.27 in 1963. Similarly, cross-country comparisons at any point in time show FIR values to be high or low according to whether a country is economically advanced or underdeveloped. In the 1960s, very poor countries like Afghanistan and Ethiopia had very low FIR values; Venezuela, Yugoslavia, the Soviet Union and India had ratios in the 0.30 to 0.40 range; Germany, France, Belgium, Norway and Australia exemplified the 0.60 to 1.00 range; while Great Britain, Japan and the United States recorded FIR values well above 1.00. (These statistics have been gleaned from Goldsmith, 1969, and Gurley and Shaw, 1967; both sources give further evidence and reference.)

There is clearly a positive correlation between levels of economic development and financial development. Why should this be so? Does the obvious association subsume an identifiable general cause and effect relationship? These challenging questions surely deserve careful thought and investigation.

As has been pointed out by Richard Porter (1966, p. 347), the association between real and financial development has attracted the attention of economists from Adam Smith onwards: 'I have heard it asserted, that the trade of the city of Glasgow doubled in about fifteen years after the first erection of the banks there; and that the trade of Scotland has more than quadrupled since the first erection of the two public banks at Edinburgh . . . that the banks have contributed a good deal to this increase, cannot be doubted' (Smith, 1910, p. 262). Yet, curiously, it is only in the last decade or so that economists—notably Goldsmith, Gurley, Shaw, Patrick—have attempted to explain the logic of the association between financial development and real economic growth. The first, and to my mind the most powerful, explanation of the relationships runs in terms of the *division of labour*, in three different aspects (cf. Gurley and Shaw, 1967, pp. 258–60; Goldsmith, 1969, pp. 391–401).

First, the use of money gives very much greater scope for the division of labour in production than is permitted by barter and other pre-monetary forms of exchange. The displacement of pre-monetary forms of exchange by transactions conducted with money is known technically as *monetization*, the potential benefits of which are recounted in introductory textbooks about money. Gurley and Shaw (1967, p. 259) point out that, while monetization outspeeds real growth initially, there is everywhere some eventual secular peak in the ratio of money to income (they suggest about 30 per cent), at which stage money transactions have become ubiquitous. The indirect exchanges that money permits eliminate the rigid transaction limits of barter and the lesser constraints of equivalencies (see Chapter 4), thus

enlarging markets over space and time and creating scope
for profitable division of labour by production type and
by production process.

Second, there is a potentially beneficial division of labour
between saving and investment (Goldsmith, 1969, pp. 392–3;
Patrick, 1966, p. 182). If economic units (persons,
households, firms, government) rely entirely on self-finance,
investment is constrained in two ways: by the ability and
willingness of any unit to save, and by its ability and
willingness to invest. The unequal distribution of
entrepreneurial talents and risk-taking proclivities in any
community means that at one extreme there will be some
whose investment plans may be frustrated for want of enough
savings, while at the other end there will be those who
do not need to consume all their incomes but who are
too inert to save or too cautious to invest the surplus
productively. For the community as a whole, productive
investment may thus fall short of its potential level. In
these conditions, the introduction of financial instruments
(at this stage, the argument requires merely facilities for
direct or primary finance and not necessarily financial
institutions) provides a bridge between ultimate savers and
ultimate investors and creates the opportunity for putting
the savings of the cautious at the disposal of the enterprising,
thus promising to raise the total level of investment and
hence of income. This argument is strongly reinforced by
the observed indivisibility or 'lumpiness' of many potentially
profitable but large investments. These substantial pieces
of capital formation are commonly beyond the financing
capacity of any single economic unit but may be supported
if the investor can gather and combine the savings of many.
As with monetization, there seem, however, to be limits
to this primary financing between actual savers and actual
investors (doubtless set by the ambit within which
information may easily be spread and communication
maintained). Gurley and Shaw notice (1967, p. 259) that,
whereas the stock of primary securities more than doubled

relative to national income in the United States during the nineteenth century, the ratio has changed little since then.

In a third sense there is beneficial division of labour in the process of financial intermediation (indirect finance) by institutions. The argument for this type of financing rests chiefly on the grounds of improved allocation of resources, although, as will be noted shortly, there are also reasons for expecting the existence of intermediary facilities to promote increases in aggregate saving and investment volumes. Just as direct finance breaks open the restraints imposed by an investor's dependence on his own saving, so indirect finance circumvents the direct link between any individual saver and an individual investor. In other words, indirect or roundabout finance conducted through financial institutions removes the 'marrying' difficulty that the direct form of finance imposes. The essence then of the allocational argument for intermediation is that different financial institutions cultivate particular finance specializations at which each institution becomes very adept. Given this specialization, a network of such intermediaries should lower the real cost of financing and, by efficiently sorting out and ranking the various investment proposals, improve the allocation of investible resources in total (see also Patrick, 1966, pp. 182–3). This should not be taken to imply any automatic or easy ranking of prospective investments according to their anticipated private or social yield. All such estimates are at one and the same time subjective, necessarily inexact, and very uncertain. Nevertheless, the capital market does sort out and arbitrate between competing demands for investible funds and will do this efficiently inasmuch as there is some relationship between the standing of the prospective borrower (as usually evidenced by past success) and his ability to invest wisely. (The uncertainties and subjectivities involved in estimating future returns, and the influences of reputation and past performance upon the allocation of funds between firms via the capital market, are concisely discussed by Richardson, 1965, pp. 295–6.)

It should perhaps be mentioned here that while all this is surely true for a closed economy, when we consider the possibility of unrestricted financing between nations it is conceivable that some countries, or even cities, may develop a comparative advantage in intermediation to such an extent that financial development in other places may be stunted. For example, it is plausible to regard the City of London as having been in such a position in the nineteenth and much of the twentieth centuries.

This is, perhaps, an appropriate point at which to notice the importance of an enforceable system of mercantile law as a necessary pre-condition to monetization and financial development. The forms of financial specialization that have just been recounted will not occur simply through theoretical perception of their economic benefits. Those who decide to accept money in exchange and to hold financial assets as wealth need the reassurance, which law and custom confer, that it is safe to do so. The role of mercantile laws and customs in financial development, especially the way in which they permit the widening of the borrowing and lending circle, has been vividly outlined by Hicks (1969, Chap. V).

From this discussion it does seem that specialization and division of labour in production, in savings and investment, and in intermediation go a long way towards explaining the association between financial development and real growth. The correlation between financial and real development has been noticed historically and argued theoretically. But the direction of causality has not yet been established. The arguments so far may be interpreted alternatively as growth responding to financial development or as growth precipitating financial development, or as two-way interaction. Is it possible now to go a step further and identify causation?

Gurley and Shaw (1967, pp. 258–60) seem to lean to the view that financial development depends on real growth, although in also acknowledging 'the retroactive impact of finance upon the real world' their discourse may be read as conceding two-way causation. Gurley has often also expressed scepticism about the universal desirability of the 'technique of finance' for mobilizing savings on the grounds that its social costs and inefficiencies may sometimes exceed its social benefits (see Gurley's essay, and partly in response, another by Goldsmith, in Krivine, 1967). Despite an early expression of agnosticism about causation, Goldsmith finally comes near to suggesting that financial development does actively promote real growth (1969, pp. 48, 400); more recently, however, he has again taken a neutral stand (Goldsmith, 1975, p. 88).

The discussion in the last few pages strongly implies, and it is my belief, that financial development generally fosters growth, but it is necessary to be more explicit about the ways in which it may do so. It seems clear that financial development in any economy will be growth-promoting to the extent that it increases the size and/or improves the utilization of the national stock of real and human capital. In other words, we need to consider the extent to which financial development (1) augments the quantities of real saving and capital formation from any given national income, (2) increases net capital inflow from abroad, and (3) raises the productivity of aggregate investment by improving its allocation. In pursuing these points in principle it must be recognized that the following arguments implicitly assume reasonably 'perfect' market conditions and rational behaviour; we do not, at this stage, contemplate such issues as the remittance abroad of domestic savings attracted to financial institutions, unevenly distributed information about investment opportunities, or non-economic discrimination by lending institutions against certain classes of entrepreneurs, which are discussed in later chapters.

There are several grounds for expecting savings to respond favourably to financial development in any form. The provision of simply primary securities (i.e. opportunities for direct lending) divorces, as we have just seen, individual acts of saving from acts of investment over both time and place, and thus allows savings to occur 'without the need for a concomitant act of investment' (Porter, 1966, p. 349). Second, the yield promised or anticipated on the ownership of financial assets may be sufficiently great to attract saving of income that would otherwise have been consumed. It is further argued (e.g. Goldsmith, 1969, pp. 395–7) that financial institutions may also raise the totals of savings and investment above the levels that would have occurred in the absence of institutional borrowing and lending, when savers and investors would be limited to direct financing. The main support for this argument lies in the observation that most savers and lenders prefer to hold claims against financial institutions rather than the primary securities issued by actual investors.

Compared with direct debt securities, claims against financial institutions are generally more liquid, more divisible and are regarded as better risks. Sometimes, too, claims against financial institutions have additional benefits; for example, the promise of an eventual housing loan is at least implied for depositors with building societies, and insurance protection is associated with lending to life insurance companies. It appears obvious that many would save and lend less, or not at all, but for the existence of financial institutions. This seems especially to be true of small unit savings—which in aggregate are significant—and of contractual or regular savings (e.g. insurance premiums and savings contributions deducted at source of income), the more so where such savings have little sensitivity to interest rates. Empirical support for the view that the existence of financial institutions raises the savings ratio can be found in the work of Hooley (1963, pp. 54–6), which shows that saving in the Philippines responded positively to development of the financial system in that country over the decade 1951–60. See also the evidence referring to various countries of South East and East Asia, cited by Rozental (1967, pp. 453–5).

Similarly, many prefer to borrow from financial institutions than from individual lenders. Institutional finance may be more tailored to the particular investment project, may be in more continuous supply, may be more flexible—should circumstances change—in amount and in terms, and may well be cheaper. To the extent that institutions handle funds that would not otherwise be lent and borrowed, because borrowers and lenders would patronize financial institutions but not deal directly with one another via primary securities, then the existence of the financial institutions truly increases the total volume of saving and investment.

Financial improvements certainly facilitate international movements of capital, although it is doubtful if they have hitherto *motivated* capital inflows to any territories that were not already so destined for other reasons. In the contemporary world, however, it is very likely and important that local financial development will deter capital outflow by providing attractive financial assets in the home economy. The brevity with which this point is made should not lead the reader to underestimate its great importance. There is abundant evidence in many countries of domestic savings being diverted from foreign to local financial assets, as the opportunities to acquire the local assets were created (see, for example, Bank Negara Malaysia, 1979, pp. 70–4).

The benefits of improved investment allocation have already been mentioned (pp. 33–4 above). As a general rule, any financial development that causes investment alternatives to be compared with one another is bound to produce allocational improvement over a system of segregated, 'compartmentalized' (Porter, 1966, p. 352) investment opportunities. Moreover, with the aid of external finance—direct or indirect—the entrepreneur may be able to break out of the confines of his own savings and undertake those discrete and lumpy investments that embody technological improvements and give rise to increased productivity (McKinnon, 1973, pp. 12–13). This argument relates, of course, to raising the aggregate rate of investment as well as to improving its allocation.

These ways in which the financial system may influence the size, composition and utilization of the nation's stock of capital, so as to promote growth of real national income, are further discussed by Hugh Patrick (1966) who goes on to advocate a policy strategy for financial development in poor countries, based on the view that financial development will promote real growth. To the growth-promoting arguments for financial development which we have expounded, Patrick (1966, pp. 178–81) adds and develops a point of such importance that it warrants fairly full recounting here.

In poor countries, much real wealth is held by individuals, under their own direct control, in such forms as land and improvements to it, agricultural and handicraft tools, livestock, stocks (especially of food), durable goods, precious metals and jewellery. We should also include here net private holdings of foreign exchange and investments, real and financial. Correspondingly, the proportion of real wealth accounted for by producers' capital is low, compared with advanced economies. This composition of wealth is due, in large part, either to lack of productive investment opportunities or to the inability of local entrepreneurs to perceive them. Patrick (1966, p. 179) argues that, as economic change throws up opportunities for productive investment, the desirability of improving the composition of *existing* national wealth, by transforming excess stocks and unproductive durable wealth into productive capital, becomes apparent.

The first job for finance in these transformations is to capture the unproductive assets. This may be done by institutions offering financial assets which are more attractive as stores of wealth than inventories, precious metals and objects, and even foreign exchange. For this to occur, it is essential that domestic financial assets offer better liquidity, divisibility, yield and real security characteristics than do the traditional forms of wealth-holding. This does not seem difficult as far as inventories of primary products are concerned, for these are subject to spoilage, storage costs and the risks of price fluctuation. It will be harder to foster the substitution of domestic financial assets for precious metals and foreign assets; exceptionally good yields and protection against inflation may need to be promised for the financial assets.

If all goes according to plan, non-productive assets will be sold for cash to various dealers (especially export merchants) and individuals will use their newly acquired cash to purchase financial assets. Thus either firms or financial institutions will obtain funds; the one for direct purchase of productive capital, the other for lending to enterprises which will then acquire productive capital.

The dealers who buy the excess stocks, precious metals, etc., must duly dispose of them in ways that lead to the supply of the capital goods sought by producers. Foreign trade offers a ready avenue for the disposal of precious metals, etc., and the relevant foreign exchange receipts can then be expended on imported capital goods. The trade route will also permit the conversion of excess inventories into capital goods, to the extent that the commodities can be sold abroad (as is usually possible, especially if the exchange rate is not overvalued). An alternative conversion mechanism for inventories is to use them as consumer goods for local workers who may be put to work making capital goods.

Patrick notes that substantial—and beneficial—shifts in the composition of national wealth have occurred historically when countries moved from specie to token money and then to the 'further refinement' of deposit money (1966, p. 180). While this last opportunity generally does not exist to the same extent in the modern age, it is still true that much of the existing national wealth of many presently underdeveloped countries takes the form of precious metals and jewellery (countries of the Indian sub-continent) or foreign liquid assets (countries in Latin America, Africa and the Middle East).

Patrick's beliefs that the financial system can exert a growth influence on the capital stock—by improving the composition of the existing stock of capital, efficiently allocating new investment among alternative uses, and raising the rate of capital formation by providing incentives for increased saving and investment—underlie his advocacy of what he terms the *supply-leading* policy of financial development in poor countries. Supply-leading denotes the conscious creation of financial institutions, instruments and services in advance of the demand for them. Supply-leading is contrasted with *demand-following* finance, in which the financial system and its services develop in response to demand for financial services by investors and savers.

> Supply-leading has two functions: to transfer resources from traditional (non-growth) sectors to modern sectors, and to promote and stimulate an entrepreneural response in these modern sectors. Financial intermediation which transfers resources from traditional sectors, whether by collecting wealth and saving from those sectors in exchange for its deposits and other financial liabilities, or by credit creation and forced saving, is akin to the Schumpeterian concept of innovation financing. [Patrick, 1966, pp. 175–6]

Supply-leading finance may not be a profitable activity, at least in the short-run, and institutions that engage in it may require direct or indirect government assistance to stay in existence. Such subsidies are likely to be just one short-run cost (more fundamentally, as will be discussed in later chapters, the opportunity cost of government assistance must be considered). Patrick's supply-leading strategy relies on the beliefs that real economic growth can be led by financial development and that the benefits of growth will outweigh, and so justify, the costs incurred in the short run by supply-leading finance.

The obvious—and to most economists the

unpalatable—nature of the short-run costs associated with subsidized financial development doubtless accounts for a generally lukewarm professional response to Patrick's ideas. (The institution-creating enthusiasms, usually unsupported by careful thought and judgement, so frequently exhibited by politicians and civil servants in less developed countries are quite another story.) Moreover, it is innately difficult to attract support for subsidizing the finance sector when in all poor countries there are, apparently, so many more important and pressing claims on the public purse; the provision of assistance to the financial sector—smacking of 'to him that hath'—seems offensive to the advocates of a more equal distribution of income and wealth.

A particularly interesting comment on Patrick's strategy proposal has been made by Stammer who, observing the somewhat retarded financial development of fast-growing Hong Kong, has questioned the need for any more than rudimentary financial intermediation. Stammer recognizes the importance to Hong Kong of a stable and convertible currency, of liberal and flexible commercial banks, of credit, marketing and commercial intelligence available through the long-established agency houses (merchant firms, commonly under expatriate control), and of non-interventionist government. Beyond this there has been little financial development, and Stammer doubts the need for it. He notices that self-finance has been abnormally important in Hong Kong. 'To all business units, from the smallest manufacturer and retailer to the giant industrial, commercial and utility company—as, indeed, with the government—retained earnings as the main source of funds for capital formation' (Stammer, 1972, p. 322). Further, where inter-unit or inter-industry financing has occurred, it has been of a direct nature, owing to the intimate networks of both the Chinese clans and the agency houses. Thus, says Stammer, the need for indirect finance through institutions has been obviated by 'a mobility of direct finance', and it may not be readily appreciated by Western economists that this informal system can achieve a good allocation of investment funds. (These points are discussed further in Chapter 6.)

Patrick is certainly not blind to the short-run costs of the supply-leading strategy (1972, p. 328 and note 4), and in a later paper he has associated himself with a more cautious, but still positive, approach to the promotion of financial development (Wai and Patrick, 1973, p. 30). However, he not only seems less than completely convinced about the short-run efficiency of internal finance as practiced in Hong Kong, but also advances two good reasons why long-run reliance on internal and/or direct finance is likely to be objectionable. First, it may lead to concentrations of wealth and economic power in few hands. 'This is not just a theoretical possibility, as the Japanese *Zaibatsu* in the 1920s and 1930s and the family conglomerates in Pakistan (and elsewhere) today attest' (Patrick, 1972, p. 328). Secondly, unless financial intermediary institutions are widely and readily available, wage- and salary-earners may lack incentives to save and outlets for their savings. Wage- and salary-earners invariably become increasingly important, and obtain collectively a rising share of national income, as early economic development occurs. Any neglect of incentives for them to save or of channels for their savings may well mean that aggregate savings and investment, and the rate of economic growth, will be less than could be achieved.

In this chapter we have noticed the historical association between economic growth and financial development, examined the logic of that association, considered ways in which financial development might promote economic growth, and referred to Patrick's supply-leading financial strategy for economic development. It is now time to go more deeply into monetary and financial conditions in developing countries.

Further Reading

As the text of this chapter suggests, Goldsmith (1969, Chapters 1 and 9), Gurley and Shaw (1967) and Patrick (1966) are mandatory reading. The other chapters of Goldsmith's book and its voluminous appendices provide a large amount of empirical reference material. Cameron *et al.* (1967, pp. 7–14, 296–310) and Porter (1966) are also strongly recommended; although these writings are focused rather narrowly on banking rather than general financial development and although Porter is cautious in his conclusions, these works are compatible in approach and judgements with the present chapter. A cooler opinion of financial intermediation, based on observations of less-developed economies in Africa, is advanced by Bhatia and Khatkhate (1975). Econometric tests of various relationships between aspects of financial development and economic growth have recently been reported by Jao (1976). These investigations, albeit limited and preliminary, do support the importance of financial development in the growth process.

Abstract literature on the theory of financial intermediation and development is just beginning to emerge: early contributions by Spellman and Gonzalez-Vega may be found in McKinnon (1976); see also Galbis (1977). Hicks (1969) is a most stimulating book which all interested in economic growth should at some stage read in its entirety; his Chapter V is relevant to our present chapter, and the work will be referred to again. Those with sufficient time and interest to read widely should refer to Cameron *et al.* (1967) and various works cited by Goldsmith (1969, pp. 401–9), and should not neglect the works of Joseph Schumpeter.

CHAPTER 4
Money

> . . . the early phases of the evolution of money have not been dealt
> with adequately either by economic history or by anthropology, and
> least of all by economic theory.
>
> [Paul Einzig, *Primitive Money*, 1949]

In textbooks on economics, descriptions and discussions
of the economic functions of money—a means of exchange,
a unit of account, a store of value—are commonplace and
often threadbare. It may therefore seem intolerably tedious
to ask the reader to embark upon yet another account
of these functions of money. The justification for doing
so is that the discussion is necessary in order to bring
out the desirability of speeding up monetization in less developed countries and to indicate ways by which this may
be achieved.

Money is unique among financial assets in that it alone
gives immediate purchasing power; in other words, it is
supremely liquid. The distinguishing characteristic of money
is that it is generally and readily accepted in exchange;
indeed, economists commonly define money as that which
discharges this function. For example, Newlyn begins his
excellent book with the sentence 'The essential function,
the performance of which enables us to identify money,
is very simple: it is that of acting as a medium of exchange'
(Newlyn, 1971, p. 1). However, to define money as that
which is acceptable in exchange is not only to adopt a
functional rather than a philosophical approach to the problem (and incidentally to give priority to one of the several

44

functions of money); it is also to take a narrowly economic view of the nature and role of money. This approach may do very well in the advanced world where economic exchange is so pervasive as to require a single item of immediate and indiscriminate acceptability. Implicitly, such an acceptable item will also be uniform, will serve as a unit of account or measure of value and will be a store of value (notwithstanding that it may change in real worth over time). But this domination of medium-of-exchange money need not pertain in economically underdeveloped countries. The less sophisticated is the economy of any society, the more likely it is that different things may serve separately the various distinct functions that are discharged simultaneously by medium-of-exchange money in advanced, commercialized societies. For instance, in very primitive societies shells or rods may serve as the medium of exchange, while cattle or commodities may be the standard, and principal store, of value. More pertinent, perhaps, is the lesser importance of payment in exchange in such societies and the correspondingly greater role of payment in compensation or gift.

Each developing country in the modern world enjoys or suffers a monetary system somewhere between the extremes of advanced and primitive money. Although many developing countries have officially adopted modern, token and general purpose money forms, vestiges of primitive or archaic monies often remain in subsidiary use; and there are still places where no dominant token medium of exchange holds sway. It is useful therefore to devote a few paragraphs to the nature and purpose of money in pre-modern societies, giving particular emphasis to the distinctions between general and partial forms of money and between commercial and other uses of it.

I trust that the discussion that occupies the next few pages will acquit this author of Paul Einzig's charge (still as generally warranted as when it was made thirty years ago) that:

even though most economists have spent very little time on investigating primitive money, textbooks on monetary history and on monetary or economic theory dutifully register in a few brief paragraphs their author's views on the origin and early evolution of money. No economist worthy of that name would think of writing, however briefly, on contemporary Chinese currency without first making a careful study of the subject and its background. Yet economists whose names are household words committed themselves unhesitatingly to views on primitive money without taking the trouble to study even such material on the subject as is easily accessible. They have devoted no original research and very little original thought to primitive money before venturing to tell their readers just how money has come into being. Most of them still live on the few casual remarks on the subject in Adam Smith's *Wealth of Nations*. They take in each others highly inadequate washing and do not even trouble to find original instances, or to invent new fictitious examples, to illustrate the well-worn conventional theory which they put forward with an amazing degree of self-assurance.

[Einzig, 1949, p. 20]

Much objection has been made to the exclusively commercial notion of money held generally by economists and to the consequent definition of money in terms of its predominant modern function in exchange (see Grierson, 1977; Polanyi, 1968; Dalton, 1967; Einzig, 1949, p. 323). These points are well taken. Money fulfils a social need, and it is rightly pointed out that its origins should be sought not in the market but in that 'much earlier stage in communal development' in which vehicles of compensation and gift were needed.

Grierson (on whose illuminating lecture I have drawn heavily) asserts that money sprang from the search for a uniform measure, or standard of value, on which to base a tariff of compensations for killing and injury. Numerous historical and linguistic examples are advanced in support of the view that the seeds of monetary systems are to be found in the evaluation of injuries rather than of commodities. It is a short step from this foundation stone to the valuation of goods and services, and the path goes via the valuation of brides and of slaves (Grierson, 1977, pp. 19–29). All this means, of course, that the non-commercial uses of money should never be overlooked—and especially not in economically less-developed societies. It follows, too, that economists should phrase the primary function of money as 'means of payment' rather than 'medium of exchange', emphasizing money's *general acceptibility*, whether in bilateral exchange or unilateral payment.

Two important questions follow from the conventional threefold classification of the functions of money into means of payment, measure of value and store of value. First, to what extent are the three functions separable? Second, which—if any—is the fundamental function from which the others derive?

It is well-known historically that there have been divergencies between the money that is used in payment, the money in which prices are reckoned and the money that serves as a store of wealth (Grierson, 1977, pp. 16–17; Einzig, 1949, gives numerous examples, as on pp. 322–5). This has given rise to the analytical concept of *limited purpose* (Grierson, 1977, p. 15) or *partial* monies (Hicks, 1967, p. 2), which serve singly any of the classical three functions, in contrast to *general purpose* or *fully developed* money, which simultaneously plays all three roles (see also Polanyi, 1968; Bohannan, 1967; Dalton, 1967). This very useful distinction between partial or specific purpose and fully developed or general purpose money clears up much confusion in the literature and avoids interminable philosophizing about the 'true' nature of money. It is plain that many references to the economic inadequacies of the various primitive or archaic monies or forms of exchange that have been characterized as pre-monetary (barter, equivalencies, etc.) are really criticisms of the limited usefulness of partial money.

Fully developed money is what matters to the economist, and by that term I mean money which *simultaneously* serves as means of payment, a unit of account and a store of value. This definition in no way overlooks the fact that money may at times be a poor store of value (as in conditions of rapid inflation) or that alternative stores of value are always available.

Economists have tended to think that exchange money has its roots in the store of value attribute. In a sense, this is logically true: Newlyn (1971, p. 2) shows that payment money is necessarily a store of value to some extent since no one immediately pays out again the whole of his money receipts. Conversely, and more fundamentally, Hicks says that acceptability in exchange requires the store of value characteristic and indeed grew out of it (Hicks, 1967, pp. 17–18; Hicks, 1969, p. 64). Noting that 'the mere capacity of acting as a store of value does not confer monetary quality, it must be the other functions which do so', he elegantly restores the pre-Keynesian view that store of value is a necessary—though not a sufficient—characteristic of money (Hicks, 1967, pp. 17—37).

Others—principally anthropologists and historians—dissent from the view that money must necessarily be a store of value: 'it is not a feature which characterizes all kinds of money . . . . Grain and stockfish have often served as money but are not good stores of value' (Grierson, 1977, pp. 15–16). It seems to me, however, a fine and crucial point against this school that grain, stockfish and other perishables *were* at least temporary stores of value in the Hicks–Newlyn senses of being very liquid and readily disposable in the short period, if not in the long.

Grierson goes on to assert that 'measure of value' is the ultimate test of money, arguing essentially that unless a *general* measure of value is held by a society the society in question is still in the stage of barter and other particularized transactions/payments. From this view it would seem to follow that generalized exchange would be held back until a general standard of value becomes accepted.

Einzig shows, however, that this latter opinion, widely purveyed in economics textbooks, is historical and logical nonsense. The supposed difficulties of barter—the need for double coincidence of wants, the difficulty of subdivision in transactions, the time cost of seeking a partner for bilateral exchange (as Sir Dennis Robertson, 1965, p. 328 once put it, 'the text books are full of the agonies of two men, one with a spare fish, and the other with a spare pair of shoes, vainly seeking one another')—have been greatly exaggerated and tend to disappear when barter is seen in its proper social context.

It is, of course, easy for a lecturer to earn the laughter of his audience by telling them about the pathetic efforts of some market gardener who has to find a barber in need of radishes before he can have his hair cut. What the lecturer and his audience do not realize is that in a primitive community the grower of radishes usually cuts his own hair, or has it cut by a member of his family or household; and that even in primitive communities with barbers as an independent profession the barber and the gardener have a fair idea about each other's requirements, and have no difficulty in suiting each other. If the barber does not happen to require today any of the products the gardener is in a position to offer, he simply performs his service in return for the future delivery of products he is expected to need sooner or later.

Even the genuine instances quoted by economists to illustrate the absurdity of barter are apt to be misleading in their implication. There is, for instance, the well-known experience of Mlle Zélie, singer at the Théatre Lyrique in Paris, who, in the course of a tour round the world, gave a concert on one of the Society Islands, and received the fee of three pigs, twenty-three turkeys, forty-four chickens, five thousand coconuts and considerable quantities of bananas, lemons and oranges, representing one-third of the box office takings. In a letter published by Wolowski and quoted to boredom by economists ever since, she says that, although this amount of livestock and vegetables would have been worth about four thousand francs in Paris, in the Society Islands it was of very little use to her . . . .

What the economists quoting these and other similar instances do not appear to realize is that the difficulties complained of are not inherent in the system of barter. They are largely anomalies arising from sudden contact between two different civilizations. A native singer in the Society Islands would not have been embarrassed at receiving payment in kind, since she would have known ways in which to dispose of her takings, or store them for future use . . . .

In many communities the necessities of life were exchanged against each other as a matter of routine. Economic units within a tribe, or even belonging to different tribes, came to be complementary to each other. In the Pacific, or on the Malayan Peninsula, fishing villages and inland villages exchanged fish against land products regularly, often at prices that remained unchanged for generations. This arrangement suited their primitive requirements. When as a result of internal progress or through increased contact with the outside world their requirements became more diversified, the need for a medium of exchange or at least a common denominator became more evident. Nevertheless, the conditions in which barter operated were even then far from being necessarily intolerable. The existence of fixed price ratios referred to above went a long way towards assisting. Likewise, the possibility of credit in connection with barter—delivering goods in return for future deliveries of goods—must have also helped to no slight degree. John Stuart Mill's much-quoted imaginary instance of a harassed tailor on the verge of starvation, trying frantically to find a baker who happens to be in need of a jacket, in order to be able to secure his daily bread in exchange for it, existed only in the imagination of a 19th century economist who, however distinguished in his own line, appears to have been unacquainted with the elements of anthropology . . . .

The difficulty of 'marrying' barter transactions in primitive communities, even after the development of a certain degree of division of labour, should not be exaggerated. The 'double coincidence' (to quote the words of Jevons) that must arise is by no means difficult to achieve in a small community where everybody knows a great deal about everybody else's products and requirements.

[Einzig, 1949, pp. 350–2]

Notwithstanding Einzig's convincing demonstration that the barter system is not a dead-weight handicap to specialization and trade, there is something in the idea of exchange and trade being positively facilitated by a notional standard, which need not also be the medium of exchange. The anthropological and historical literature bristles with examples (see the references cited by Grierson, 1977, Polanyi, 1968, and Dalton, 1967), but strangely economics in general and development economics in particular has overlooked this large range of exchange arrangements which lies between the extremes of bilateral barter and fully developed (general purpose) money. The only reference I have found in the modern literature of economic development is over a decade old and seems to be little known (Levenson and Randall, 1966). The authors of this paper dispute that barter is the norm in non-monetized economies, and they employ the term 'equivalencies' to identify a system of well-known exchange ratios, set by law or custom, between a few key commodities and all others. Commonly, cloth, grains and metals were the key goods in terms of which other commodities were valued. No single commodity was necessarily the sole means of payment or sole unit of account; the existence of multiple standardized units of account allowed for widespread and highly developed specialization in production, trade and commerce, and government receipts and payments, 'even where units of account do not also serve as stores of value' (Levenson and Randall, 1966, p. 325). Changes in the supply of and demand for commodities could alter the equivalencies over time, but the system remained workable so long as relative prices did not change too rapidly. Moreover, equivalencies permit intertemporal transactions such as the rendering of labour or perishable commodities for requital in some other form at some other time (as is illustrated in the previous quotation from Einzig). Any such 'stored up' claim is in essence a financial asset, though probably not a transferable or negotiable asset.

If, as history thus suggests, systems of barter, equivalencies and partial monies have not prevented the emergence of specialization and trade and the associated growth of productivity, why should developing countries be in haste to adopt general purpose money? The answer is that fully developed money gives much more scope, if not positive encouragement, to specialization, trade and growth. The important point about general purpose money is that, because it can perform, for any one person, any of the various distinct functions discharged separately by partial monies, it simultaneously facilitates—for the community as a whole—exchange, calculation, measurements, wealth-holding, lending and borrowing. Partial monies, etc., work, but they are very limiting; fully developed money increases the potential of the domestic economy and links it to the world economy (see Bohannan, 1967, for an example of such an expansion of a primitive economy).

Moreover, the transactions costs of general purpose money are very much less than those of partial monies. Brunner and Meltzer in a recent important paper offer a modern and rigorous restatement of the individual benefits and social benefits of using money. Their notable contribution, however, is to demonstrate that 'the use of money encourages the development of the market system by lowering the costs of acquiring information and transacting'. Although Brunner and Meltzer identify money with medium of exchange, they implicitly mean general purpose money, which they see, correctly, as 'a substitute for investment in information and labour allocated to search' (Brunner and Meltzer, 1971, pp. 786–800).

It is general purpose money which Eric Furness had in mind when he wrote:

> When the individual is paid for his goods and services in money he can choose from an immense range the goods and services he wants to take in exchange; he can choose the time at which he acquires these commodities; he can decide with ease what portions of his income to consume and which to save; and he can choose how to invest his savings. And ... it is of the utmost importance that savings can be made and transferred in the form of money, because only in this way can the savings of the many individuals in society be transmuted into the capital goods needed for economic growth. [Furness, 1975, p. 6]

The scope for further monetization is still very considerable in most less developed countries. One should not be deceived by observations that virtually all inhabitants of poor countries use money to some extent into thinking that non-monetary economic activity has diminished to unimportance. The jam may be spread widely, but it is often still spread thinly. Fisk reminds us that non-monetized production and exchange continue to play a large role in the rural areas of the underdeveloped world, notably among the producers of food but also in cloth-making, house-building, and the provision of local water, fuel and transport.

> In fact ... the majority of the population outside the main towns depends very heavily upon non-monetary production for a large part of the essentials of living. The subsistence sector as a group of people wholly outside the monetary sector may have become sufficiently small to be ignored in most countries, but the monetary sector, similarly defined (i.e. only those wholly independent of non-monetary economic activity) would also be very small in most underdeveloped countries. [Fisk, 1971]

If monetization is such a positive aid to economic development, it is clearly important to promote the process. And once growth is under way it will, of itself, raise further the demand for money. We may quote Brunner and Meltzer in support of the latter point:

> The magnitude of the net social productivity of money is not constant but varies with the degree of uncertainty about market conditions .... Large fluctuations in economic activity also raise costs of acquiring information and the productivity of money. Our analysis implies that *the demand for mediums of exchange is higher in periods of rapid change* than in periods of gradual or relatively steady change. The longer the period of steady, gradual change continues, the lower the productivity of money and the smaller the demand for assets that reduce costs of acquiring information by serving as mediums of exchange. [Brunner and Meltzer, 1971, p. 800; italics supplied]

The scope for monetization (in other words, the displacement of partial monies, etc., by general purpose money) will be considerably determined by the existing nature of demand for various services which money provides and/or functions which money performs. It is surely mistaken to view the demand for money in less developed countries from the standpoint of demand for money theories—notably of the type of Keynesian liquidity preference and its descendants—which have been forged in and tested for advanced economies. This type of theory, and its related empirical work, focuses on marginal adjustments to interest rates, prices, incomes and asset portfolios, in the light of fairly

generally accepted ideas about people's motives for holding
fully developed money within the context of the already
monetized economy in the short period. In considering the
demand for money in less developed economies, it is by
no means clear (*pace* Brunner and Meltzer, 1971, p. 784)
that we can even hope to make an operational distinction
between the motives for holding money (such as anticipation
of interest rate changes) and the demand for the functions
(such as store of value) which money performs. I have
therefore elected to discuss the subject in an intuitive way,
preferring eclectic—even *a priori*—theorizing to rigorous
model-building and econometric testing. While this seemingly lax approach may offend the purer social 'scientists',
and could scarce be defensible if refined ideas and relevant
testable data were available, I do not think it is too sinful
a way to go about the job when there is no theoretical
consensus about (indeed, few attempts at a theory), and
negligible empirical investigation of, the demand for money
in underdeveloped countries.

In low-income societies it is probable that the store of
value function is relatively more important than the other
roles of money than is the case in advanced societies. Moreover, it is the desire for money as a store of value that
may be best played upon to accelerate monetization (increase
the demand for fully developed money). As the people in
developing economies become acquainted with new and durable goods, it becomes obvious to them that many desirable
commodities cannot be obtained from current savings in
any relatively short production and consumption period,
but must be financed from the cumulative savings of a
number of such periods. It is equally obvious that a number
of items which may serve as stores of value (partial money)
in closed societies or for short periods will not suit that
purpose in more open, expanding, societies or in the longer
run. Purposeful saving then requires a store of value which
(1) will either be directly acceptable in payment when eventually applied to that function or convertible into means

of payment and (2) will not deteriorate rapidly. As the horizons of their spending plans lengthen, people therefore move away from illiquid or perishable assets towards financial assets of high liquidity—and the most liquid asset is fully developed money. Moreover, people may be motivated to produce more output so as, more rapidly than otherwise, to amass savings in order to buy appealing new goods; and the new goods will almost certainly have to be bought with fully developed money. We are describing here part of the dynamic process of social change—the conversion of a relatively closed, rigid, static society into one that is more open, flexible, productive and growing.

> From a policy point of view, the path to economic development in a society of transitional subsistence production units lies to a very large extent in increasing the level of participation in the monetary economy, for only with the catalysis of money do the full advantages of specialization, division of labor, and large-scale capital formation, upon which most economic development depends, become accessible. For this reason, the response of the subsistence production units to the opportunities and incentives offered by contact with the monetary sector, and the means available for intervention to accelerate and enhance that response, are of particular theoretical and practical interest. [Fisk, 1975a, pp. 75–6]

The use of general purpose money as a store of value promotes the division of labour between saving and investment, thus probably both raising the investment : income ratio and improving the allocation of investible resources. (Strictly speaking, this point applies, in some degree, to saving held in the form of any financial asset and not solely in money. But in a developing economy, general purpose money will be the first financial asset met by most people.) And general purpose money serves also—as has already been emphasized—as a measure of value and means of payment. Any community which is moving from subsistence production or a limited form of specialization and exchange towards a widespread and pervasive exchange economy will have many incentives to adopt general purpose money. We may use here to advantage a model developed by E. K. Fisk

(1964) which illuminates the role of monetization in the transition from subsistence to market production and suggests some ways in which demand for money is engendered.

A key concept in Fisk's analysis is that of the *utility of money for spending*. (General purpose money is not referred to as such by Fisk—he uses the term 'cash'—but fully developed money is necessarily implied in his analysis, since cash is required in exchange for certain incentive goods and services, must be storable, and needs to be of uniform unit value.) The demand for money to spend, and hence the amount that a subsistence producer will want to earn, will depend very much upon his opportunities for spending it. In this sense, money needs or depends on a market in order to reap utility (whereas, as we have seen, markets can function—albeit restrictedly—without money). Money is of little use to the subsistence producer unless it gives him ready command over commodities he wants and does not already have in sufficient quantities. Until then the 'utility of money' will be low. In Fisk's words, 'At 5/- a bottle, beer may be acceptable as an occasional luxury and worth the money, but when the cost is 5/- plus a six-day walk, the relative utility of the 5/- as a means of obtaining satisfaction is greatly reduced' (Fisk, 1964, p. 166). Fisk uses as an indicator of the utility of money the amount of labour that any subsistence economic unit will devote to earning any specific sum.

The greater is the readily available range of purchasables, the greater will be the utility of money for any individual. However, the provision of purchasable goods and services to a hitherto non-monetized community may depend upon entrepreneurship. And if it does, some minimum level of prospective money sales will be necessary before any entrepreneur will attempt to provide new purchasables to such a community.

As the prospective sales value in any area depends on the available amount of spending money in the area and so, ultimately, on the money income of the area, it is of course possible that an area with little or no money income would never attract an entrepreneur from an outside, advanced, region. However, if some contact with the outside advanced world is established the subsistence economy will start on the road to rapid transformation (see the Appendix to this chapter, where Fisk's argument about the growth relationship between utility of money, labour input and income is set out). Fisk's virtuous circle story of increasing utility of money interacting with rising levels of production and income begins with the occasional visits, to the pre-monetized group, of an itinerant trader offering a modest range of consumer goods for cash sale. He will make his first call when he judges that the pool of spendable cash in the area—say a remote village—seems likely to provide enough sales to justify his visit. The trader makes available to the village community goods that hitherto were not readily obtainable; this increased availability of goods will raise the utility of money and cause people to seek more of it by producing more saleable output. The consequent and continued expansion of their money income will raise the potentially spendable stock of money in the area. Sooner or later this will prompt some entrepreneur to open a village store which offers, for cash, 'a wider range of goods available at all times' (Fisk, 1964, p. 169). The utility of money therefore increases again, stimulating the villagers to produce yet more saleable output in order to earn more cash income. As this occurs, more and more shops will be established, thus again raising the utility of money; and so on. In sum, the greater the range of goods and services readily available for purchase, the greater will be the utility of money to peasant producers and the more they will wish to earn. The more money they earn, the more attractive it becomes to merchants to improve 'the range, quality and accessibility of goods and services available for purchase in the area ... The utility of money will therefore be some function of total income in the area' (Fisk, 1964, p. 169).

Fisk's analysis also brings out that the utility of money

rises in discrete, discontinuous jumps and—because the virtuous circle may turn vicious at various times—suggests
that incentives may be desirable in order to push monetization and economic development from one jump-off point
to the next. He proposes that any or all of the following
'artificial' policy measures should be imposed from outside
(i.e., by government): an increase—by persuasion or force
—in cash production of the area; an increase in the cash
return per unit of labour; and an increase in the utility
of money brought about by the subsidized provision of
saleable goods and services (Fisk, 1964, p. 172).

It is evident that Fisk's analysis of the demand for money
in the early stages of monetization, and the policy proposals
to which it leads, concentrate on the spending service which
fully developed money provides. But, in the light of our
earlier discussions, it should be apparent that the store of
value and non-commercial characteristics of money may
also be played upon to raise the demand for general purpose
money and promote monetization.

D. W. Stammer (1970) has noticed that demand for money
as a store of value will extend its utility, as also will the
desire to hold money for status (the demand for money
for status is logically separate from the demand for money
as a store of value, but Stammer collapses the two into
one). A paper by C. A. Blyth (1969) is at least suggestive
that the urge to earn cash income is prompted by more
than the mere desire to spend on attractive consumer goods.
Blyth not only draws attention to the tendency—in villages
on South Pacific islands—for marginal propensities to save
money to increase as village money incomes increase (the
store of value effect?), but he also notes that 'prestige expenditures', on gifts, gambling, churches and so forth, 'are
very responsive, to changes in [money] income' (Blyth, 1969,
p. 367). This may reasonably be interpreted as some justification for our view that the demand for money in developing
societies has its roots in more than the need for a medium

that is both acceptable and necessary in exchange for commodities.

It is fairly generally agreed among economists that the reasons for holding money may be divided broadly into transactions and assets motives. Our earlier discussion, of course, suggests that this terminology must be interpreted very loosely since, for example, 'transactions' embrace payments generally and not just in market exchange, while 'assets' may be desired for social status as well as for earning power and capital gain. Nevertheless, these qualifications need not prevent us from proceeding to discuss analyses based on the division between 'transactions' and 'assets' motives for holding general purpose money.

We may begin by disposing quickly of the transactions motive. Theoreticians agree, and empirical work confirms, that the transactions motive for holding money depends principally on the level of current income and the rate of change of prices, actual or anticipated in both cases. (This summary statement is not, of course, intended to be read as dismissing the influence of permanent incomes, expenditure levels and rates of interest which Baumol, 1952, and others have drawn to our attention.) Adekunle (1968) adopts a generalized 'expectations' approach to the demand for money which avoids distinguishing between actual and anticipated income and price levels. For the purpose of the decision to hold money, incomes and prices are always 'expected', but the nature of the 'expectations function' may vary from place to place and time to time. Adekunle argues that the expectations will be more static the shorter the length of 'the representative economic horizon', and that shorter economic time horizons have been observed to pertain in less developed than in developed economies. It follows, he claims, that income expectations will be relatively static in less developed countries and the expected value of the income variable will depend predominantly on its current measured value. Adekunle's view that 'in forecasting income and rates of change in prices, one would expect greater weight to be given to recent experiences in less developed than in developed economies' seems to be verified by his empirical tests (Adekunle, 1968, pp. 226–30, 245–6).

It is further agreed that the income elasticity of the demand for money is universally positive and is higher in less developed than in developed economies (Thirlwall, 1974, pp. 107–8). Two complications, however, are evident. One— which will be discussed in more detail later on—is that empirical tests of the relationship between desired money holdings and levels of income have generally used a broader concept of money than has been employed so far in this book. The other, linked to our previous paragraph and of a fundamental nature, is that the income elasticity of money demand embraces more than the transactions motive for holding money: the asset motive is also related to the level of income.

As has already been remarked, money is but one of many alternative forms of holding wealth or storing value. The available asset forms are either physical or financial, and fully developed money is distinctive in the latter class. We have earlier stressed the supreme liquidity of this general purpose money, which is simultaneously a store of wealth and an immediately useable means of payment. The asset demand for money is generally reckoned to be positively related to real income. As Adekunle suggests (1968, pp. 231–3), this is a reasonable view, even though (not surprisingly!) it has not yet been possible empirically to disentangle the observed positive income elasticity of demand for money into transactions and asset motives. It does seem clear that the supreme liquidity of money makes it a very attractive asset in developing economies. To start with, there are in these economies few alternative financial assets of any form, let alone of a highly liquid nature, and not many physical assets embody liquidity; hence the strong demand in these countries for assets such as jewellery, which, though lacking the means of payment characteristic of fully developed money, rate highly as stores of value and consequently embody certain degrees of liquidity. Second, the shorter decision-time horizons, and the more uncertain economic and social conditions, that prevail in less developed than in developed economies seem to generate a stronger liquid asset demand for money in the former countries than in the latter (this point joins, of course, to the preceding one about the limited availability of alternative liquid assets in the poorer countries). Adekunle quotes Friedman and Schwartz with effect: 'the major virtue of cash as an asset is its versatility. It involves a minimum of commitment and provides a maximum of flexibility to meet emergencies and to take advantage of opportunities. The more uncertain the future, the greater the value of such flexibility and hence the greater the demand for money is likely to be' (quoted by Adekunle, 1968, p. 232). These points certainly give intuitive support to the view that the asset motive for holding money is a powerful component of the high income elasticity of demand for money observed in developing economies. This is likely to remain true despite Adekunle's caveat that existence near the minimum level of subsistence may make it impossible for people to forgo even the scant returns that may be obtained from holding illiquid earning assets rather than money.

It has been conventional to treat the asset demand for money as competitive with the demand for other assets and to focus, therefore, on the substitution effects between money and alternative assets as determinants of the desire to hold money as an asset (see Adekunle, 1968, pp. 233–4 and the references cited therein). The substitution approach to the question leads one to compare the liquidity, risk and real yield on various alternative assets and to emphasize expected marginal changes on the values of relevant variables, in particular the expected rate of inflation. Adekunle suggests, but it can be put no stronger, that 'for the less developed group substitution possibilities relating both to financial and to real assets seem to be important'. He also believes in the importance of real asset substitutes for money-holding in areas where income is near the subsistence minimum and consumption consists predominantly of necessities. 'This means that money holdings will be particularly sensitive to the yield on real assets' (Adekunle, 1968, pp. 253, 236). By contrast, R. I. McKinnon approaches the demand for money in a way which specifically rejects the asset substitution model, at least so far as developing economies are concerned. (McKinnon, 1973, Chapter 5, presents a general critique of conventional theory.) He offers the alternative idea that the demand for money, in developing economies ('fragmented economic environment'), is complementary to the demand for physical capital goods. In order that the importance of McKinnon's novel approach be appreciated, it is necessary to spend a few paragraphs in outlining the essence of his ideas.

McKinnon first emphasizes the imperfect, distorted, uncertain and 'fragmented' economic conditions that generally pertain in low-income countries. (See McKinnon, 1973, Chapters 2 and 3, in which fragmentation is defined as follows: 'firms and households are so isolated that they face different effective prices for land, labour, capital and produced commodities and do not have access to the same technologies.' Modern fragmentation has been 'largely' due to governments, and hence the concept goes beyond the familiar idea of dualism arising from the implantation of an export enclave into a hitherto subsistence economy.) McKinnon then argues that under such conditions money has a peculiarly important role to play in improving the quality and increasing the quantity of capital formation. But the usefulness of money depends on people's willingness to hold it and this in turn is influenced, among other things, by the price level. Specifically, in McKinnon's analysis 'money's attractiveness depends on some combination of the percentage rate of inflation, $\dot{P}$ . . . , the nominal interest rate on bank deposits, d, and the "convenience" of holding money . . .' (1973, p. 39). It must here be pointed out that McKinnon works with a broad definition of money, inclusive of interest-bearing deposits as well as demand deposits and currency. Individuals, households and firms adapt their holdings of real money, says McKinnon, to their anticipated real returns on holding money. The anticipated real rate of return on money may be written as $d - \dot{P}^*$ where $\dot{P}^*$ is the anticipated rate of inflation. Once economic units have established their expectations about this real rate of return on holding money, a stable demand for real money balances may be inferred in relation to any level of income. McKinnon (1973, p. 40) promises 'evidence that firms and households in poor countries are quite sensitive to $d - \dot{P}^*$ in determining their preferred ratio of money holdings to income'. (The evidence referred to is supplied in McKinnon's Chapter 8 but, as will be shown, is not wholly convincing.)

We have presented, to this point, a view which suggests that inflation would be harmful to the process of monetization. And McKinnon goes much further, arguing that inflation can retard the rate of growth of output, through its adverse effects on propensities to save and invest. Moreover, given McKinnon's premise that the demand for real money balances and the demand for physical capital are highly complementary, he believes that the conditions that make real money attractive to hold also encourage physical capital formation and vice-versa.

McKinnon's assumptions about the fragmented nature of poor economies, the generally small size therein of private firms, the general lack of finance external to the firm and the lumpiness of investment all imply that substantial totals of personal (equity) purchasing power are required whenever investment is undertaken. Hence, the average ratio of real money balances to income will increase if the desired rate of investment, and so the related volume of prerequisite savings, increases at any level of income. 'Average cash balance holdings, therefore, are positively related to the propensity to invest (save) under the formal constraint that all investments are "self-financed"—as indeed some always are in practice' (McKinnon, 1973, p. 58). Emphasizing the non-static nature of the demand for money, McKinnon brings out that the accumulation of self-owned money balances is a preparatory means, over the relevant necessary period of time, to the end act of physical capital formation. Money, to use his word, is a *conduit* through which accumulation of an investible sum occurs.

McKinnon conceives of an average demand to hold money, the determinants of which include the proportion of income invested (I/Y), the transactions motive for holding money (governed by current income, Y) and the real rate of return on the asset money ($d - \dot{P}*$). If we write ($M/P)^D$ to represent the desired stock of real money (i.e. nominal money deflated by a comprehensive price index of goods), the money demand function is

$$(M/P)^D = f(Y, I/Y, d - \dot{P}*)$$

McKinnon points out that the conventional neoclassical demand for money function contains a term r, the real rate of return on physical capital, in lieu of the investment: income ratio (I/Y) in his function. Of course, he says, the use of a single real rate of return on capital that is also the uniform opportunity cost of holding money is misleading in the underdeveloped world where actual rates of return vary greatly at, and within, the margin. The rate of return to physical capital can be conceived of only in an average sense, $\bar{r}$, 'with a given dispersion around it measuring the variable productivity of capital among firm-households' (McKinnon, 1973, p. 59). If $\bar{r}$ should rise in response to some exogenous economic change, then desired investment would increase; this would occasion a rise in I/Y and so, in terms of his equation, would promote increased demand for real money balances. In the poor, fragmented economy where firms depend upon self-finance, a rise in the average rate of return to physical capital increases, rather than decreases, the demand for real money because enterprises will set out to accumulate money in order eventually to undertake new investment. Thus

> the traditional portfolio approach treats money and capital as substitutable forms of wealth holding in a quite static sense where the accumulation process per se is ignored. However, if money is viewed as a conduit through which accumulation takes place—rather than as a competing asset—the demand for money rises *pari passu* with the productivity of physical capital. [McKinnon, 1973, p. 60]

Further, says McKinnon, self-financed investment will increase over a significant range of opportunities if the real return on holding money increases. This effect occurs because the increased return on holding money reduces the opportunity cost of internal saving for the purpose of eventually purchasing capital goods. (It should here be remembered that McKinnon works with a broad definition of money. If money is more narrowly regarded as excluding interest-bearing bank deposits, then it would only be possible to raise $d - \dot{P}^*$ by reducing the general price level or, more correctly, by creating expectations thereof.)

The above analysis has its logical limit, namely, the point at which the real return on holding money has risen to equality with a firm's best anticipated return, at or within the margin, on self-financed investment. In other words, the 'competing asset' effect overwhelms the 'conduit' effect once the real return on holding money exceeds that anticipated from capital formation. In the underdeveloped economy, however, there is every reason to believe that the limiting point is remote and that increases in the real rate of return on holding money may be promoted without jeopardizing investment. This is because of the importance of intramarginal investment opportunities arising from the fragmented nature of underdeveloped economies. The investment possibilities for the individual business are not confined to the investment margin of the whole economy but include also some intramarginal 'quantum investments in new technologies', which may displace traditional methods of production (but which may not have been undertaken previously for want of finance). The 'lumpiness' of such investment in the fragmented economy means that the average return to physical capital need not fall, and may remain substantially above $d - \dot{P}^*$, as the total volume of new investment increases. The lumpy, discontinuous nature of investment opportunities confronting the individual enterprise provides another argument for ensuring that money becomes and remains an attractive store of value. For otherwise sheer poverty will discourage people from making consumption sacrifices in order to finance lump-sum investments. It is thus extremely important that inflation be prevented and McKinnon, with broad money in mind, advocates also high rates of interest on bank deposits.

The 'conduit' argument is not the only reason for complementarity between the demand for money to hold and that for physical capital. McKinnon seems to have overlooked the important point that firms need liquid working capital and that the demand for money balances for this purpose grows (absolutely, but not necessarily proportionally) with the scale of a firm's operations. It may be, however, that McKinnon implicitly subsumes this point under transactions demand or alternatively, as may perhaps be read into his first sentence on p. 87, that he regards monetary working capital (i.e. distinct from stocks and work-in-progress) as in essence similar to real investment and therefore part of it. This possible explanation, however, seems contradicted by his frequent and generally careful other emphasis on the physical nature of real investment. In any case, it does seem that money working capital is such an important complement to physical capital as to have deserved explicit notice. This is especially so for those cash-crop farmers in underdeveloped countries who have abandoned all subsistence production in order to specialize in marketable non-food crops. These farmers require money balances (or need to be able to obtain credit) with which to buy their food and other requirements (see Myint, 1965, pp. 47–8, 70).

What has empirical work to say for these various theories

about the demand for money in underdeveloped economies? It must first be said that there is very little published empirical work on the subject. Adekunle's study has been referred to, his broad conclusion being that 'interest rates, current real income, and expected rates of change in prices seem to be the appropriate variables in the money-demand function of these [less developed] countries' (Adekunle, 1968, p. 253). Most of the other relevant work is cited by Thirlwall (1974, p. 108). All concur that the income elasticity of demand for money is higher in less developed than in more developed economies. A pregnant remark appears in the standard modern textbook on the demand for money: 'in certain countries where the financial structure is relatively less sophisticated, for example, Chile and Argentina, the income elasticity of demand is well above unity, suggesting that in these economies the motives underlying money holding encompass much more than transactions and precautionary considerations' (Laidler, 1977, p. 157). Actual estimates of income elasticities of demand for money vary, even within developing countries, according to the definition of money employed. The elasticity value is generally much higher when a broad definition of money (i.e. including interest-bearing deposits) is taken. As Thirlwall observes, the much higher elasticity of demand for broad than for narrow money is probably related to the substitution of interest-bearing deposits for other forms of saving (including currency and demand deposits) as the financial system develops and the yield obtainable on interest-bearing deposits becomes generally apparent. In this context, interest-bearing bank deposits resemble other financial assets rather than narrow money.

As such, a high income elasticity of demand for money, taking a broad definition of money, cannot be taken as indicative of an extensive release of resources for investment. The resources would probably have been freed to some extent by the act of saving in a different form. [Thirlwall, 1974, p. 108]

Published empirical work does not yet permit any general inferences about the demand function for general purpose money narrowly defined (M_1). Chapter 8 of McKinnon (1973) does not directly test the money demand function of Chapter 6; this is a disappointment because we learn nothing tangible about the influences of transactions, complementarity and substitution effects even on the demand for broadly defined money (to which McKinnon's money demand function relates). We can, however, squeeze out of McKinnon's book the notion that less liquid interest-bearing deposits are much more sensitive (rising rapidly in periods of price stability and declining equally fast in periods of inflation) than narrow, liquid money (M_1) to changes in the price level 'Because time and savings deposits are not directly usable, as a means of payment ...' (McKinnon, 1973, p. 105). Similarly, an extremely interesting study by Trescott (1972) shows that in Thailand over a twenty-year period M_1 has been much more stable in relation to the growth of national income than M_2 (broader money) and other near liquid assets. For liquid financial assets, broadly defined, the Thai public displayed income elasticity of demand 'substantially greater than unity' over the twenty-year period, in which real gross national product increased sixfold, currency holdings increased twofold, demand deposits fifteenfold, savings bank deposits twentyfold, government securities holdings twentyfold and time deposits two hundredfold (Trescott, 1972, p. 264). Finally, the rising trend value of income velocity of circulation (implying income inelastic demand for M_1) observed in the Philippines (1946–65) has been attributed to rapid growth of interest-bearing deposits and other near-moneys (Treadgold, 1969).

It is obvious that in Thailand there were shifts in the pattern of income-induced demand for financial assets, most notably away from M_1 towards near liquid financial assets. Trescott attributes the very substantial growth of other asset holdings relative to narrow general purpose money to: stable price expectations, owing to tight monetary and fiscal policies after 1955; restrictions on the import of non-monetary gold, in which there had hitherto been a large local market; substantial increases in rates of interest on financial assets; and a great extension of branch banking (Trescott, 1972, pp. 270–5). Nevertheless, the income elasticity of demand for M_1 (currency and demand deposits) remained stable, at about unity, over the period, although after 1955 the income elasticity of demand for currency fell while that for demand deposits rose to an apparently offsetting degree. The demand for M_1 seemed unaffected by rate of interest changes, and Trescott infers that M_1 demand is essentially for transactions purposes only. One cannot be sure, however, that the store of value demand for narrow money dried up wholly in Thailand in the period under consideration or that it would do so similarly in other economies reaching the same stage of development. This is because substantial basic structural changes in the economy may blur the impor- tance of money as a store of value. In the Thai context of 1947–67, Trescott rightly makes much of the shifting composition of the national income, away from agricultural– rural sources towards industrial/service–urban sources.

> Nonagricultural income has increased heavily in the relatively urbanized, monetized 'modern' sector of the economy. Much of the increase has come in the form of business and property income, accruing to the relatively well-to-do. Our findings imply that the relation between liquid-asset demand and GNP will be unstable to the extent that the composition of GNP is unstable.
>
> [Trescott, 1972, p. 268]

Structural change is at the heart of economic development, but it would be mistaken therefore to infer that the demand for narrow money is unimportant. For monetization is bound up with and facilitates structural change, among other things. If a store of value demand for money can be identified in the agricultural sector, it is important to capitalize on that in promoting monetization in those countries in which agriculture is still predominant, that is, in almost all underde- veloped countries. The fact that the agricultural sector de-

clines in importance as economic development proceeds is
a red herring, as also is controversy about the stability
of the demand for money. One can do no better than endorse
Adekunle's acknowledgement of that controversy as high-
lighting 'a process whereby, as an economy develops, these
money substitutes [alternative financial assets] become more
and more important in the demand-for-money relationship
and some will argue, ultimately render the relationship use-
less in tracing the effects of changes in the stock of money'
(Adekunle, 1968, p. 236).

It is time to sum up this somewhat circuitous tour of monetary philosophy, history, theory and evidence. Fortunately,
a few major landmarks are evident. First, inflation may
retard severely the spread of monetized transactions in an
economy that still relies, to any significant extent, on subsistence production, barter or other pre-monetary forms of
economic organization. By calling into question the worth
of money as a store of value, inflation inhibits the displacement of partial by general purpose monies. Since monetization facilitates specialization—in production (by affecting
goods and factor markets) and between saving and investment—which generates increased output and consumption
per head, it follows that inflation is harmful to the economic
growth of any society that is still in the process of monetization. Secondly, and more positively, it is desirable to promote
monetization of those countries in which general purpose
token money is not pervasive. It follows, thirdly, that the
makers of economic policy should study the motives for
which people adopt general purpose money and the circumstances in which they are prone to do so. It seems here
that wider and more readily available opportunities to effect
monetary purchases of goods and services is important.
However, and fourthly, economists have hitherto given insufficient attention to non-exchange payments which may
nevertheless engender transactions demand for money. And
fifthly, in the asset (store of value) demand for money,

status and other social motives, complementarity, and working capital requirements should be considered, as well as the relative yield variable which has virtually dominated the asset approach in demand for money analysis to date. The neglect, by economic theorists, of these various important considerations is reflected in the poverty of empirical conclusions about the demand for money in underdeveloped societies. Not much more has been discovered than that the demand for narrow money is closely related to income, with an income elasticity of about unity, irrespective of the income levels over which elasticity is calculated. It is surely time that the econometricians attempt to employ more imaginative money demand functions. McKinnon has given them some ideas to play with, and a few more may be gleaned from this chapter.

Further Reading

There is a large anthropological/ethnological literature on primitive and archaic monies which is distinct from the economic literature on money; of the latter, only a small part relates to money in underdeveloped societies. Between the separate disciplinary fields there are few reconciliatory links. Grierson (1977) gives a brief and authoritative account of the non-economic literature and his essay is replete with further references. Brunner and Meltzer (1971) is to my mind the best succinct modern economic analysis of the nature and uses of money, although Newlyn (1971) is still to be recommended. It will be evident that I have been influenced by Hicks (1967, 1969), especially by his views on the importance of money as a store of value. Incidentally, Hicks's superb lectures on 'The Two Triads' (1967) are designed to reconcile—successfully, in my view—the threefold characteristics of money with Keynes's three motives for holding money. (More generally, Hicks has been taken to task by Harris, 1969.) Einzig (1949) made a gallant attempt to knit together the theories of economists and the observations of anthropologists, ethnologists and historians; his book is still required reading for scholars. Briefer reconciliations of economic theory and anthropological, etc., observations have been attempted by Karl Polanyi (1968) and those associated with him: Dalton (1967) is the best representative work of this school.

A work of broad perspective, built on a wide reading of secondary sources, is Morgan (1965); this book is recommended for junior students.

A modern work dealing with money in present-day developing countries is McKinnon (1973) which is recommended especially for its seminal ideas on the demand for money (Chapters 4–6). A related work, but not to my mind so persuasive, is Shaw (1973). Fisk (1964) is well worth attention for his ideas on monetization. Adekunle (1968) and Trescott (1972) are two useful contributions to the undercultivated field of empirical studies of money in developing countries. A just-published study by Fry (1978) of ten Asian developing economies finds no support for McKinnon's complementarity thesis. However, Fry concedes that in the countries studied financial development has proceeded to such an advanced stage that modern financial assets other than M_2 money (as well as, of course, indigenous non-institutional assets) may be used as repositories of funds being accumulated for purposes of eventual real investment.

APPENDIX

E. K. Fisk's Model of the Transition of Producers from Pure Subsistence to Part-Time Participation in Monetized Transactions

The focus of analysis is a group of self-sufficient producers (the subsistence unit), enjoying what Fisk calls 'primitive affluence'. In other words, the customary needs of the group are easily satisfied by inputs of labour and natural resources that fall well short of available supplies. Spare capacity exists in the sense that, with given resources and techniques, output could readily be increased simply by working longer hours. But in the absence of local need or external demand for additional output, the group has no incentive to devote effort to producing it. The incentive for the unit to expand production above the customary level comes from contact with the outside world: it brings new goods to the attention and desire of the subsistence group, and it provides a cash market for the produce of the group. The strength of the incentive to the subsistence unit to engage in additional/supplementary production for sale in the outside market (or to offer wage labour to outside employers) will depend on a comparison of the utility of money that can be earned with the disutility of the additional labour needed to earn it.

As has been explained in the text above, the utility of money to the subsistence producers depends upon their opportunities for spending it, and the greater is the utility of money to them the more of it they will wish to earn. The utility of money can be expressed within a labour supply curve 'in terms of the amount of labour that the subsistence unit would consider it just worthwhile to devote to earning any specific income. . . . there could be a large number of curves indicating the different level of utility [of any cash income] as the goods and services available for money improve' (Fisk, 1964, p. 167).

In Figure 4.1, cash income for the subsistence unit (Y) is measured on the vertical axis while the horizontal axis measures the labour input of the group (L). Curve U_1 represents the situation when the utility of money is very low. The subsistence unit will be prepared to give some labour in excess of subsistence requirements in order to earn a little spendable money but will quickly reach the point where the marginal utility of cash income falls below the marginal utility of leisure, at which stage the group will not be pre-

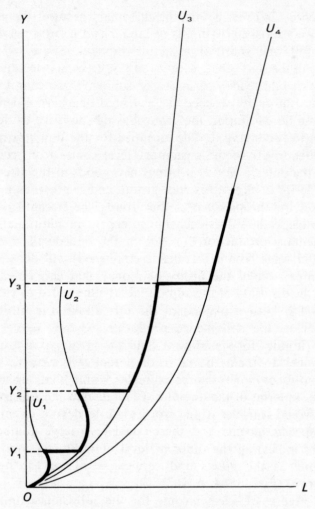

FIGURE 4.1 Utility of money.

pared to offer any further labour in order to earn additional cash income even though opportunities to do so may exist.

Subsequently, the *U* curve will turn backwards, reflecting that the effect of any increase in the cash return will be to reduce the total labour input. (The *U* curve may be identified as a group version of the familiar 'backward-bending supply curve of labour', which applies universally. Other things being equal, any labour supplier—group or individual—will withdraw effort sooner or later as the rate of reward for effort rises. Some of us may wish to climb very high on the vertical axis but we all have our turning point on the horizontal.) If a greater range of purchasables were readily available to the subsistence unit, the utility of money would be greater and the group would therefore be prepared to offer more labour hours to gain a given cash income. Given an income level, say Y_1, this situation would be represented by a point on curve U_2 (where the utility of money is always greater than under U_1 conditions); subsequent extensions of the utility of money income Y_1, calling forth successively more labour, could be represented by relevant points on curves U_3, U_4, and so on. The U curves as a set represent alternative labour supply curves at successively higher levels of utility of money.

Suppose that Y_1 represents the amount of group money income that prompts an itinerant trader to visit the subsistence group and offer new goods for sale. The availability of these goods will raise the utility of money and cause curve U_2 to become operative above income level Y_1. When total cash income rises—as a result of the input of more labour along the supply curve U_2—let us say to Y_2, a shopkeeper may be sufficiently encouraged to establish a full-time store in the area. The further and more readily available goods and services so proffered will again raise the utility of money and bring labour supply curve U_3 into play. Further rises in the cash income of the subsistence unit, Y_3 etc., will prompt further entrepreneurial initiatives (the establishment and expansion of shops, bars, cinemas, etc.), which in each case will raise the utility of money and bring labour supply curves U_4 etc. into operation. We may in Figure 4.1 trace out the U path (heavy line) which shows the course of labour inputs as the cash income of, and the utility of money to, the subsistence unit increase.

In Figure 4.2 we superimpose on the diagram of Figure

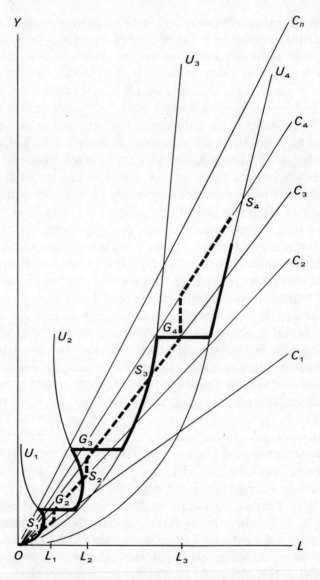

FIGURE 4.2 Utility of money and cash return for labour effort.

4.1 the rays OC_1, OC_2, OC_3, etc. These successively steeper lines from the origin represent progressively increasing cash returns per unit of labour. Cash return per unit of labour effort is:

$$\frac{\text{(Gross cash receipts} - \text{Cash costs)}}{\text{Labour input}}$$

Assuming constant returns to scale in production and taking the price at market centre (or port, in the common case of an exportable commodity) as given, then the variable element in cash return per unit of labour consists of the costs (in money and/or labour) of getting produce from the 'farm gate' to the market centre. These are the costs of processing, packaging, transporting, storing and marketing the produce. Facilities for these services are especially scarce and expensive in primitive economic regions in the early, tenuous stage of contact between subsistence groups and the advanced economy.

In Figure 4.2, ray OC_1 represents the (constant) rate of cash return per unit of labour effort when the subsistence unit enjoys little contact with the external advanced economy, derives no cost-saving externalities from the facilities of the latter, and has no incentive spontaneously to introduce scale-economizing methods. There are, however, a number of subsequent ways in which the unit cash costs of subsistence production may be reduced, thus raising the cash return per unit of labour. Suppose, for example, that a government road is built to join the subsistence area to a large market centre. This in itself will make travel between the two points easier and quicker and the transport costs attached to marketable produce may be further and considerably reduced if the government runs a bus or lorry service along the road. This kind of external benefit will effect a once-and-for-all cut in unit costs of production and present the subsistence unit with a better rate of cash return per unit of labour, say ray OC_2. Suppose, further, that this easier communication with the market encourages the subsistence group to increase its marketable production to a scale that would make it worthwhile for the group to install simple facilities for processing, grading and packing the produce before sending it to market. This would greatly reduce costs compared with the earlier stage of transporting unprocessed, ungraded and heavier raw produce to market. The cash return per unit of labour jumps now to rate OC_3. And so on for further cost-reducing methods introduced by the subsistence unit or cost-reducing externalities flowing from the outside world. The various increases in the rate of cash return per unit of labour will not occur smoothly but will take place in discontinuous jumps as either external benefits occur more or less by chance or, more commonly, as certain thresholds of group output and cash income are reached, at which it becomes worthwhile for the subsistence group to implement scale-economizing services in marketing and processing or for outsiders (government or entrepreneurs) to introduce services that confer economies on the subsistence unit. The points L_1, L_2, L_3 etc. on the horizontal axis represent the levels of labour input (and, by implication of abundant land and constant returns to scale, production) at which cost-reducing innovations occur. The dotted line traces out the path of cash return (the C path) as the unit rate of reward for labour effort leaps up each time a cost-reducing service comes into effect.

Consider now the relationship between the C path and the U path described earlier. The C path (heavy dotted line) shows the total cash income that the group has the opportunity to earn for increasing levels of labour input over time; the U path (heavy unbroken line) describes the supply of labour that the group will, over time, just offer to earn various levels of cash income. (I emphasize 'over time' because the process is one of continuous economic and social change.)

When the C path lies to the right of the U path (as, for example, between points S_1 and G_2) the amount of labour needed to earn a given level of cash income is greater than the amount of labour that such a cash income would justify on utility of money grounds. Hence the economic forces represented by the C path provide no incentive to increase the level of labour input and there will be contraction to S_1. S_1 is a point of stagnation, as also are S_2, S_3, S_4, etc. On the other hand, when the U path lies to the right of the C path (as, for example, between G_2 and S_2) for any income in the relevant range, the amount of labour that will be offered on utility-of-money grounds is more than the minimum labour necessary to earn that income; product and income thus rise in response to the 'excess' labour input. In these conditions, market forces provide an incentive for labour input to rise up to the next point where the paths intersect, viz. S_2. The origin and points G_2, G_3, G_4, etc., are therefore labelled 'growth points' by Fisk.

The development problem is to lift the subsistence region over the humps (e.g. $S_1 - G_2$) where there is inadequate incentive to increase marketable output. For this purpose, Fisk proposes the three measures of external government policy that have been noted in our main text, viz.: (1) an artificial increase in the level of production for sale (persuasion or force); (2) an artificial increase in the cash return per unit of labour (provision of scale-economizing facilities); and (3) an artificial increase in the utility of money (provision of better spending opportunities). He points out that

All three methods have been attempted in various places and at various times, though seldom in concert to obtain the greatest effect and often on an inadequate scale. The model makes it clear that, unless intervention is on a scale sufficient to force the subsistence unit right over the hump to the next growth point, natural growth cannot be resumed. It also shows clearly the advantages and economies to be obtained from concerted three-point intervention rather than a piece-meal approach. [Fisk, 1964, p. 172]

CHAPTER 5
The Money Supply

In so far as one may safely generalize about the large and diverse number of underdeveloped countries, it is essential to emphasize the important, if not indeed central, influence of the balance of international payments upon the domestic volume of money. Modern money, in the general purpose sense, came first to many of today's less developed countries from the outside world in payment for goods, services and tributes. In the terminology of balance-of-payments accounting, these payments could be traced either to exports or to capital inflow, the latter embracing not only official capital, such as tributes and the spoils of war, but also private investment capital in the form of coinage used to purchase local labour and materials for use in the export industries frequently established by foreign entrepreneurs. In this sense, a favourable balance of payments at one and the same time promoted monetization and provided a stock of money.

Some countries, no doubt had so little external trade as to have been virtually closed economies but possessed natural deposits of gold, silver, etc., from which sufficient coins could be wrought as monetization occurred. But those conditions obtained in few of the presently less developed countries. More commonly, the stock of money either originated wholly from abroad—through trade and investment—or was a mixture of local and foreign coinage. Certainly the former British colonies—including those in America—were often starved of coin, in some cases to the extent that gold and silver coin and bullion had to be reserved exclusively for external payments, with a consequent retardation of domestic monetization. The general historical condition in today's less developed countries—extending well into the twentieth century—was that the stock of money consisted predominantly of coinage and that its volume was chiefly, if not exclusively, determined by the balance of international payments. The stock of coin represented simply an accumulated physical surplus, over time, of incoming over outgoing international payments.

The eventual establishment of banks in a country meant that its stock of money ceased to be such a simple function of the balance of payments. For banks could add to the money supply by making loans which would create circulating bank notes or deposits, provided that the public were prepared to regard these bank liabilities as money equally with gold, silver and copper coins. However, the banks had to bear in mind the possibilities of depositors wishing to convert deposits into currency, and of depositors and bank note holders wanting to convert these claims into internationally acceptable money. The banks had, therefore, to maintain sufficient reserves of international money and local cash to satisfy any of the public's convertibility desires. So long as domestic money in a developing country was freely convertible into international money, the real limit on the banks' powers of credit creation was their ability to provide international money on demand.

Even when a country reached the bank money stage of financial development, it was still common for a high proportion of bank deposits to originate via the balance of payments. A favourable balance of autonomous international payments, whether effected by the import of coin or bullion or by international bank credits, first added directly to the domestic money supply. Secondly, the balance-of-payments surplus increased the international reserves of the banking system (wholly when effected directly into a domestic bank account and partially to the extent that coin or bullion entering the country in other ways was eventually deposited in a bank). The banks were thus provided with increased liquidity on which to base credit expansion and the wherewithal to meet any consequential demands by depositors for international money. Thus, even after an economy advanced from coin money alone to a combination of coinage and bank money, the balance of payments was the most important influence upon the supply of local money; and it remained so when, as in modern times, the private import of coin and bullion virtually ceased. Not until very recent years, marked by the emergence of more independent governments bent upon active credit policies and of more bank lending being directed towards non-trade activities, did the balance of payments begin to lose its dominating influence over the domestic money supply in most developing countries. It is therefore worth spending a few paragraphs on further description of the relationship between the balance of payments and the volume of local money, leading to a useful framework for analysing the determinants of change in the money supply under typical modern conditions.

With few exceptions, underdeveloped countries are open economies (many are small open economies), economic dualism is common, their financial development is stunted, and their exchange rates are fixed (or infrequently adjusted). On the basis of these observations, one may reasonably use as an expository device a generalized structural model which bears a fair resemblance to many underdeveloped countries today, and to many more at some stage of recent history (usually, at least to the point of political and economic independence). Typically, the economy contains, at one extreme, a large subsistence sector, composed of peasant farmers, fishermen and handicraftsmen, who go about their age-old occupations regardless of fluctuations in the money supply and rates of interest. At the other extreme may be found an export sector (often largely foreign-owned or financed) whose production is subject to overseas demand which lies, of course, beyond the influence of any local monetary authority. Not uncommonly, exports account for a substantial proportion of gross domestic product and investment takes place largely within the export sector. Investment is therefore influenced more by world market prospects for exports than by local monetary conditions. Indeed, in some cases one can go further and suggest that private investment is/was determined chiefly by foreign entrepreneurs in the light of international market and money conditions.

In such circumstances it is only the residual amount of domestic monetized production which is potentially responsive to any local monetary policy. In other words, we are left with construction, services and local manufacturing as the activities which might show orthodox responses to discretionary changes in the local money supply. In total, in an open underdeveloped country these industries are unlikely to account for a large share of economic activity.* It follows that, regardless of the intent of any local monetary authority, the scope for monetary expansion by way of bank lending to the private sector will be limited, at least initially. (As will be seen in later chapters, there may be scope in the longer term for lending to indigenous, small-scale, export producers whose efforts may be hampered by lack of credit; the present discussion, however, takes a narrow range of financial institutions with conservative lending attitudes as given.) Nor can government in a poor country, no matter what it may desire, expect to make great investment play with bank credit because public spending plans must also be subject to the constraints imposed by inelastic supplies of local real resources and by the balance of payments; public spending that defies these constraints leads inevitably

---

* While this broad description would not conflict with observation in most developing countries, statistical confirmation is hard to come by, owing to the imprecise and incomplete estimates of domestic product (especially so far as subsistence or non-market production is concerned) of developing countries in general. Some 'back of envelope' sums with available data for Papua New Guinea (1977) and the British Solomon Islands (1967) suggest that in each case only about a third of total output could be regarded as neither subsistence nor for export nor export-related.

to inflation. Further, the high marginal propensity to import and the scarcity of financial assets characteristic of such countries means that any domestic monetary expansion will be subject to considerable external drain. And so the balance of payments will remain the dominant element in the creation of local money, the more so if institutional arrangements prohibit, or severely curtail, the possibility of any generation of local money via the discretionary lending activities of a local monetary authority (as was the case under the currency board system common in colonial times, and as is still true of those countries who have elected to maintain high, if not indeed full, foreign exchange reserve backing for their local currencies).

While the conditions just described may seem rather unfamiliar to readers brought up in advanced economies, they were indeed common in underdeveloped countries until at least the 1960s and they reasonably describe the essentials for those many poor, albeit independent, nations whose economic welfare still depends critically upon exports and foreign investment. The general income-determination considerations for economies of this type have been drawn out by Newlyn (1969) and Furness (1975, pp. 193–202); the monetary aspects alone will now be outlined. (A fuller exposition of the operation of a typical 'dependent' monetary system may be found in Drake, 1969a, Chapter 4 and pp. 54–63.)

When the balance of international payments (i.e. the net proceeds of trade with, and autonomous capital flows and transfers from, foreign countries) is positive, its effect is to create claims on banks in the recipient country (bank money) and to endow the banking system with an equivalent volume of foreign exchange reserves. It is necessary here to make a point of considerable historical and analytical importance. The text has just referred to the foreign exchange reserves of 'the banking system'. By this term I mean all banking institutions, both central and commercial. Prior to the establishment of any central bank, the commercial banks held most of a nation's foreign exchange assets and undertook (in the absence of any exchange controls) to redeem domestic money for foreign exchange on demand at the going rate of exchange. As well as the banks, some countries had currency boards that were obliged to interchange local currency and foreign money at a fixed rate; and it was not uncommon also for governments, public authorities, firms and individuals to hold foreign currency balances. Strictly speaking, all of these various holdings of foreign reserves—together with any available lines of international credit—collectively constituted the nation's stock of foreign exchange reserves, analogous to the centralized official holdings of most central banks today. Moreover, notwithstanding the existence nowadays of local central banks, in some developing countries the commercial banks remain free to hold their own foreign exchange reserves and are not obliged to surrender, to the central bank, foreign currency received through trade and foreign investment activities of depositors. To take care of these various possibilities in what follows, we envisage that the commercial banks and the central bank may hold independently their separate foreign exchange assets (at this point we let the independent foreign exchange holdings of government and business drop out of sight as unimportant) and, correspondingly, we regard any fluctuations in commercial bank foreign exchange reserves as part of the net monetary movement in the balance-of-payments accounts. (In familiar tabular presentations of the balance of payments it is customary to rule a line under all autonomous international receipts and payments in order to add up these items and separate them from the equal and opposite accommodating change in a country's international reserves which is produced by the autonomous transactions in total. Under conditions by which a country's holdings of international reserves are centralized in the hands of an official central bank, fluctuations in commercial banks' foreign balances are included among autonomous capital flows so that accommodating—'below the line'—reserve changes refer only to changes in the foreign reserves of the central bank. By contrast, in countries where the commercial banks are permitted to deal freely in foreign exchange and hold independent foreign exchange balances, it is sensible to treat such balances as part of the nation's stock of foreign assets and to regard fluctuations in them as accommodating—'below the line'—transactions.)

The domestic money supply (bank deposits component) increases, in the first instance, by the amount of any balance-of-payments surplus. The equivalent increase in the reserves of the banking system provides the basis for a further, multiplied expansion of bank deposits via bank lending. The limits to this multiplied expansion of bank deposits depend not only on leakages, any minimum (customary or legal) reserves/deposits ratio observed by the banks and the volume of new reserves generated by the balance-of-payments surplus, but also on the willingness of the banks to make local loans and advances. There may be a point where the banks, however liquid they may be, do not think it desirable to undertake further lending locally, for want of sufficient demand for credit from customers whom the banks regard as creditworthy.

At this point, the balance of payments comes into the story again. It has been noticed historically in many countries that bank lending was closely correlated with the fortunes of foreign trade and investment (see, for example: Drake, 1969a, Chapter 4; Newlyn and Rowan, 1954; Newlyn, 1968). A favourable balance of payments meant that export industries were experiencing strong demand and/or that foreign investment capital was flowing into the country. In either case, producers then sought bank credit in order to expand output, while importers sought credit in order to cater for the increased demand for imports (consumer or capital goods) which followed, or was associated with, the increase in output and incomes generated by export growth and foreign investment. The generally higher level of activity also caused local construction, food-producing and service activities to flourish. The banks were well able to meet demands for credit for any of these purposes, because the balance-of-payments surplus had provided them with excess reserves.

Conversely, a balance-of-payments deficit meant a reduction of money supply and bank reserves, was associated with a general decline in the level of domestic economic activity, and implied a poor outlook for exports and a diminution of foreign investment. The banks had less opportunity and incentive to lend, and indeed often sought to reduce their levels of outstanding credit. These observations suggest a model in which the balance of payments is the main element in monetary change, with bank operations likely to magnify monetary changes in the same direction as the balance of payments, rather than offsetting the monetary (and activity) effects of balance-of-payments fluctuations. There was a so-called 'classical link' between the balance of payments and the local money supply.

However, there are no convincing *a priori* reasons why bank lending should inevitably fluctuate automatically in sympathy with the balance of payments. Certainly an autonomous balance-of-payments deficit would reduce the liquid reserves of the banking system; but branches of international banks were common, if not dominant, in many underdeveloped countries and they could surely have relied on their head offices to support any desired expansion of lending in a particular country by providing any necessary liquid reserves. In the days when expatriate banks had virtually unlimited freedom of operations in any single underdeveloped country, any international bank calculated and considered its liquidity position in a total sense, without undue concern for its liquidity in each country in which it operated. It would certainly have been possible for the banks in many countries to have managed their lending policies so as to offset the monetary consequences of swings in the balance of payments. But there was scant incentive for them to do so in economies that were dominated by international trade and investment and in which only a minority of economic activities was likely to show much response to variations in domestic credit conditions. Bank credit fluctuated in sympathy with international trade and investment not because of the liquid reserve consequences for the banks of changes in the balance of payments, but because lending opportunities were concentrated in the international trade sector.

So much for the model to which a common historical pattern gives rise. We need now to reconsider this model in the light of more recent events and assess its relevance to present conditions. We must also consider the ways in which the balance of payments and other determinants of monetary change affect the level of activity and income in today's less developed countries. But before entering these fields of discussion it is necessary to set out a framework for observing and analysing the sources of change in the money supply.

As is well understood, the components of modern money—currency and bank deposits in the hands of the public in any country—are liabilities respectively of the central monetary authority and the commercial banks. Since assets equal liabilities (including net worth) for any and every enterprise, the monetary liabilities of these monetary institutions must necessarily change whenever there is any change in their net assets (total assets minus the sum of non-monetary liabilities and net worth). Expansions or contractions in the volume of money can therefore be discovered and measured by calculating changes in the net assets of the monetary institutions. Further, the proximate sources of change in the volume of money may be traced to observable changes in particular categories of assets of the monetary institutions, notably net external assets (the change in which reflects the balance of payments) and domestic earning assets (the change in which reflects the balance of bank lending operations with the private and government sectors). None of this is to suggest that by observing changes in external and domestic assets of the monetary institutions we are able to explain the ultimate causes of money supply fluctuations (see also Furness, 1975, pp. 110–16). The recorded values of liabilities and assets of the banking system represent, after all, the outcome of a multiplicity of individual decisions about whether to buy or sell, borrow or repay, save or lend, hold currency, bank deposits or other assets and so on, and all either within the home economy or—to any permitted extent—abroad.

In short, the demand for money enters also into the determination of any equilibrium quantity of it and into the disposition of that quantity between the currency and bank deposits components. Nevertheless, it remains importantly true that the simple distinction between external and domestic sources of money supply is analytically illuminating. This is especially so for the many open underdeveloped countries which, for structural and institutional reasons, find that their quantities of money are powerfully influenced by external forces. Not only does any balance-of-payments surplus/deficit automatically create/extinguish an equivalent amount of domestic money, but also (in contrast to most advanced countries, which enjoy the institutional means to neutralize the effects of balance-of-payments fluctuations upon bank reserves) in open underdeveloped economies there has been a tendency for secondary domestic expansion/contraction to follow in the wake of the balance of payments. Moreover, because of the open nature of these economies, domestic credit expansion itself has considerable repercussions on the balance of payments.

A number of writers have set out frameworks of 'sources of change in the money supply' designed to reflect the fundamental division between external and domestic sources. (This is not the place to debate the relative merits of different forms of presentation, which can be found in Drake, 1969a, pp. 44–9; Wilson, 1957; King, 1957; Newlyn and Rowan, 1954; Hicks, *et al.*, 1957; Dorrance, 1970; Newlyn, 1968; and Furness, 1975, to cite a few.) We may here set down the bare essentials again (Table 5.1) and in doing so notice

TABLE 5.1   *Sources of Change in Money Supply[a]*

		$m
	Changes in net external assets of:	
	Commercial banks	117
	Central bank and/or other monetary authority	−40
equals (1)	*Total change in the net external assets of monetary system*	77
	Changes in loans and advances of commercial banks	315
plus	Changes in government borrowing from commercial banks	−30
plus	Changes in government borrowing from central bank/monetary authority	181
equals (2)	*Domestic credit expansion/contraction*	466
(1) plus (2)		
equals (3)	*Total change in financial assets of monetary system*	543
	Changes in inter-bank liabilities	8
plus	Changes in cash held by commercial banks (liability of monetary authority)	30
plus	Changes in other liabilities (net worth, etc.)	8
equals (4)	*Total change in non-monetary liabilities of banking system*	46
(3) minus (4)		
equals (5)	*Change in total monetary liabilities* of which:	497
	Change in currency outside banks	90
plus	Change in demand deposits[b]	134
equals (6)	*Change in money supply* (M_1)	224
plus	Change in fixed deposits	190
plus	Change in savings deposits	83
equals (7)	*Change in total monetary liabilities* (M_3)	497

[a] Illustrative figures referring to a defined period of time.

[b] Any change in official demand deposits can be deducted from item 6 to show the change in the volume of privately-held money.

the further point that domestic credit creation includes central bank lending (normally to government) as well as commercial bank credit activities.

Item 1 in Table 5.1 represents, of course, the balance of international payments, and it would be desirable to identify individually the various current and capital items that contribute to that balance and so to the change in external reserves. However, it is usually difficult to identify much more than items of visible trade for most underdeveloped countries, whereas net changes in the external assets of the monetary institutions can be measured precisely. Similarly, it may be difficult to trace the revenue, expenditure and financing flows underlying item 2, which represents the residual borrowing/repayments of the government and the private sector requiring recourse to the banking system. For practical reasons, therefore, the balance sheet approach to identification of sources of change in the money supply must generally be preferred to the more appealing approach based on disaggregated statistics.

When the relevant statistics for any underdeveloped country in any period are organized in a framework of this type, the important, and often dominant, role of the balance of payments will usually be evident (Furness, 1975, pp. 116–34 gives several African examples). The reasons for expecting this pattern are basically twofold: first, the openness of these economies means that exports, imports and capital flows necessarily loom large in relation to total monetized transactions; secondly, there is limited scope for non-inflationary domestic credit expansion chiefly because of the inelasticity of supply of real resources in so many underdeveloped countries, which limits the promotion of greater production through increased demand based on domestic credit expansion. (This latter point is reinforced to the extent that inflexible institutional arrangements may also inhibit the discretionary creation of money.)

Should domestic credit expansion, to whatever extent allowable, be attempted without regard to real resource constraints, either the balance of payments will suffer and/or inflation will ensue. These propositions are brought out very clearly in the work of J. J. Polak (1957) (see also Polak and Boissoneault, 1960; Polak and Argy, 1971; Newlyn, 1969; 1971, pp. 153–8; Furness, 1975, pp. 206–14). Polak's model and the early statistical investigations based upon it indicate that, with a constant velocity of circulation, a high and stable marginal propensity to import and a fixed exchange rate, the ratio of loss of external reserves to any given expansion of domestic credit approaches near to unity within at most three years. Since every credit expansion by the domestic monetary system would lead, under the given conditions, eventually to a corresponding loss of reserves, 'it might seem to follow that a country could not afford any permanent expansion of internal credit without endangering its balance of payments' (Polak, 1957, p. 34). However, domestic credit expansion can be sustained if it should be accompanied by a lasting improvement in the balance of payments. Further, and of central importance, the Polak analysis shows that the loss of foreign exchange reserves is reduced to the extent that money balances increase faster than income, i.e. to the extent that velocity of circulation slows down. Should this occur, a greater rate of domestic monetary expansion would be possible for any given level of reserves; indeed, other things being equal, a greater rate of domestic monetary expansion would be necessary in order to avert deflation, insofar as people should seek to achieve any desired higher marginal money : income ratio by reducing their rates of expenditure.

We have now reached the stage where we may move to a general discussion of the money supply, velocity, price level and output relationships, bearing in mind the analytical distinction between external and domestic sources of change in the money supply, and the underlying importance of the balance of payments.

In open underdeveloped countries, a sustained balance-of-payments surplus appears to be a necessary condition of sustained monetary expansion. Where discretionary domestic credit expansion is possible, it needs to be accompanied by a *continuing* tendency towards a balance-of-payments surplus if inflation and severe losses of external reserves are to be avoided (Polak, 1957, pp. 34–5). And where discretionary credit creation is inhibited by institutional rigidities the need for a balance-of-payments surplus is even more fundamental. Indeed, it has been shown that those underdeveloped countries which operate/operated automatic (usually colonial) monetary systems based on the balance of payments subject their economies to a potential *deflationary bias* owing to the lack of mechanisms for discretionary creation of local money. The deflationary tendencies of money supply systems which, as with the colonial currency boards, operated under fixed exchange rates and high—if not full—external reserve backing for domestic currency,* were noticed many years ago (e.g. Myint, 1954; 'Analyst', 1953; Hazelwood, 1954). An early expression of the idea was formulated during the postwar restructuring of the Philippine monetary system:

> When a system requiring a 100 per cent reserve against the note issue is applied to a growing economy, it may logically be expected to impart to it a deflationary bias. In order to create the larger money supply required for an increasing population and an ever-expanding domestic trade, it would be necessary for the country to have a persistently active balance of payments, which in itself would be a costly luxury for an under-developed economy. [Grove and Exter, 1948, p. 939]

The argument has been developed in a fuller form by the present author (Drake, 1969a, pp. 59–63); a fairly terse restatement will here be sufficient.

The starting point is that, under a currency board type of system, the *currency* supply is wholly determined by the

---

* Logically, not even a high ratio of external reserves to currency on issue is necessary once the currency is fully expanded in relation to a given volume of external assets. Thereafter, notwithstanding that the currency issue may in part—even large part—be supported by domestic government securities, some increment in external assets is necessary before any more currency may be issued.

balance of payments, because local currency can be issued only in exchange for acceptable foreign money at a fixed rate. In these circumstances, the currency supply will not be able to expand in step with growing domestic production unless there is also secular growth of external reserves, through a trade surplus and/or net capital inflow.

Of course, the local money supply consists of bank deposits as well as of currency. Bank deposits may increase directly through the balance of payments; and the banking system through credit creation may also expand the deposit money component independently, but not regardless, of the state of the balance of payments. The banks cannot disregard the balance of payments because their lending is based upon liquid assets (consisting of interchangeable local currency and foreign exchange reserves) which cannot in total grow without a continuing balance-of-payments surplus. So bank credit would, sooner or later, reach a maximum level, determined by any given volume of liquid reserves in the banking system in conjunction with any liquid reserves : deposits ratio adhered to by the banks. In the absence of any further growth of reserves via balance-of-payments surpluses (the only possible way), there is an upper limit to the total quantity of money, and not merely to its currency component.

The essence of the deflationary bias theory is that—given a fixed exchange rate and high, inflexible external reserve backing for the domestic currency—there is a problem of insufficient elasticity of the money supply whenever the output of the economy expands without any simultaneous improvement in the balance of payments. The argument is strongest when framed in terms of an expansion of output in the non-trade sector ('Analyst', 1953, p. 47), for local output sold on the home market is not accompanied by an influx of foreign currency earnings which may be converted to an equivalent increase in the volume of local currency. However, the argument does not depend on such a restrictive assumption. It is necessary only to hypothesize growth of domestic product (tradeable output or not) without any simultaneous surplus in the balance of payments for the deflationary bias to come into play. It is the lack of a *continuing surplus* on the balance of payments which prevents secular growth of external reserves and so restrains monetary expansion. Such a situation is perfectly consistent with, for example, growing exports, so long as imports or capital outflow are growing equally and so prevent the emergence of a balance-of-payments surplus.

To put the gist of the last few paragraphs simply, whenever the people of a country wish to acquire more money they must give goods, services or property rights to the money issuers; when the country runs a currency board type of system, they must give (net) goods, services and property rights to foreigners.

The argument can be expounded in terms of the familiar tautology $MV \equiv PT$; where M is the quantity of money, V the income velocity of circulation, P an index of all prices and T real domestic product. The deflationary bias argument is that, if real output T grows without a corresponding surplus in the balance of payments so that M cannot be increased (once the banks are 'fully loaned'), then if V is constant, P must fall. Alternatively, with V constant and if P is inflexible downwards, the growth of T will be restrained because M cannot grow without a continuing surplus in the balance of payments. The straitjacket would become even tighter in the event that there should be any fall in the velocity of circulation—for instance, as a result of increasing monetization.

On the other hand, as the spread and refinement of banking and credit habits generate greater transactions efficiency and give rise eventually to a widening range of liquid assets, the velocity of circulation of narrow money may increase. Moreover, so far as the public prefers to hold money in the form of bank deposits rather than currency, the banks may raise the deposit creation ceiling for any given total of currency in the economy. Most importantly, bank deposit expansion via the bank lending process may proceed without a supporting autonomous balance-of-payments surplus to the extent that the head offices of international banks would undertake to provide foreign reserves to cover the drain on liquid reserves occasioned by the lending activities of their branches in any individual country. (It should not be forgotten, however, that these last arguments about the possibility of obtaining monetary elasticity through bank credit creation assume implicitly that the banks are willing to lend because they expect it to be safe and profitable to do so.) If a domestic capital market exists, it may further be expected that monetary tightness would raise interest rates and encourage non-bank capital inflow. There are other loopholes in the system as well as some extraneous escape routes (Drake, 1969a, pp. 60–1); but the basic monetary tightness of the currency board type of system cannot be disputed. Peera has considered the deflationary bias argument and conducted some limited empirical tests of it; he found that, although some erstwhile British colonies escaped its constraints, the deflationary bias hypothesis 'receives some support from the evidence covering a period near the end of the colonial era' (Peera, n.d.). In short, the logic of the deflationary bias argument is sound and it is an empirical question as to how far the banking system in any country can and chooses to loosen the straitjacket of the currency board system.

Countries that inherited currency boards from their colonial days have generally sought to loosen the constraints of that system by institutional changes. Chief among these has usually been the establishment of a local central bank, with autonomous power to create obligations that serve as liquid reserves for the banks. This institutional attempt to break the grip of the balance of payments upon the supply of money has often turned out to be no real solution. Indeed, for a number of countries it has been but a siren song, enticing government and monetary authorities along a ruinous path of unchecked deficit finance and bank credit creation leading to inflation and chronic balance-of-payments difficulties (cf. Birnbaum, 1957; Newlyn, 1977).

There are very real limits to any attempt to moder: te external influence on the money supply. These limits are imposed by the basic underdeveloped and open nature of so many poor countries. Neither governments nor private investors can, by local spending unsupported by capital inflow, generate local capital formation to a greater extent than local, under-utilized, real resources allow. Where such resources are in limited supply, external resources are not provided, and the marginal propensity to import is high, the loosening of institutional constraints so as to permit domestic credit expansion leads only to balance-of-payments difficulties.

We must digress for a moment from the long-run implications of this line of thought in order to note, and then put aside, the once-and-for-all surge of domestic credit expansion that occurred in many developing countries at some time between about 1950 and the 1970s (and may still be in prospect for a remaining few countries). This has been described as 'a unique event similar to that which took place in England in the nineteenth century' (Newlyn, 1968, p. 157). The historically unexpanded state of bank deposits, or, in other words, the existence of excess bank liquid (mostly external) assets, could be traced to limited demands for bank credit, stringent security requirements originating in British banking practice, the lack of bank branch networks, and the lack of local financial assets which could have provided the banks with local earning alternatives to loans and advances. When, however, the banks in many hitherto dependent and little-monetized economies began to lend to a much wider range (by both size and activity) of borrowers, on security conditions more appropriate than before for developing economies, and through a wider network of branches, the banks' excess reserves were rapidly dissipated. This run-down of bank liquid reserves (local cash plus net external assets), resulting from sustained domestic credit expansion irrespective of the state of the balance of payments, led the banks of many countries into an overdrawn external position (as has been noticed and discussed, for example, by Newlyn, 1968, pp. 156–9, and Drake, 1969a, pp. 51–3). The important point for the future is that, once the banking expansion has occurred and the accumulated excess reserves have been expended, domestic credit expansion can go no further without the banking system first acquiring fresh reserves. Newlyn and Drake both argue that banking systems in underdeveloped countries can no longer expect to sustain further expansion of local credit on the basis of overdraft support from offices abroad. Leaving aside any particular difficulties associated with each case, bank reserves can increase only through (1) a reduction in the public's demand for currency, (2) reserve creation by a monetary authority, or (3) a surplus in the autonomous balance of payments. We thus return to the question of the influence of the balance of payments on the local money supply.

The long-run answers to the problem of how to reduce the importance of external forces on the local money supply are to be found, to the extent that answers exist, in variations in the prospensity to import (given a fixed exchange rate), or in the velocity of circulation of money, or in exchange rate changes. Our interest is primarily in the last two variables, which should be under the close watch, if not the reasonably direct influence, of the monetary authorities.

As economic development proceeds, it will normally be accompanied by a decline in the relative share of non-monetary output (arising from subsistence production and barter, etc., transactions) in total output. As Bloomfield has pointed out, this shrinking relative share will tend to cause the demand for real money balances to grow faster than total real income; in other words, the elasticity of demand for money with respect to total income is likely to exceed unity, and, other things equal, the velocity of circulation will fall. The differentiation of production, the spread of banking habits and the relative expansion of purely financial transactions—all associated with economic development—will also contribute to the outcome (Bloomfield, 1956, p. 247.* It follows that, unless the supply of money is also permitted to grow at a rate correspondingly in excess of the growth rate of total real output, deflationary pressures will emerge.

The desire for increased money balances may be satisfied, and any slow-down in the growth of production avoided, by expanding domestic bank credit at a rate appropriately faster than the rate of growth of real output. If the correct rate of credit expansion is struck, it can be carried through without threat to external reserves or risk of inflation. Structural and political considerations will doubtless determine the mix of domestic credit expansion as between commercial bank lending to the private sector and the provision of deficit finance to government. In any event, by responding to and satisfying the secular rise in the demand for money, the domestic banking system will increase its role in money formation.

Whether or not the local monetary institutions respond to the increased demand for real money relative to real income by expanding domestic credit, there is likely initially to be a fall in the observed velocity of circulation (a rise in the observed money : income ratio).† This outcome implies that the financial sector is not well developed and that there are few money substitutes. At a later stage of development, however, where financial habits and institutions have become so diversified as to provide a range of money substitutes or 'quasi-money', and the earlier pressure of demand for narrow money has bred transactions econo-

---

* This may seem to contradict the argument on p. 95, but in the present case we are assuming the absence of 'money substitutes'. I shall return shortly to a reconciliation of these arguments.

† My own preference is for the notion of the ratio of money to income, which does have behavioural content. The velocity of circulation is an artifact, has no life of its own, and often leads to confusion; however, the term is so embedded in the literature that it is judicious to employ it now and again.

mies in its use, the demand for money relative to income may decline and the velocity of circulation of money may rise. These considerations lie behind the observations reported by Thirlwall (1974, pp. 106–9) and his statement, 'Typically what happens is that initially velocity falls as income grows and then rises in the later stages of development.'

It may be thought that the time period over which velocity of circulation first falls (chiefly owing to monetization) and then eventually rises again (owing to transactions efficiencies and the emergence of modern quasi-money) would be rather a long one. This need not be so: the forces that pull velocity in different directions may in fact occur simultaneously, so that any cursory observation of stable income velocity of circulation may blind the observer to underlying counter-pulls between monetization, on the one hand, and more intensive use of money stock, on the other. This type of monetary behaviour was noticed by the author and M. L. Treadgold in respect of Papua New Guinea during the period 1964–73. Over these years, a remarkably stable income velocity of circulation was observed in Papua New Guinea. At the same time, very rapid monetization occurred: non-market production shrank from about one-third to less than one-fifth of gross domestic product at current prices. The apparently surprising stability of V turned out on closer inspection to reflect the fact that the shrinkage of the share of non-market output in GDP (causing a rising demand for money for transactions purposes) had been offset by a rising velocity of circulation in the money economy (resulting from a falling demand for money relative to cash income). In other words, although the money economy grew faster than GDP as a whole, it used money more intensively than before, thereby preventing the fall in overall velocity that would otherwise have been expected to result from the process of monetization.

The following algebra may help to clarify the relationships discussed. The symbol V represents income velocity of circulation, M the volume of money, Y the gross domestic product, and Y_m the gross product of the money economy. By definition $V = Y/M$, which may be re-arranged as

$$V = \frac{Y_m}{M} \cdot \frac{Y}{Y_m} = \frac{Y_m/M}{Y_m/Y}.$$

In words, the overall income velocity of circulation is a product of the income velocity of circulation in the money economy (Y_m/M) and the inverse of the share of gross domestic product originating in the money economy, or the degree of monetization (Y_m/Y). Thus it is evident that a stable value of V may be associated with simultaneous increases in both the velocity of circulation in the money economy and the degree of monetization of the economy as a whole, as was observed in Papua New Guinea.

We have now arrived at the point where we can best consider alternative forms of monetary control. In doing this we must have regard also to the question of choice of exchange rate regime. We shall begin by assuming the existence of a generally fixed exchange rate, which accords with, at least, all but the very recent experience of most developing countries.

The extreme type of fixed exchange rate is the use by one country of the currency of another as a medium of exchange. This arrangement implies, of course, that the former country has no monetary independence of the latter. Thanks to the writings of Johnson (1972) and Harberger (1972), economists are perhaps most familiar with Panama as the exemplar of a country completely dependent upon the money of another. But—*pace* Johnson—Panama is far from 'unique or virtually so among the independent nations of the world with respect to its monetary system'. Liechtenstein, Liberia, Monaco, Botswana, Lesotho, Swaziland, the British Virgin Islands and Papua New Guinea use, or have used until recently, the currency of another state. Some independent states in the South Pacific use the currencies of Australia or New Zealand, while the CFA Franc persists in some African states.

Apart from the apparent affront to national independence, the use of another country's money (the currency itself being in circulation or in hoards, and bank balances being denominated in it) has two economic disadvantages. First, the government of the dependent country has no control over the volume of money, which depends upon accumulated surpluses in the balance of payments and commercial bank lending: the authorities acting alone therefore can neither provide fiduciary finance for local investment nor insulate the local economy against price fluctuations originating abroad. Secondly, currency in circulation constitutes an interest-free loan to the country whose currency is used.* There is thus a loss of resources of the value of the net investment return that could have been gained by local ownership of the currency reserve.

Against these disadvantages must be set the benefits of using another currency and forming part of a larger monetary system. These benefits will vary in degree with the size and economic structure of the lesser economy, most specifically with the relative composition of its output between

---

*When any community holds currency (notes and coin) it in effect makes an interest-free loan to the party who issues that currency (correspondingly, when people acquire current account deposits in a bank, they make interest-free loans to the bank). Perhaps the point can be put with simple clarity by saying that, where people render goods and services to a government in exchange for the currency issued by that government, the government acquire the real goods and services and the people in return acquire pieces of paper and metal which, though highly useful for the conduct of transactions, yield no interest to the holders. By contrast if people accept interest-bearing government bonds in exchange for real resources, they would obtain interest on the bonds as well as acquiring a claim against government of the capital value of the bonds.

When a community holds the currency issued by its own government, the interest-free loan is an internal matter and the government may use the real resources that it obtains, as a consequence of the community's decision to hold money, in ways that may benefit the nation. In other words, the interest-free loan is within the national family. But when the community holds currency issued by an outside government, the interest-free loan is made to the outside government.

tradeable and non-tradeable goods. The literature on optimum currency areas—notably McKinnon (1963), Mundell (1961) and Corden (1972)—deals with the relevant considerations in detail. For our purposes it suffices simply to list the potential benefits of using a superior currency. These are as follows: the advantages of using money are secured at virtually no provision cost; no resources need be devoted to managing the domestic money supply, manufacturing and issuing the currency component of it, or managing an exchange rate; there is no possibility of inflation arising through the financing of government deficits by a local monetary authority; there are no difficulties about foreign payments, at least in so far as the superior currency is internationally acceptable. (It should perhaps be observed that the government may be able to finance deficits by borrowing from a commercial bank and that commercial banks may choose to offset, by credit expansion to government or the private sector, any decline in money supply of the dependent territory arising from a deficit in its balance of payments; in any such event, the ability and willingness of the banks so to act will be governed by the state of their cash reserves over their whole international field of operations. In other words, the dependent territory is, from the banks' point of view, similar to a minor region of the country that provides the currency.)

In general, the use of a superior currency also reassures foreign investors about their ability to repatriate capital and/or profits and so encourages inflow of foreign capital for investment purposes. This encouragement is greater the more important is the superior currency in international exchange and the less threatened it appears to be by exchange rate depreciation. More particularly, as Johnson noted in the case of Panama, use of a superior and internationally popular currency may benefit the tourist trade of the dependent territory and enhance its prospects of becoming a regional financial centre.

Finally, a country that makes use of a superior currency

(or fixes its exchange rate firmly to another currency) and that also has, in its total market supplies, a high ratio of tradeable to non-tradeable goods ties its price level to price levels in the country of the superior currency. (More generally, a country that fixes its exchange rate against gold, the SDR or a basket of foreign currencies ties itself to international price levels in some average sense.) This means that the common currency guarantees domestic price stability *provided foreign prices are stable*: the high proportion of tradeable goods, whose prices are internationally determined, in the home market obviates the possibility of inflation arising domestically. On the other hand, if foreign costs and prices are less stable than those at home and general price disturbances originate abroad, then the common currency will automatically transfer those prices to any dependent economy that has a high ratio of tradeables to total market supplies. In these circumstances a separate currency, variable in exchange value, would provide the means of insulating the economy against imported inflation.

Next to the extreme form of hard money and fixed exchange rate that the use of an external currency represents comes the currency board system. This allows a country to enjoy the symbolic value of its own currency and to avoid the opportunity cost associated with the use of another currency (the interest-free loan to the country whose currency is used). As practised until recent times in many present or erstwhile colonial territories, the system usually incorporated a fixed exchange rate against the currency of a metropolitan power, and required the backing of 100 per cent foreign reserve investments against notes and coins issued locally. However, as we shall soon see, it may be possible to have some degree of flexibility about each of these requirements without sacrificing the essence and all the benefits of the currency board system.

The principal merit of the system is that, consistent with the maintenance of externally backed money and a fixed exchange rate (in other words, consistent with reassuring both domestic money-holders and foreign traders and investors that the local authorities will neither generate monetary inflation nor depreciate the exchange value of the currency), the country may earn revenue from investing the currency reserve. Currency is a circulating, non-earning asset. Those who choose to hold currency elect not to hold or enjoy the goods and services on which the currency could be spent. These real resources instead pass essentially to the command of the supplier of currency. In a closed economy, whoever provides currency obtains goods and services in exchange from those who wish to acquire currency; in an open economy using external money, the local inhabitants must send resources abroad in order to import currency in exchange.

This is the essential nature of the interest-free loan which the amount of currency in circulation represents. The adoption of a currency board whereby local currency is issued by the board in exchange, at a fixed rate, for foreign currency tendered to it (and vice-versa) means that the inhabitants of the country now hold local notes and coin and the board holds the foreign currency which has been earned by the net export of goods, services or property rights, i.e. by a balance-of-payments surplus. But whereas the local population would hitherto have held physical foreign currency that earned no interest, the currency board need not do so. Secure in the knowledge that most currency put into public circulation will stay there, the board has no need to maintain a wholly liquid, let alone physical, reserve of foreign currency to meet any demands for conversion of domestic currency into foreign. It will suffice for the currency board to hold a fraction (experience shows that one-third is generally more than adequate) of the currency backing in liquid assets against conversion contingencies. The remainder of the foreign money constituting the currency reserve may be invested in income-earning assets (for safety, predominantly securities issued by the governments of strong economies). In addition to the interest income thus secured, the currency board, being a money-changer, can exact a small commission income on all exchanges into and out of local currency. (The commission revenue, of course, would go to the currency board and would represent a redistribution from the private to the public sector rather than a net gain to the nation. Although both foreigners and local citizens would contribute to the commission income, a small country with given terms of trade would inevitably have the commission costs shifted on to it via higher import prices and lower export prices, expressed in local currency.)

Against these forms of income must be set the costs incurred by the currency board in order to arrive at its net disposable income. The board's costs relate to its own administration (staff, office accommodation, etc.), the printing of notes and manufacture of coins, and the costs of issuing, distributing and redeeming the notes and coin. The costs of administration should be modest. Johnson (1972, p. 225) puts it with a nice colour:

> a currency board has the great advantage over a central bank that its operations can be made fairly automatic, so that it need not require a comparable expenditure on both administrative staff and prestigious directors and a governor able and obliged to attend the annual meetings of the International Monetary Fund and make fittingly portentous speeches prepared by high-priced research staff. Nor does it require an impressive building. It should be possible to run a currency board with a small staff and one to three commissioners who need to meet only two to four times a year.

The costs of manufacture and circulation of currency will vary according to the *per capita* income, degree of monetization and geography of the country. A city-state with relatively high average income, such as Singapore, may expect to make good use of notes of high average denomination and long average life, which is the cheapest currency to provide and service. At the other extreme a very poor, vast country, ill-served by distribution networks and requiring low unit value currency, will make most use of coins, which are much more expensive than notes to produce, and low-denomination notes, which wear out quickly. (Against this, however, are Johnson's points that notes circulating in remote rural districts might remain outstanding for many years and that valuable bank notes may induce attempts at forgery, which it may be difficult and costly to prevent or police.)

In sum, the currency board system provides all the advantages of using an external currency while avoiding the loss of interest on currency holdings. A significant net interest return should be captured since the operations of the board are automatic and inexpensive.

The disadvantages of the currency board system, in its most rigid form, all relate to the fact that the local authorities cannot directly manipulate the currency supply (though in some circumstances they may be able to influence the total money supply via controls/influence over the commercial banks). Thus, the authorities cannot direct the currency reserve (which represents savings of the public invested in the holding of currency) into local asset formation but must instead hold foreign reserves. Secondly, contra-cyclical monetary policies cannot be engineered by any discretionary creation/extinction of money via the currency board. Thirdly, the system suffers from a built-in deflationary bias whenever the output of the economy expands without any simultaneous improvement in the balance of payments. Finally, the fixed exchange rate embodied in the currency board system limits severely the scope of any very open economy for fending off price changes originating abroad. All this presumes a currency board of the most rigid institutional form (but note, as Johnson, 1972, p. 288, points out, that 'even a carefully set up and limited currency board could be converted by a determined and irresponsible government into a temporary source of easy finance for its programme'). Let it be assumed, however, that a responsible government would 'play by the rules', in which case some possibly desirable flexibility should perhaps be introduced into the currency board system. We will indicate how this can be done shortly. First, for ease of exposition and understanding, it may be timely to refer briefly to the other extreme in monetary management, namely an independent and autonomous central bank.

The conventional independent central bank may select its own assets, create money without limit by buying local securities, hold virtually all the national stock of foreign exchange, and control the nation's exchange rate by buying and selling foreign currency as a monopolist. With complete freedom of investment policy, a central bank would in principle have the scope for considerable monetary and financial influence: first, through its ability to vary the money supply, in the interests of stabilization or development or both; secondly, through buying and selling local financial assets, thus stimulating the growth of the capital market. There are some further advantages of a full-blown central bank which should not be overlooked (central banking will be discussed more fully in a later chapter). Most important are the monetary control and the stimulation of local financial development which may be obtained by the imposition of variable liquid asset ratios and/or local asset ratios over financial institutions in the country and by a thorough system of licensing and inspections imposed at least on the commercial banks (and preferably on all financial institutions). By these methods a newly established central bank could first capture, for subsequent investment at its own discretion, part of the resources (foreign exchange) sold to the banks by the public in exchange for bank deposits. This would imply, secondly, some transfer of monetary authority to the central bank and a corresponding loss of independence by the commercial banks. (This redistribution of foreign exchange assets, perhaps desirable for control purposes, does not necessarily imply any increase in the volume of foreign reserves available to the nation.) Thirdly, and most important, the need of the banks to acquire local assets, in greater proportion to their deposits, would be expected to have beneficial effects on the supply of domestic credit, the development of the local capital market, and on domestic capital formation. However, these changes would require the new central bank to assume responsibility for convertibility of the currency and to be able to meet the foreign exchange needs of the banks on demand (or otherwise resort to exchange controls). It is by no means certain that it is always a wise move for a fledgling central bank to assume responsibility for the maintenance and management of a country's foreign exchange reserves when these responsibilities are already being borne satisfactorily by the private banking system (see Johnson, 1972, p. 227; Maynard, 1970, p. 124).

The potential advantages outlined above would require very great administrative resources in the central bank. Not only is it costly to staff these activities, but it may also be very difficult to do so in countries where indigenous managerial and financial skills are among the scarcest resources. The greater the autonomy of a central bank, the greater is the commensurate risk of domestic inflation arising through any unwise use of its discretionary investment powers. Moreover, excessive issue of currency, in exchange for government securities, would sooner or later undermine the central bank's ability to convert local currency into foreign currencies at any fixed rate. The further possibility of a variable exchange rate is thus raised.

The introduction of a variable exchange rate (an adjustable peg system) would add another tool of economic policy. In principle, any country may resort to exchange rate variation as a means of balance-of-payments adjustment, although the measure would probably be of little use for that purpose in a very open economy, characterized by a high ratio of traded to non-traded goods in the monetized economy; this is because resources devoted to subsistence production cannot, in the short run, be readily switched into the production of tradeable goods within the money economy. (However, these remarks should not be taken to exclude entirely the possibility of a devaluation stimulating some increase in the output of tradeable goods in any very open economy;

for an example see Lewis, 1979, p. 21.) But the same 'open-ness' which frustrates the use of exchange rate variation for balance-of-payments adjustment makes it an effective measure for dealing with price fluctuations originating abroad. In a very open economy, the local currency may be devalued in order to counteract foreign deflation or reval-ued in order to insulate the home economy against imported inflation. Used in this insulating way, the variable exchange rate may be a particularly valuable policy tool. But the scarcity of local economic expertise might make it difficult to administer a variable rate in many developing countries; and any mismanagement of the exchange rate would interfere with the efficient allocation of resources and would inhibit the growth of income in general and of the foreign trade sector in particular. The exchange risk which the introduction of a variable rate introduces might deter much needed foreign investment from entering the country. Indeed, foreign inves-tors might decide that a local central bank with full discretion would pose too great a threat to the actual convertibility—as well as to the exchange rate—of anticipated profit or capital remittances from the country.

It is obvious that for many countries neither extreme rigidity nor total discretion is appropriate for the monetary system in their present state of economic and social develop-ment. Some compromise system may be sought which would embody a mixture of desirable attributes and could be administered by the small number of skilled personnel. As net capital inflow and domestic willingness to hold money would be gravely prejudiced by rapid inflation and balance-of-payments difficulties, the system devised should lean to-wards the 'hard money' principle. But hard money need not mean a rigid and wholly automatic currency system; rather, it may be consistent with some modest but important elements of official intervention.

Even within a currency board type system of currency issue it would be possible for the monetary authority to have some degree of autonomy in managing its investment reserves; specifically, a currency board might be allowed to hold a modest and limited proportion of local government securities in its portfolio. The effects of this would be to create a means of overcoming the deflationary bias to some extent, and to provide the government with some financial resources (mostly, but not entirely, of a once-and-for-all nature) for development or stabilization expenditures; the funds so provided to government would be by no means negligible and would increase in step with growth of the cash economy.

To the extent that a monetary authority (be it currency board, central bank or whatever) has powers of asset control, licensing, etc. (as outlined above) over the commercial banks, it can exercise a good deal of monetary influence. A system of central banking in which the bank has a high degree of influence over the commercial banks but lacks the central power directly to create currency (or may exercise such power only within very narrow limits) is not without effective precedent. In Malaysia such a system worked very well during the 1960s at a time when the economy was growing rapidly, from quite a well developed base (see Drake, 1969a, pp. 69–72).

The control of inflation must be a major aim of economic policy. It is of the greatest importance to realize that inflation brings an additional danger to a developing economy, over an above all its more generally recognized undesirable effects. This danger is that inflation may so sap public confidence in the adoption or continued use of money that monetization of the local subsistence economy could be arrested. Monetary systems of the currency board type which embody full or high external reserve backing for the currency have inbuilt safeguards against inflation of domestic origin. However, they have no provisions for keeping imported inflation at bay. Foreign inflation may impose severe problems on any country which relies to a very heavy degree on imported consumer and producer goods. One important element might therefore be added to the quasi-automatic currency system, namely an adjustable exchange rate. This would confer the valuable policy advantage of a weapon for insulating the economy against overseas inflation. But it would also introduce problems of exchange risk and the maintenance of convertibility, as well as the major difficulty of administering the exchange rate.

Consider the mechanism by which convertibility of the local currency would be guaranteed under a 100 per cent external reserve currency system and a fixed exchange rate. In such circumstances, the liabilities of the *currency issue fund* would consist of currency on issue, and its assets would be external reserves. While it appears tautological that the assets and liabilities of such a fund would always be of equal value if currency were bought and sold at a fixed exchange rate, this need not be the case in practice. The reason is that the various external assets that the currency fund may own (gold, foreign currency balances, foreign securities, IMF credits) may fluctuate in value in relationship to one another, and so some will not be of constant value in relation to the local unit of currency. The value of the currency fund assets may fluctuate, at times falling below the face value of the currency in circulation. In that event some provision would be necessary to make good the deficiency and restore the 100 per cent external asset backing. It was the practice in currency board systems to bolster the currency fund with an annual appropriation from the currency board's interest and commission incomes. This ensured that the fund's assets were always in excess of the face value of currency in circulation. Assets held in excess of currency liabilities then appeared in the balance sheet as '*Excess of assets over liabilities account*'.

This system, which took care of modest fluctuations in the local value of external reserves when the exchange rate was fixed, could easily be adapted to provide for convertibility of local currency in the face of any larger fluctuations arising through conscious variation of the exchange rate. In the internal accounting of the monetary authority it would be necessary to have an *exchange rate adjustment account*, in supplement to the central currency issue fund. An exchange rate adjustment account would be funded, first, from annual appropriations from income of the currency board and, secondly, by using the adjustment account to absorb the notional profits or losses arising from devaluations or revaluations of local currency. The ease with which this system could be operated depends very much upon the degree and the frequency of exchange rate adjustments. Assuming that adjustments were neither drastic nor frequent, it would be reasonable to expect that, in the long haul, credits to the exhange rate adjustment account consisting of devaluation 'profits' plus annual subventions from income would be sufficient to cover debits arising from revaluation 'losses'. Thus convertibility could be assured under a variable exchange rate system, with little more difficulty than under a fixed exchange rate regime.

In the absence of a workable exchange rate adjustment account, the aftermath of any exchange rate variation under a currency board type of system would be that monetary mechanisms would impart to the economy secondary influences promoting inflation (or recession) at times when the exchange rate adjustment itself had already set inflationary (or deflationary) tendencies in motion. These secondary influences, which would have similar effects on the direction of price level and national output changes as the exchange rate variation, may well be desirable in many cases. Indeed, if the impacts of the secondary influences can be predicted accurately, a smaller than otherwise variation in the exchange rate would be sufficient to produce the desired price level and output adjustments. On the other hand, if the secondary influences should be underestimated, a given exchange rate variation would turn out to be over-corrective. Consider a devaluation of the local currency. This would directly cause domestic inflation by raising the local price of tradeable goods. In addition there must be added a monetary effect also likely to foster inflation. As a consequence of devaluation, external reserves would become worth more in local currency; hence the ratio of currency reserves to currency liabilities would rise above the statutory figure and would permit a once-and-for-all issue of currency, which could be used for government spending. Conversely, an appreciation of the currency would be strengthened, above its ordinary deflationary pressures, by the fact that currency would have to be withdrawn from circulation (via a budget surplus) in order to restore the pre-existing statutory ratio of external assets to currency in circulation.

It is thus apparent that a variable exchange rate not only poses possible difficulties about convertibility, but also brings mechanical problems that would exacerbate, perhaps undesirably, the inflationary or deflationary pressures arising from an adjustment of the exchange rate. However, these problems are not as formidable as they may seem. Provided that variations in the exchange rate are neither drastic nor frequent, the difficulties may be avoided by the maintenance of an exchange rate adjustment account. Of course, while the exchange adjustment account system would promise convertibility of the local currency into foreign currencies, it would not give any protection against exchange risk. Some degree of exchange risk has to be a fact of economic life. It need not deter overseas investors if the exchange rate is administered responsibly and sensibly.

There remains the problem of administering the exchange rate. This is of no small moment in any country where financial and economic skills are scarce, even though it is hard to envisage that a variable exchange rate—used primarily for insulating local market prices from foreign price changes—would need to be changed very often. Nevertheless, someone in the developing country must decide upon changes, for it is inconceivable that an independent country could leave decisions about the value of its currency in the hands of any outside power or institution. It seems both right and feasible that local personnel be trained, under experienced expatriate guidance, in the formulation and administration of exchange rate policy. The required guidance could be provided by officials seconded from overseas central banks and/or the International Monetary Fund. It is clearly desirable too that exchange rate decisions be taken as part of general economic management and that those responsible for the exchange rate (whether expatriates or locals) bear wide responsibilities in the Treasury and central bank.

Adequate external reserves could still be ensured, even without a fully backed currency and fixed exchange rate, provided that the exchange rate adjustment account were to be used in the manner suggested. This statement, of course, refers only to currency. Reserve backing for the commercial bank deposits component of the volume of money would not be guaranteed, nor would it be required so long as the monetary authority refrained from assuming large discretionary powers of currency creation and control of the liquid reserves of the banks. Under a quasi-automatic currency system, the onus falls on the commercial banks to maintain, or be able to obtain from abroad, sufficient liquid reserves to support the volume of deposits they permit to be created. Historically, commercial banks have borne this responsibility quite satisfactorily. Only a bank's failure can render deposits inconvertible (as well as illiquid), but failures should be unlikely in a properly licensed, regularly inspected and well administered system. The gist of all this is that the overseas assets and international lines of credit of the commercial banks may be regarded as 'below the line' for balance-of-payments purposes. In other words, bank deposits are convertible into both local currency and foreign exchange because the banks, in the final analysis, will honour them with foreign exchange. (In the long run, of course, the central bank may wish to acquire the foreign exchange holdings of the banks and itself assume total control of international reserves and all responsibility for convertibility.)

The drift of the recent discussion is that most developing

countries need to choose between maintaining a fixed exchange rate or adopting some sort of adjustable peg exchange rate system: the alternative of a floating exchange rate has been ignored, by implication as unsuitable. In my view the floating rate system is unsuitable for most developing countries, and it is perhaps timely to make explicit the objections to that system.

A good examination of the exchange rate alternatives facing developing countries today, when the currencies of the major industrial countries are more or less floating, may be found in a recent paper by Crockett and Nsouli. These authors adumbrate those common characteristics of developing countries which limit the scope for, and the effectiveness of, exchange rate variation, namely: highly specialized production, inability to affect export or import prices in foreign currency, inelastic demand for imports and supply of exports, need for net capital inflow, and rudimentary financial systems. They emphasize also that the floating rate system could not work freely unless and until foreign exchange markets are sufficiently well developed to cope with a good volume of both spot and forward transactions (Crockett and Nsouli, 1977, pp. 125–7, 141). Finally, Crockett and Nsouli (p. 139) remind us that 'independent floating cannot be construed as freeing the country from "discipline" in the pursuit of monetary and fiscal policy', principally because any expansionary monetary policy, relative to the rest of the world, would force down a country's exchange rate, thus giving further impetus to inflation and leading to adverse public reaction. It may be repeated here that in small open economies, where tradeable goods constitute a high proportion of total market supplies, exchange rate disturbances may reduce the liquidity value of domestic money, causing the inhabitants to avoid it and try either to hold foreign balances or to revert to non-monetary transactions. In short, under the conditions commonly found in underdeveloped countries, there may be little money illusion about the domestic currency.

No less powerful an advocate of flexible exchange rates than Harry G. Johnson has put the same viewpoint inimitably.

> One is accustomed to thinking of national moneys in terms of the currencies of the major countries, which currencies derive their usefulness from the great diversity of goods, services, and assets available in the national economy, into which they can be directly converted. But in the contemporary world there are many small and relatively narrowly specialized countries, whose national currencies lack usefulness in this sense, but instead derive their usefulness from their rigid convertibility at a fixed price into the currency of some major country with which the small country trades extensively or on which it depends for capital for investment. For such countries, the advantages of rigid convertibility in giving the currency usefulness and facilitating international trade and investment outweigh the relatively small advantages that might be derived from exchange rate flexibility. (In a banana republic, for example, the currency will be more useful if it is stable in terms of command over foreign goods than if it is stable in terms of command over bananas; and exchange rate flexibility would give little scope for autonomous domestic policy.) These countries, which probably constitute a substantial numerical majority of existing countries, would, therefore, probably choose, if given a free choice, to keep the value of their currency pegged to that of some major country or currency bloc. In other words, the case for flexible exchange rates is a case for flexibility of rates among the currencies of countries that are large enough to have a currency whose usefulness derives primarily from its domestic purchasing power, and for which significant autonomy of domestic policy is both possible and desired. [Johnson, 1972, p. 206]

The final consideration for a developing country that chooses a fixed, or adjustable peg, exchange rate system is whether to fix or peg to a single foreign currency, to a basket of currencies, to gold or to the SDR unit (itself valued in terms of a basket of sixteen main currencies) of the International Monetary Fund. Crockett and Nsouli come down in favour of some form of pegged exchange rate for most developing countries. Pegging to a single currency is generally sub-optimal, except for those developing countries who have very close economic links with the country to whose currency they are pegged. Crockett and

Nsouli prefer pegging to the SDR basket because the other alternative of each individual developing country pegging to its own import-weighted basket opens up a large problem of cross-rate variations among the developing countries as a group (since each will be pegged to a different basket) which would not exist if the developing countires all pegged to the SDR basket (Crockett and Nsouli, 1977, pp. 131–7, 141).

We return finally to the fundamental importance of price stability in developing countries. It is essential to sustain domestic and foreign confidence in the value of local money: the one in order to foster monetization and financial development, the other to encourage international trade and investment. These forces will accelerate economic growth faster than any attempt to do so chiefly by domestic monetary expansion. As has been emphasized throughout this chapter, where real resources are scarce, domestic credit expansion leads inevitably to inflation and loss of external reserves. Fundamentally, what the money and banking system can do for development is constrained by the size, nature and structure of the money economy. This is not to say that the monetary authorities should eschew attempts to promote monetization, ease any deflationary bias in the monetary system, improve the financial structure and diversify the economy, as I have argued (see also Maynard, 1970, p. 127). Nor should it be forgotten that fiscal policy can be used in the pursuit of stabilization and diversification. But one must avoid any delusions about money magic. It is not, I think, concluding the case for price stability and tight control over domestic credit creation on too strong a note to recall Johnson's wisdom:

> Monetary history is full of cases where governments hungry for money that they wanted to spend on projects they considered desirable obtained the money not by taxes but by pressing their central bank to buy more government debt than was prudent from the point of view of defending the stability of the currency. As a result in such cases, the central bank runs its international reserves and liquidity

position dangerously low, and the government is driven into exchange and trade controls and eventually into currency devaluation. Both involve not only deceit and robbery of the domestic public, whose money is reduced in value by a sort of arbitrary tax imposed on it, but perhaps more important the destruction of foreign confidence in the currency and in the country and its government, which is harmful especially to foreign investment in the country's economic development. [Johnson, 1972, p. 227]

Further Reading

Running through this chapter is an emphasis on the open nature of most underdeveloped economies, the historical simplicity of their monetary systems, and their dependence upon a favourable balance of payments for the provision of local money. These characteristics are notably seen in those many countries which operate(d) automatic currency systems based on external reserve backing and a fixed exchange rate. The currency board system, which is the best institutional embodiment of these practices, is the subject of a very large literature, going back many years. Perhaps the best single examination of the principles of that system is by Hazelwood (1954); a succinct summary analysis and list of references may be found in the work of Nevin (1961). There are numerous descriptions and analyses of the system as operated in individual countries, for example Newlyn and Rowan (1954), Drake (1969a).

The work of J. J. Polak and his associates synthesizes monetary formation and income determination analyses, emphasizing the importance of the balance of payments and the consequent limitations on domestic credit expansion in underdeveloped economies (Polak, 1957; Polak and Boissoneault, 1960; Polak and Argy, 1971). The Polak model has been expounded by Newlyn, 1969; 1971, pp. 153–8; and with particular clarity by Furness, 1975, pp. 206–14.

Doubtless owing to the fashionable resurgence of monetarism in the last decade, the Polak model has been widely interpreted as a 'monetarist' view of the process of income determination in dependent economies. This interpretation is too casual and leads one to think that those who espouse it can know little of the economic and financial structure of open, dependent underdeveloped economies. For many years Walter Newlyn held out—virtually alone—a 'Keynesian' interpretation of Polak. He has lately been joined by Eric Furness (1975) and, with great effect, by Bruce Bolnick (1975). Bolnick's penetrating article does more than demonstrate afresh that the Polak model may be compatible with Keynesian views about income determination: with admirable scholarship and precision he also clears up a good deal of incidental confusion and drives home the central point that, in economies of the type under consideration, changes in income and the volume of money occur simultaneously and through the same causes, thus justifying the Polak conclusion that 'control over bank credit creation and over foreign trade and capital flows should be the targets of monetary authorities in developing countries' (Bolnick, 1975, p. 335). Bolnick's article deserves full and careful reading by those interested in the synthesis of income determination and money formation analysis, but perhaps pp. 332–3 and 335 should be especially commended for the manner in which they relate the particular structural features of dependent, underdeveloped countries to the aggregate variables of conventional macroeconomic models (see also Furness, 1975, pp. 212–13 on this last point).

Developing countries need to make monetary arrangements that will provide for development and cyclical stabilization without undue risk of price level inflation. These themes are well discussed in general by Bloomfield (1956) and Nevin (1961). As is evident in the text of this chapter, monetization and financial development generally are bound up with these subjects.

Exchange rate flexibility appears to be an obvious way of loosening the monetary rigidities in developing countries. Whether or not a fixed or flexible exchange rate is best for any given country is for the reader to judge in context. He will find guiding principles in the literature on optimum currency areas, in which Corden (1972) is especially recommended. The recent essay by Crockett and Nsouli (1977), which leans—correctly in my view—away from floating exchange rates for underdeveloped countries in general, gives a good discussion of various degrees and forms of fixed peg and adjustable peg exchange rate regimes. Lewis (1979) has just published a stimulating essay which calls attention to the dangers that less developed countries run into by adhering to inflexible exchange rates; but while Lewis's arguments suggest the need for less developed countries to contemplate adjustable exchange rates they do not, to my mind, make a case for floating.

Finally, Maynard (1970) has given an excellent, and brief, case study illustrating many of the ideas that I have dealt with in this chapter; at more length, Letiche (1974) has described and analysed changes in the monetary system in East Africa (Kenya, Tanzania and Uganda).

CHAPTER 6

Informal Finance

From the earliest times, those who consumed less than their current production/income have sought ways of storing the consequent savings. This is true of all underdeveloped societies, and the many stores of value that have evolved have included rudimentary financial assets as well as real assets. The term 'unorganized' finance is commonly applied to these financial arrangements, doubtless in order to contrast with the well organized formal borrowing and lending conducted through modern financial institutions. As has been well said by Rozental (1967), p. 456), however, 'unorganized' is a misnomer for activities which, 'unofficial' or 'informal' or even 'illegal' though they may be, are often very highly organized. In this work, therefore, the term 'informal' has been preferred.

Inasmuch as savers have acquired informal financial assets, the issuers of them have either undertaken real expenditure (in the case of direct finance) or have sought others to whom to lend (indirect finance). With all these possibilities in mind we are led to ask: in what forms are savings typically stored in developing countries? what forms of informal intermediation occur? what forms of lending are favoured by those financiers or middlemen who profit by lending out their own surpluses and/or the savings which they have acquired from others? for what purposes are informal loans sought? what rates of interest apply in the informal finance market?

Of its nature, informal finance is not captured in the typical flow-of-funds matrix presented in Chapter 2. Conceptually, informal finance transactions would have a place in that matrix (which would then need finer division of sectors and rows) if they could be identified. But in no aggregative sense can this be done. This is most unfortunate, since 'it is reasonable to assume that it is the unorganized sector, with its high interest rates, that finances the bulk of total credit requirements in most of the Asian countries' (Chandavarkar, 1971, p. 62); and it seems likely that, the less developed the economy, the greater the ratio of informal/unorganized to formal/institutional finance (Wai, 1957, pp. 83–4, 87).

We are here concerned not with hoards of currency nor with savings deposited in financial institutions, but with the portion of unconsumed income that finds its way into non-institutional assets. Saving in this form comes from what might be loosely described as the household sector of the economy, though that sector also includes many simple businesses and those family farming activities that overlap the 'household' and 'business' categories of social accounting. Although the participation in informal financial activities of people in the rural economy is most obvious, urban dwellers also take an important part. Notwithstanding that urban workers enjoy small regular incomes, from which small regular amounts of saving may arise, and have easy access to and some familiarity with financial institutions, they are still active in informal finance. The incomes of rural people are generally less regular and often smaller than their urban fellows, but from time to time a favourable leap in income may permit the acquisition of a relatively substantial asset. The assets that the saver acquires will be governed not only by the size and regularity of his income, but also by its form (cash or produce) and his earning status (producer, wage/salary employee, casual worker). The disposition of his savings is also likely to be influenced by location, social class, ethnic group, religion, etc.—in other words, any individual's savings habits are very much subject to the socio-cultural environment in which he finds himself.

In rural areas, unconsumed income is likely to be devoted

to farm improvements, stocks of produce, cash hoarding, loans to other members of the community, the acquisition of livestock, land, building materials, tools and equipment, and precious metals, stones and ornaments. It is evident that, while some of these assets may constitute 'capital formation' to the economist, others do not and at first sight may seem a wastefully unproductive use of savings. This, however, is by no means certain: the problem must be analysed at the aggregate and not the individual level; what matters is whether the ultimate sellers of the unproductive or second-hand assets (gold, silver, ornaments, land and pre-existing livestock and equipment), and those who borrow choose finally to use the funds obtained for consumption or capital formation. (Indeed, even if the funds are hoarded, saving will still release resources for capital formation in the economy as a whole.) To take the case of land, for example, Hunter (1967) has shown quite clearly that it is logically wrong to condemn land-buying as 'debilitating' from the development point of view. Land purchasing may be good, bad or neutral with respect to economic development. It all depends on who makes the purchase and how he finances it, in conjunction with who sells and what he does with the proceeds. Hunter has demonstrated that there are a sufficiently large number of outcome combinations to erode any *a priori* belief that land transactions will be wasteful or inflationary. Similar considerations apply to the acquisition by savers (rural and urban) of gold, silver, ornaments and other valuable durables.

There are no firm and reliable estimates of the volume and value of precious metals and stones held in the developing countries, but there are many indications that the demand for these assets is very widespread (Bonné, 1957; Swift, 1961; Gamba, 1958; Chandavarkar, 1961; Panikar, 1961). It is doubtful, however, if the demand for these assets is of great aggregative importance in the flow sense. For example, Chandavarkar suggests that in India in the period 1950–8 the acquisition of gold accounted for only about 3·6 per cent of household savings and 0·2 per cent of national incomes; and although Panikar and Bonné both give the impression that the cumulative stock value of private gold hoards in India is very large, this would not necessarily be inconsistent with a low rate of acquisition of gold out of the year-to-year flows of current income. Gamba quotes United Nations estimates which put the ratio of private gold hoards (a stock) in some parts of Asia at about 10 per cent of the relevant national income (a flow). On the whole, one is led to believe that, while only a small share of current income is used to acquire precious metals, etc., the historic accumulation of these assets is considerable and may have some valuable alternative use. We are thus led to ponder why individuals seek those asset forms and why, having acquired them, there is an obvious collective reluctance to relinquish them in favour of either alternative assets or consumption.

It seems that the demand for precious metals and stones is of a precautionary nature and is rooted in long historical experience of these assets as stores of value with a high degree of liquidity. The precautionary motive seems to be verified by the common observation that gold, say, is sold in times of distress and in times of seasonal shortages of cash. Swift has drawn attention to the seasonal pattern in Malaya, where both festive seasons and the agricultural cycle influence the relative demands for gold, etc., and cash. The interchange of these assets is facilitated by goldsmiths and pawnshops, which

> thrive just before the Festival of Hari Raya Puasa, and to a lesser extent before the Festival of Hari Raya Haji. The trade will be in both directions. On the one hand, there will be people redeeming and purchasing so that their display on the big day may be as fine as possible. On the other hand, individuals less fortunately placed will be raising cash so that they may obtain more important items such as sugar and meat. [Swift, 1961, p. 25]

The existence of pawnshops and of sale–repurchase practices among jewellers is of crucial importance in conferring liquidity upon precious metals, stones and ornaments. Swift describes these arrangements in Malaya (e.g. the practice of gold articles being sold to the public on the understanding that they may be returned to the shop for cash at around 90 per cent of cost price). Such buy-back arrangements and pawnbroking are virtually universal, and these practices may perhaps be regarded as carrying some seeds of a market for financial assets. The wide and ready availability of these facilities for moving between gold, etc., and cash makes gold, etc., almost as liquid as money balances while at the same time causing them to be perceived generally as a superior store of value.

> A visit to the Cairo gold market, for instance, during the daily rush hours . . . is quite instructive to the economist. The fellahin of the villages arrive with their bank notes and return after a few hours with their choice of coined gold or gold jewellery. The motive of the hoarders is not just to substitute one form of wealth with another, but to increase the degree of safety of their savings without reducing the liquidity of this investment. Gold fulfils this purpose but also fits other purposes well. The custom has become established owing to the satisfactory experience of many generations acting in the same way. For the same reason, appeals to the peasants to use banking facilities for their cash surpluses have so far had only a limited effect. [Bonné, 1957, p. 198]

It is no surprise that gold, silver, precious stones and ornaments are regarded as better stores of value than the coin, notes and bank balances of any individual country. The precious metals and stones have universal worth, and a high value in relation to bulk (large values are easily hidden and cheaply transported). Moreover, financial assets may be unattractive because of unfamiliarity or distrust, or because financial institutions appear forbidding (because of formal, impersonal ways) or cumbersome and slow, or are remote. As all history shows, those who live in fear of a natural disaster or war prefer to store their wealth in forms that are instantly and easily transportable and negotiable, should it become necessary to start a new life elsewhere. It is beyond our purpose to consider why the appeal of gold, etc., transcends time and space; suffice it to observe that the virtual universal negotiability of these assets rests not only on individual beliefs that others will find them valuable but also on the satisfaction (psychic income) that comes from the possession and display of the jewellery and ornaments into which most of the precious metals and stones in underdeveloped countries have been fashioned. This important 'durable consumer good' attribute is not obtainable from other stores of value. Indeed, Chandavarkar (1961) goes so far as to claim that the hoarding of gold, etc., is primarily motivated by this attribute.

The precautionary element in the desire to acquire gold, etc., has so far been considered in relation to expected misfortunes (episodic, trend, cyclical or seasonal) in a world of implicitly stable prices. It is also possible that gold, etc., may be desired as a hedge against inflation and/or in expectation of capital gain. Gamba (1958, p. 38) suggests that notes and coin may be more vulnerable to inflation than gold, etc.; but, as Gamba himself recognizes, relative values may move in the other direction in times of deflation. More fundamentally, Chandavarkar doubts that gold, etc., is very consciously sought as a hedge against inflation. He argues that peasants in poor countries are already protected from inflation to the extent that their incomes arise from subsistence and other non-monetary activities, that many underdeveloped countries have enjoyed price stability over long periods, and that the typical resident of a developing country is not so aware of the cost and risk of inflation that he would consciously seek assets that are unlikely to depreciate in real value.

Finally, the demand for precious metals and stones may be stronger in Islamic countries than elsewhere because orthodox Islam, which forbids the acceptance of interest, may discourage the holding of many types of financial assets.

It is not a sustainable argument that the hoarding of gold, etc., is deleterious to economic growth (Chandavarkar, 1961, offers a full discussion; the views of Hunter, 1967, on land acquisition are also largely applicable). It would seem, therefore, to be an unwise policy to attempt to suppress the widespread and continued demand for precious metals and stones in underdeveloped countries (even if it could be done successfully). Rather, it seems more sensible to recognize the inducement role of gold, etc., in encouraging a rise in the production of commodities for the market, in fostering saving and in promoting monetization (Chandavarkar, 1961, p. 145); it thus seems better to regard the acquisition of these assets as a desirable step up the ladder of financial development. The peasants who reach the stage of storing value in gold, etc., instead of either consuming all their incomes or saving in the form of storing surplus crops, are developing the habits that lead eventually to the acquisition of money and financial assets, thus in time allowing indirect finance through intermediaries to displace the more restricted allocation of investible funds that occurs under self-finance and direct finance. As economic and financial development proceed, it is to be expected that gold, etc., will be relinquished in favour of interest-bearing financial assets; in due course, and in roundabout ways, the privately held precious metals are likely to be transformed into reserves of the monetary system (see Chapter 3).

We turn now to the informal financial assets which proliferate in most underdeveloped societies. Since these do not take the form of marketable instruments, are seldom negotiable and sometimes are not even recorded on paper, it seems best to discuss them in terms of the types of borrowing/lending relationships in which they arise. Informal financial assets may be created by person-to-person loans or through some system of loan associations (credit clubs); both forms are very common in rural and urban areas in developing countries. A good example of the range and character of informal finance is contained in Table 6.1, which reproduces Rozental's categories of informal urban finance in Thailand. Although this table refers in its original context specifically to urban finance, the categories also have rural relevance in most

TABLE 6.1 *Informal Finance Markets in Thailand*

Type of market	Supply	Demand	Monthly rate of interest (%)
'Penumbra' of commercial bank	Compradores, bank officers, branch managers, agency partners	Businessmen	$1\frac{1}{2}$–2
Wholesalers	Landlords, rich merchants, highly placed individuals	Traders	2–3
Trade credit	Foreign exporters, large corporations, and others	Manufacturers	1–4
Rotating credit societies	Various		3–5
Retailers	Individuals (often wives of officials and traders)	Small businessmen	5–10
Small	'Unofficial' pawnshops, gold shops, night watchmen	Households	10 and over

Source: Rozental (1970a), p. 249.

countries. Indeed, the further inclusion of small-scale commercial credit (via storekeepers, crop buyers, landlords and moneylenders) and interpersonal credit (relatives, friends, neighbours) would make the table exhaustive of informal credit possibilities.

To lenders, informal loans offer the attractions of a generally higher rate of return than on formal securities, secrecy (advantageous, for example, in avoiding taxes), and being undemanding and uncumbersome administratively. The chief apparent disadvantage is the riskiness of this form of lending (*inter alia* the loans are generally unsecured), but the actual risk may be small insofar as each borrower's circumstances and reliability may be very well known to any lender who confines his activities to a small circle of friends and acquaintances. For many borrowers the informal loan is the only possible source of credit: commonly the borrower does not have the standing or the collateral to be considered for formal credit from a financial institution. However, even borrowers of standing at times find informal loans attractive because of the speed and/or secrecy with which they can be raised. Many also want to borrow for purposes which formal lending houses would regard as unwise. In this last respect, the fact that there is often no need to divulge the purpose for which an informal loan is sought is a further attraction of that type of credit.

Much attention has been given to the fact that informal credit arrangements are characterized by large numbers of borrowers and lenders dealing in relatively small amounts. The multiplicity of informal borrowers and lenders and the small size of loans have been well explained by Barbara Ward (1960) in terms of the limited size of the circle of knowledge possessed by any one creditor.

> The successful working of a system of commercial primary production by peasants requires the existence of a credit system that is not only extensive but also highly personalized. But if credit is to be advanced only to personal acquaintances, then there is a limit—and a fairly low limit—to the number of clients any one creditor can have. [Ward, 1960, p. 157]

Although Ward's perceptive analysis is couched in terms of rural credit, it also adequately explains much urban credit.

Ward devotes several pages to establishing the important starting point that middlemen are needed in underdeveloped export-producing societies to organize the collection and sale of marketable produce, and to provide for the distribution of imported consumer goods down to the smallest consumer units. This need is due partly to the difficulties of transport and communication in an underdeveloped economy, but more fundamentally to the small average size of the many independent producing and consuming units. These units are involved in the money economy as both sellers and buyers but they have little behind them in the way of stores of liquid wealth. Hence credit is crucially important to them.

The small producer needs cash or credit for the acquisition of those productive inputs and those foodstuffs that are not obtainable within the subsistence sector. With no money savings and with, very often, an uneven or seasonal flow of cash earnings, he must rely on credit. The small-scale consumer unit (distinguished only for expositional purposes from the producer unit, for commonly they are two sides of the one) also usually needs credit. Leaving aside petty cash outlays in street markets or for minor services, expenditures fall into two broad categories: (i) irregular, infrequent and relatively major cash purchases (e.g. of a boat, motorcycle, sewing machine, the wedding of a son/daughter); (ii) regular purchases of necessities such as imported foodstuffs, groceries and fuels. In the absence of cash savings, expenditures in category (i) will need to be financed by a cash loan from someone who knows and trusts the consumer (the sellers of the goods in this category will usually be specialist retailers in larger towns who cannot be expected to give personal credit to the purchaser). Expenditures of category (ii) 'because they are necessarily recurrent and localized and consist of goods which can be successfully stocked only in a permanent building and by at least a relatively full-time and experienced trader' (Ward, 1960, p. 158), lend themselves to revolving personal credit accounts.

Village shopkeepers supply credit for category (ii) purchases, very often advance the cash for category (i) transactions, and not uncommonly are also the buyers of peasant produce for export (in which case the value of exportables is credited to the producer's account, offsetting the debits for materials and consumer goods). We are here concerned only with retail and/or producer finance, but it is perhaps worth mentioning that the ultimate sources of this credit in under-developed economies are the great import–export merchant houses located at the major ports. From these firms, a veritable chain of trade credit extends through regional wholesalers and town stores down to the village shops and itinerant traders who deal finally with the producers and consumers.

It should not be thought that village lending is the exclusive preserve of shopkeepers and produce buyers. There are also those individuals or groups who make a full-time job of moneylending. Perhaps the best known are the *chettiars/chettyars* (colloquially, '*chetties*' '*chettys*' or '*chitties*'), a Tamil cast of moneylenders who have spread from Madras State in southern India throughout South and South East Asia. The *chettiars* went out as agents, each with a certain sum of money to start business. They normally also had lines of credit with their principals in Madras and were able to gain further finance from the British colonial bankers who had great faith in the shrewdness, integrity and reliability of the *chettiars*. The overseas *chettiar* received salary from the firm in India and share in the profits of his enterprise. After an agreed period, usually three years, he handed the agency to a successor and returned to Madras. In the twentieth century, many *chettiars* remained in South East Asia and began their own businesses, relying on the experience and funds they had built up as agents. The *chettiar* financial network is intricate; it reaches into the cities and towns as well as the villages, embraces all occupational and ethnic groups among its borrowers, and provides large credits as well as small.

Small-scale credit is needed, but it is not to be expected that banks or other financial institutions would be interested in supplying it: the would-be borrowers are unknown and apparently unreliable; they have no acceptable collateral to offer; and the unit costs of processing and administering loans would be prohibitively large in relation to the small average size of loans. Moreover, the banks very often operate under interest-rate ceilings, officially imposed or collectively agreed. In short, this type of credit would not be profitable for banks. It is, however, profitable—often highly so—for those lenders who can select borrowers who may be relied on for payment. Here the village shopkeeper/middleman/moneylender comes into action. He is in an unrivalled position to know the resources and character of those in his local circle, and his informal loan methods are not unbearably costly per loan unit or in total. But the number of loans he can carry is determined by the size of his own resources, which are not likely to be large. The lender, therefore, is twice limited in the number of debtors he may contemplate: by the small amount of loan capital at his disposal, and by the need to have close and accurate personal knowledge of each and every one of his debtors. (In those rural societies where it is customary for borrowers to pledge land and/or its product to creditors, each creditor is further limited by the small number of farms he can effectively supervise.) It follows, says Ward, that a wide distribution of credit can be achieved only by a relatively large number of creditors, each supplying small sums to a limited circle of trusted borrowers.

Corroborative evidence comes from Nisbet's interesting first-hand study in Chile. He found that rural moneylenders operated within a two-mile radius of their home villages, while shopkeepers gave credit over a larger area, in some cases up to a radius of twenty miles from home, depending upon population density and the nearness of other shops. Nisbet agrees that moneylenders and shopkeepers have, and need, close personal knowledge of their borrowers' circumstances. He observed that each lender carried between approximately one hundred and one thousand borrowers, that formal contracts and loan security were not used, and that in general there was no *bilateral* documentation of loans. The farmers interviewed by Nisbet 'displayed an appalling lack of knowledge of lenders and of the terms offered', usually being unaware of alternative informal lenders or rates of interest. This ignorance Nisbet attributes to a lack of education, economic and geographic immobility, narrow ideas, and the fact that moneylenders, being illegal in Chile, are secretive about their operations (Nisbet, 1967, pp. 80–2).

Ward's paper brings out the value of scarce information, i.e. the knowledge of who are, and who are not, good credit risks.

> Indeed, it might be suggested that the similarities between some of the methods of entering into a credit relationship in peasant producing populations and in the West are closer than might be expected. If a private individual here in England wants to borrow money or open a credit account, he too has to establish his credentials, and in the last resort this means that he too depends on personal knowledge on the part of his creditor. This applies to loans from building societies and even from the banks which do not have a multiplicity of branches stretching into quite small villages for nothing. It applies still more to the multitude of more or less 'private' mortgages negotiated by solicitors on behalf of their clients. It could be argued that this function of the local solicitor in England (together with others that also require his personal acquaintance with his clients) largely explains the otherwise rather surprising multiplicity of small legal firms existing in every small town in the country. There is certainly a very large proportion of creditors to debtors in these 'private' relationships. [Ward, 1960, p. 163]

The credit arrangements just described—via shopkeeper, middleman, moneylenders or 'friends'—are all of a person-to-person nature. Also informal, and still relying for successful operation on close knowledge of debtors, are those many and various group loan arrangements which collectively may be styled *money loan associations*. Some alternative terms are *money associations, mutual loan associations, mutual credit clubs* and *tontine*, which is the Westernized term for Chinese *wui*, or *kuthu*, a Tamil term. There are a multitude of different language and dialect names for these group finance systems and much variation on the basic theme (see Gamba, 1958; Freedman, 1961; Geertz, 1962; Campbell and Chang, 1962; Rozental, 1970a for names and descriptions of these activities as practiced in many parts of Asia). So common is this informal institution that printed books, setting out the rules and providing columns for recording contributions and payments, are available (Freedman, 1961, p. 40; Gamba, 1958, p. 40). Incidentally, the practice is by no means confined to underdeveloped countries; it was well known, for example, in Melbourne offices and retail stores in the 1930s under the name of 'suit clubs'—the man drawing the pool invariably using it to purchase a new suit of clothes. It is probably because of the postwar flowering of easy consumer credit in Australia that the suit clubs have disappeared.

The common theme of the money loan associations is that a group of people—almost always well known to one another—meet regularly to pool agreed amounts of money and take turns to 'draw' (appropriate) the whole pool. Mutual trust—based on knowledge of character—is essential. 'The members needed to trust both the promoter and one another not to decamp after drawing the pool. It therefore fell to the promoter to recruit his group in such a fashion as to inspire confidence' (Freedman, 1961, p. 40). The need for mutual trust usually means that the members have a common bond in class, village origins, dialect group, clan or employment. They meet regularly and frequently (once a month is usual) to pay in contributions. At each meeting the pool of contributions is taken by one member, each getting the pool once only in turn determined by bidding or by lot.

The lottery method of allocation is preferred by contributors who like a gamble. The simplest system is of regular, flat-rate contributions, with no interest being paid on contributions or charged for use of the pool. Hence the earlier one draws the pool the longer interest-free use one has of the lump sum and the shorter is the period that one makes non-interest-bearing contributions; conversely, the later one draws the pool the longer one pays into it without either reward or use of the lump sum. It is clearly advantageous to obtain an early draw. Consequently, the promoter invariably has first draw, this being the reward for his enterprise.

Where the pool is auctioned, interest on the pool sum is paid, in effect, by each borrower on the pool sum for the term he has the use of it, and interest is received by each contributor on his contributions. Complexities arise in that (1) each member of the group is both contributor (receiving interest) and at some stage recipient of the pool (paying interest), and (2) interest payments are frequently not explicit, but implicit in the size of contributions and pool. As before, the promoter generally has the benefit of first draw and in some variations also receives an organizing fee. An example, borrowed from Freedman, may clarify these points.

> Suppose that there are nine members and a promoter. At the first meeting each member paid the promoter $10. At the second meeting tenders were submitted, the pool going to the highest bidder. Suppose the successful bid was $2; then the bidder collected $10 from the promoter and $8 (i.e. $10 minus 2) from each of the eight other members, a total of $74. The process was repeated at the third meeting. Suppose the highest bid was again $2; then the bidder collected $10 each from the promoter and the previous successful bidder and $8 from each of the seven other members, a total of $76. It will be seen that the amount of the pool (loan) increases progressively. The period over which the loan is enjoyed, however, is reduced progressively. This latter circumstance is likely to outweigh the former, so that one would expect, other things being equal, that the amount of the successful bid would decrease progressively. Extraneous factors, of course, might cause the bids to diverge from such a regular pattern, while any sudden lack of confidence in the organization might lead members to bid high even towards the end of the series. If, for the sake of simplicity, we assume a flat rate of bidding of $2 throughout, then the very last member (who, of course, made no bid) came away with $9 \times 10 = \$90$, having paid $74 in instalments. If the meetings were at monthly intervals, the last member had invested $74 over a period of nine months and made a profit of $16 at the end. The first succesful bidder, on the other hand, had paid out $90 in instalments during the period and had the benefit of a loan of $74 for a period of eight months. [Freedman, 1961, pp. 40–1]

An early draw of the pool provides earliest use of the common fund, at the cost of maximum interest paid; conversely, a late draw means less interest paid but entails a wait for use of the pool. The system appeals to both borrowers and lenders—the needy borrower should bid high to get the pool early, while the lender should bid low, or not at all, in order to get the latest and largest pool possible. The attractiveness of the associations to lenders is evidenced by the fact that many contribute to a number of different loan associations, finding this outlet for their spare funds more attractive than interest-bearing deposits with institutions.

In the example quoted, the last person to draw the pool earned a return (simple) of over 14 per cent per annum on his contributions, while a similar rate of interest was paid by the one who drew the pool first. However, the lender probably earned more and the borrower paid less than the interest rates attached to alternative uses/sources of their funds. The borrowing rate is invariably higher than that charged by financial institutions, but, of course, most borrowers from loan associations could not command institutional credit (or at least not for the amounts and terms involved) and generally have only moneylenders or pawnbrokers as their alternative sources of finance. A good example of this type of borrower would be the hawker or petty shopkeeper who uses the pool to augment his working capital. It is appropriate here to emphasize that the money loan associations may be an important source of business finance and are by no means used only to provide consumer credit. This is especially true in Thailand, where a survey of urban business finance conducted by Rozental revealed that 30 per cent of the firms surveyed (mostly small retail establishments) had recourse to this form of finance (Rozental, 1970a, Chapter 7).

The money loan associations have been observed throughout Asia and in Africa and are very important within the social groups that use them. Some indication of the economic size of the associations may be given by the fact that in Singapore, between July 1953 and February 1954, police were called in to investigate abscondments involving $1,814,000 (=$US600,000 approximately) by organizers of Chinese *tontine* (Gamba, 1958, p. 40). Although this example is now somewhat dated, the money loan associations still flourish and will only be displaced, if ever, by financial institutions that can offer attractive rates of interest to lenders and cheap, simple, easily accessible forms of small credit.

> It is important to recognize the fact that these practices are general and that they form an integral part of the life of many thousands of individuals, even among those who are quite well educated. These methods of borrowing are efficient and speedy, as well as easily understood by people at all socio-economic levels. They do not involve the signing of papers nor any complex organisation. Furthermore, they rely for their operation and success on mutually accepted standards of honesty, and on trust between individuals, because they belong to the same class, . . . province or village. [Gamba, 1958, p. 142]

In general, money loan associations are most prevalent in urban areas where there are greater concentrations of people in regular wage employment. But they also flourish in the rural districts among plantation workers, railway employees, etc., who enjoy regular incomes, and they are not unknown among peasant farmers (cf. Geertz, 1962). The associations are particularly popular among lower-grade clerical workers, shop assistants, domestic servants and wage-labourers on agricultural estates. It has often been remarked that the initiative in forming an association often comes from the supervisor or foreman in any group of workers.

This might be the most appropriate place to insert a little piece of historical evidence, namely the annual cash receipts and expenditures summary for 1893 of a twenty-five year old clerk in the Malayan Railway Service who had emigrated from Ceylon. (I came across this item among the old records of a Singapore merchant firm. There seems no reason to doubt the authenticity of the evidence.) The figures, in Straits Settlements dollars, are as follows:

Income

Salary and overtime	466.95
Receipts from *kuthu*	50.00
	516.95

Expenditure

Consumption	241.91
Kuthu contributions	75.00
Remittances to Ceylon (Rs. 215)	90.00
Repayments to *chetty*	
($25 loan over 5 months @	
interest 2·75 per cent per month)	28.50
Loans to other people	45.00
Undecipherable	12.20
	492.61
Balance unaccounted for	24.34
	516.95

Notice that, in addition to transactions relating to the money loan association (*kuthu*), the clerk was simultaneously both lending to acquaintances and borrowing from a *chettiar* moneylender.

The economic advantages of the money loan system are many: it is a good way of rolling tiny amounts of saving into larger, more deployable sums; it improves individual financial responsibility, as people are generally likely to be more careful in spending the pool than the smaller individual contributions; it engenders entrepreneurial, managerial and financial skills (in both contributors and pool promoters); it provides a form of insurance, since in case of hardship it is possible to draw the pool at short notice.

Geertz convincingly emphasizes the role of the money associations as a socio-economic bridge between the financing habits of traditional societies and the financial forms of commercialized societies. He points out that, moving through the spectrum from simple to complex money associations, the social emphasis diminishes as the economic intensifies. Where the rural associations in Java pay much regard to the meeting and entertaining aspects of the association and simple if not scant attention to the question of interest, the well developed urban associations in Singapore, Korea and Vietnam are very sensitive to the interest rate, disburse the pool by auction rather than by lot, have large memberships and (often) paid administrators. Movement along this spectrum involves harnessing familiar motivations and applying them to unfamiliar purposes. Loyalty, understanding and trust originate in one's traditional group identity, and it is on this foundation that faith in more general financial promises may be built. Geertz argues that the money loan associations provide a means of using customary patterns of co-operation, mutual support and communal responsibility to regulate emergent economic and financial activities.

> The fact that the members of the association all have neighbourhood, kinship or other particularistic ties with one another acts to prevent fraud and evasion. The fact that the money is delivered immediately upon collection to the winner, so that no one has to be trusted to hold cash belonging to anyone else for any period of time, reduces the likelihood of embezzlement. The feasting aspect softens the harshness of the economic calculation aspects and prevents them from under-mining customary ties. The form thus combines an activity functional to a commercial economy—the concentration of monetized resources in larger units—with a maintenance of traditional moral values. [Geertz, 1962, p. 262]

The money associations, like the pawnshops, etc., have a most useful role to play in introducing and habituating people to financial forms and methods. From this start, people may move on to formal institutions such as banks, co-operative finance societies, consumer credit houses, etc. In the course of economic development informal financiers and loan associations may become redundant. Meanwhile, however, their valuable role in financial development needs recognition and encouragement. As I shall argue in the final chapter, it is also desirable to take advantage, where possible, of these informal practices in attempting to foster integration between informal and institutional finance.

The lending style of shopkeepers/moneylenders, pawnbrokers and money loan associations is on the whole extremely informal. Minimal records are maintained, legal documentation is negligible. Loans do not take the form of a bank money credit but are usually disbursed in currency or, as in the case of shopkeeper loans, in goods. The pawnshops, of course, take as collateral the items surrendered to them in pledge (jewellery, radios, clothing and so forth), and other moneylenders take collateral where it is possible to do so. For example, on relatively large loans the borrower may pledge land, crops, livestock, gold, jewels or an automobile. (The *chettiars* have always preferred secured loans; gold, mortgages and promissory notes being favoured as collateral. Inevitably, native land passed into *chettiar* hands by the forfeiture of mortgages, to the consequent dismay of governments who then sought to curb the activities of the *chettiars*.) But as most loans are of small amounts and made to people who cannot provide acceptable collateral they are necessarily unsecured. In passing, it is worth noting that pawnbrokers' tickets, the only transferable paper emanating from informal loan activities, are often sold to third parties for cash, and so may properly be regarded as marketable financial instruments. (Indeed, some people make a profitable business of buying up pawnshop tickets for trivial sums and then redeeming and selling the goods.) Here is a seed of financial development.

Informal financing, in the forms so far described, is by no means wholly direct in nature; i.e., the lenders are not invariably restricted to their own resources: they may also 'retail' funds entrusted to them from other sources. For instance, 'the pawnbrokers, through time, have become also similar to investment bankers, accepting cash from friends and relatives and investing it in the business. The pawnshops, furthermore, are heavily backed by some of the Chinese commercial banks' (Gamba, 1958, p. 53). This example suggests that the pawnshops may be a promising point of integration between informal and institutional financing. Rozental (1967, p. 458) is of the same view. Pawnshops sponsored and/or regulated by government may be an important vehicle for distributing credit supplied by government down to small-scale producers and consumers while at the same time habituating such people to the benefits and norms of institutional finance.

Rozental has drawn attention to the fact that a good deal of credit obtained from shopkeepers, moneylenders, pawnbrokers, money loan associations, family and friends goes on consumption spending or to low (national) priority investments (Rozental, 1967, p. 456). These uses of credit, however, are surely inevitable. In all societies some people do live precariously or spend recklessly or invest unwisely but still desire credit for these purposes; in advanced economies, for instance, a lot of personal saving finances dissaving by others or 'sub-optimal' investment. The real question is whether in underdeveloped societies small credit needs are best met in the traditional informal ways or whether those ways should be stamped out and replaced by government/institutional credit. It is perhaps unfair to put the question in terms of such extreme alternatives, for I shall argue for the middle course of sustaining traditional financial practices while at the same time promoting their gradual integration with the formal, institutionalized financial sector. However, others have been highly critical of traditional finance and have argued vehemently for its eradication. Such views are usually based upon the alleged wickedness of moneylenders and middlemen, as evidenced principally by the extremely high rates of interest that they charge for loans. It is appropriate, therefore, that we now devote some space to the subject of interest rates.

'High' interest rates on informal/unorganized financial transactions in underdeveloped countries are generally acknowledged. The facts are attested by a very large number of official reports—almost every country can point to an inquiry into credit conditions—and academic publications. Much of this literature is of a hand-wringing tone, buttressing something of a conventional wisdom that high interest rates are 'bad' for development and indicative of 'wickedness' among suppliers of credit. Nominal rates of interest on informal credit certainly run—and seem always to have run—into double figures, 'ranging typically from 24 per cent per annum to 50 per cent and above' (Chandavarkar, 1971, p. 61). The figure of 300 per cent per annum can be found several times in the literature (From the vast literature, selective reference may be made to Wai, 1957; Gamba, 1958; Nisbet, 1967; Usher, 1967, whose articles contain abundant evidence of very high nominal rates of interest and also give reference to many official acknowledgements of the existence of such rates. Table 11 by Wai, pp. 140–2, and Table IV by Usher, reproduced here as Table 6.2, are especially noteworthy.) It is worth noting that these are lenders' rates charged upon informal loans. There is

TABLE 6.2 *Summary of Thailand Interest Rates*[a]

	(%)
Personal loans from money lenders in Bangkok	300
Private loans among civil servants	120
Money lenders' rates to farmers—North and North East	60–120
Money lenders' rates to farmers—Central plain	15–60
Loans to farmers from other farmers—North and North East	40
Loans to farmers from other farmers	19
Private loans among businessmen	15–18
Rates of commercial banks on loans and overdrafts	10–15
Earning: price ratio of shares	12.5
Co-operatives lending to farmers	10
Net return on stockholding of rice	10
Land rent/land price, North and North East	5–10
Time deposits (12 months) of commercial banks	7
Bank of Thailand rediscount rate	5
Land rent/land price, central plain	3–5
Demand deposits of commercial banks	0–1/2

[a] Per cent per annum, circa 1964.

Source: Usher (1967), p. 278.

no evidence available about deposit rates offered by money-lenders, though it is generally believed that 'moneylenders do not usually accept deposits, and in the event of acceptance the rates are far below those for loans' (Chandavarkar, 1971, p. 63).

These observed nominal rates are certainly high relative to rates charged by financial institutions (in both advanced and underdeveloped economies), though less so in recent years of the high, world-wide inflation which has pushed many institutional rates of interest into double figures. Unfortunately, no very recent observations of informal interest rates in developing countries are available, but there is some suggestion that they are not very sensitive to inflation, or at least much less sensitive to it than are institutional rates; and if this be true the differential between informal and institutional rates will have narrowed lately. A more pertinent observation (following Chandavarkar, 1971, p. 62) is that informal loan rates in developing countries may not invariably be unduly high in relation to rates charged on comparable loans (i.e. unsecured and for consumption) in advanced economies. The security aspect leads to another observation (Wai, 1957, p. 104) that moneylenders tend to charge higher rates on small loans than on large loans and on short-term than on long-term accommodation. The explanation for this apparent inversion of interest rate conventions is that large and/or long-term loans are likely to be made against collateral security whereas small, short-term credit is invariably unsecured.

The considerations raised in the previous paragraphs should lead us to reflect upon the economic reasons for the nominally high rates of interest on informal loans. 'Wicked exploitation' by moneylenders has been alleged but supply and demand (capital scarcity), cost and risk must also be taken into account.

According to Wai (1957, pp. 80–1, 107–8), high interest rates result from chronic excess demand for credit. Low incomes permit little saving and lending by individuals, informal lenders do not own large resources and cannot readily draw further loanable funds from the organized, institutional, financial sector. In short, there is a general shortage of capital in underdeveloped countries; the need for credit is endemic in a poor society because of its social and structural characteristics, notably the inadequate gap between consumption and income.

The cost element in informal interest rates cannot be ignored. Credit is expensive to administer when average loan size is low and operating economies of scale unavailable. Commercial banks, organized to scale-economizing operations, have invariably been deterred from competing with informal credit because unit costs of loan administration are prohibitively high in relation to small loans. Thus the field has been left clear to the moneylenders whose operational costs are low but whose scale of business is necessarily limited by the need to know each debtor. Nisbet's study found that 97 per cent of informal loans in his sample were for amounts of less than $US1,000 and 78 per cent for amounts lower than $US200. By contrast the average size of farm loan granted, at the same time, by Chile's largest commercial bank was $US10,000 approximately. Incidentally, half of the informal loans in the same sample were for consumption purposes (Nisbet, 1967, pp. 78–80, 87).

High risk is often argued to necessitate high rates of interest on informal loans. U Tun Wai, for example, takes this view and claims that 'defaults tend to be larger in unorganized money markets' (1957, p. 109). Moreover, as we have seen, collateral security is rarely available for informal loans (another factor deterring competition from banks). However, the high default rate is by no means invariably observed—many examples of low default can be found—and it can be argued the *sine qua non* of successful informal moneylending is an intimate knowledge of the creditworthiness of debtors, such that default should be rare.

Interest rates must also be assessed in real, not nominal,

terms. For example, Nisbet's study in Chile revealed some interesting, and entirely rational, behaviour in the informal credit market under conditions of inflation. Categorizing lenders as 'commercial' or 'non-commercial' (relatives, friends, etc., of the borrowers), Nisbet found that the real interest rates on loans tended to depend on the type of lender: commercial lenders usually reaped positive real rates of interest, within a range of 27 per cent to 360 per cent per annum, whereas non-commercial lenders tended to receive zero, or even negative, real interest rates. Non-commercial lenders, in fact, tended to lend in kind and seek repayment in kind so as to avoid the risk of real losses associated with cash loans and repayments under inflation. Indeed, given the general reluctance in Chile to hold cash, commercial lenders also preferred repayment in kind, whether the loan was given in kind or cash (Nisbet, 1967, pp. 74–8). In any informal loan market, irrespective of any general inflation in the relevant economy, nominal interest rates on loans are often inflated by hidden charges. Examples abound in all countries; suffice it to mention the common practices of deducting interest from a loan at the moment of advancing, thus raising the effective rate of interest on the sum actually taken by the borrower; overvaluing advances in kind; undervaluing repayments in kind.

The fact that lenders in the informal credit markets are so often price-setters while borrowers are generally price-takers has led to a popular view that high interest rates reflect a degree of monopoly power held by the suppliers of credit. (Chandavarkar, 1965, provides a succinct statement of the economic and social conditions that make for non-competing moneylenders; see also Bottomley, 1964, pp. 432–5.) There is undoubtedly some truth in this view: witness the fact that many small borrowers have no real alternative to a single local source of credit. But to recognize this truth is not to say that all suppliers of informal credit enjoy monopoly profits, even when nominal interest rates appear to be high. Bottomley, while admitting the existence of monopoly profits, has argued that 'administration charges, together with the premium for risk, are probably the major determinants of the high level of interest rates which obtain throughout the underdeveloped world' (Bottomley, 1963, p. 646). We have already noticed that commercial banking institutions have refrained from invading the small loans market because of the high unit costs attached to the granting and supervision of small loans and the riskiness of such loans when they are neither supported by security nor based on personal knowledge of the debtor's reliability. It should also be noted that official attempts to displace moneylenders by government-sponsored co-operative credit societies have not been widely successful, for either the co-operative has to charge high interest rates if it is to be a commercially viable enterprise or the government must subsidize the co-operative in order to hold down the loan interest rate (e.g. Drake, 1966; Usher, 1967; more will be said about co-operatives in the next chapter).

While in the longer term economic development will enhance the ability of borrowers to approach lending institutions (the argument—see Bottomley, 1964—is based on increased farm productivity leading to increased rural surpluses, permitting the build-up of assets which would serve as loan collateral, and on the general education improvements that make people aware of institutional alternatives to local monopolistic moneylenders), in the short run the only way that any monopoly powers of informal moneylenders can be eroded is to increase the competition in the informal loans market by expanding the volume of credit and the number of suppliers. It has been further argued that increased competition will—by causing surviving lenders to operate more efficiently at higher capacity—bring down the administrative cost element in loan charges (Bottomley, 1964).

It is futile to attempt to depress informal interest rates by regulation 'because the moneylenders perform a genuine economic service in the unorganized credit market which the government cannot provide' (Myint, 1970, p. 140). This is true for both rural and urban areas: it is the type of credit needed (small, unsecured amounts), rather than the location or the economic activity of the borrower, that provides the opportunity for the moneylender. Any increase in the supply of informal credit requires, in effect, facilitating the access of would-be moneylenders to funds from the formal financial institutions. It is crucially important, however, that this strategy should be associated with increased competition in the informal loans market. For otherwise any existing monopolist would prefer to continue to restrict the supply of loans while enhancing his monopoly profit by availing himself of cheaper 'wholesale' credit from an institution, so lowering his costs. It remains, of course, an empirical question in any area whether apparently monopolist lenders (e.g. a single shopkeeper in a village) do behave consciously in classical textbook fashion, restricting the supply of loans and holding up the interest rate, thereby reaping maximum (monopoly) profits, as Bottomley (1964, p. 432) assumes. It is alternatively possible that credit is so scarce that the competitive market-clearing rate of interest is very high. Ward's empirical work seems to support the latter view. A policy of increasing the supply of informal credit (provided that this is not inflationary) and encouraging linkages to institutional finance seems desirable, irrespective of whether or not monopoly is already present.

In fact, there are already many points of contact between the informal and formal loan markets. The proper policy is to increase and strengthen these links so that a fuller integration of the two financial sectors can be achieved. Usher (1967) has suggested that a greater degree of integration between informal, formal and even international finance markets exists than is generally believed. He is certainly right to object to the narrow view that village rates of interest are determined entirely by local forces, uninfluenced by rates elsewhere in the country or abroad;

but his argument is complex and may perhaps be regarded as peculiar to Thailand, where exportable rice production and related activities account for such a large part of gross domestic product.* More generally, the great importance of bill of exchange finance and trade credit (well known and widely observed to run between banks, large export-import firms, wholesalers, retailers, produce buyers, producers and consumers) in primary-producing, export-oriented developing countries suggests that there is considerable scope for strengthening the links between the informal and formal finance sectors.

Finally, it is necessary to say a few words about another type of informal finance which is quite different in size and characteristics from the types so far discussed. This is the informal financing that occurs within large *Groups*, which operate conglomerate activities in the modern sector of any developing economy.

'Groups flourish in countries that have chosen to pursue economic growth within the framework of a private but not necessarily free or competitive enterprise system' (Child, 1976, p. 124). Groups are common in Asia, Latin America and Africa. As Leff (1976, p. 99) observes, 'Much of the private industrial sector, and particularly the activities that involve large capital investments, are in practice Group oper-

---

* In essence, fluctuations in rice prices—as well as changes in interest rates and other costs—affect the rates of return obtainable from both landholding and rice-storing (a potentially profitable activity since mature rice is always more valuable than young rice). The rates of return determined on rural land and rice stocks held by peasants put ceilings on the rates at which the peasants will be prepared to borrow to finance the growing and/or holding of rice and a floor under the rate of return that they will contemplate from alternative investments. Any rise, for example, in the world rate of interest transmitted by the chain of credit to peasant farmers would raise the cost of storing rice until maturity and so, subsequently and other things equal, would reduce the supply and raise the price of 'old' rice. 'The evidence is consistent with a pattern in which world rates of interest are transmitted through letters of credit or trade credit to the annual appreciation of the rice price and from there to the rate of return on landholding. This interpretation implies a far greater integration among world markets than is generally supposed to exist' (Usher, 1967, p. 277).

ations. The Groups in fact constitute a mechanism for mobilizing and pooling entrepreneurship and technical expertise as well as capital in large-scale, modern activities.' The main distinctive features of a Group enterprise are as follows:

(1) it is run by people with a strong common bond—usually of a tribal, clan or other ethnic nature—which transcends the mere nuclear family;
(2) its industrial and commercial interests extend into several product and service markets, sometimes even embracing its own bank;
(3) its original capital comes from within the Group and is expanded through the reinvestment of profits.

The last feature leads to the important point that accumulated capital funds are shifted between the different industrial and commercial activities conducted by the Group (see Chapter 3 above, p. 41). Leff goes on from this point to argue that the Groups 'perform the principal functions of a capital market' (Leff, 1976, p. 99) and, as we have seen previously, Stammer (1972) has suggested that the Groups may obviate the need for a diverse and widespread set of financial institutions.

Leff (1976, p. 99) points out that, 'Because of the Groups' inter-activity capital flows, the concept of "self-finance" takes on a special meaning: cash flow generated in one activity can be used to increase the capital stock in other, widely diverse activities.' However, this means that intra-Group financing does not create negotiable financial assets. Hence (1) there is no augmentation of the national supply of marketable financial assets (securities); and (2) the Groups themselves do not acquire financial assets which may be traded at will, and so they may be moved eventually to acquire foreign financial assets in order to avoid an illiquid and unbalanced investment portfolio consisting predominantly of real domestic capital. Intra-Group financing may thus constitute a double handicap to domestic financial development—diminishing the supply of securities that would otherwise be created via financial intermediation, and diverting demand for securities to foreign capital markets.

Bound up with the question of group finance are distributional problems and issues of monopoly/oligopoly power in product and factor markets. From a purely financial viewpoint, however, the Group system may be beneficial in economies where the financial system is little developed, provided, of course, that the Groups do not 'foreclose the possibilities for future evolution toward a pattern of capital markets with broader public access' (Leff, 1976, p. 113). The ripe time for Groups comes and goes, as has been well said by Child (1976, pp. 124–6). There is a clear need for more research about the Groups themselves and the economies in which they operate before either encouragement or discouragement of them can be advocated in general. Virtually nothing is publicly known about the structure, size and ramifications of any Group; there are no good quantitative estimates of the resources handled by Groups in any country; their relationships—perhaps influential—with governments and the ways in which Group operations are related to fiscal, tariff, exchange and investment policies do not appear to have been documented in any country. Until knowledge is gathered on such subjects, we can say no more than that, while the Groups may provide valuable financial mobility in economies that are deficient in intermediaries, the Group system should not be regarded as an adequate substitute for more general and widespread financial development. The role of the Groups is at best auxiliary or transitional.

Two main policy points emerge in this chapter and need to be identified now; they will be pursued again in a general framework in Chapter 9. First, informal finance and the rudimentary financial assets it generates have an important place in the process of financial development. Informal financial activities both promote monetization by encouraging the holding of money and money-debt in place of traditional real assets, and represent a step beyond mere monetization towards the further economic benefits that flow from fuller financial development (see Chapter 3). Informal finance habituates people to the spreading of expenditure over time and place and inculcates skills in financial management. The great merit of these informal activities is that they have evolved naturally and spontaneously, in response to needs.

> The very existence of such activities under the common handicaps attached to them demonstrates their vigor and their acceptance. To remove them by policy decree would either not be effective, or if effective, would merely leave unattended a keenly felt economic need. The latter can be justified only in those relatively rare cases where it can be shown that such activities are detrimental to important social goals and values. [Rozental, 1967, p. 457]

Rozental himself recognizes that informal finance promotes—at least in the short run—consumption and low-social-priority investment. This 'cost' however must be weighed against the long-term benefits of financial development. Financial habits and skills are not easily imposed, or grafted, on a traditional society. They grow faster and stronger when they are built upon, and develop naturally from, traditional practices. I therefore believe—and would claim the support of Geertz and Rozental in this approach—that traditional financial practices should be fostered *as a means of financial transition.* In other words, people should not be actively discouraged from informal financial activities, but they should be encouraged to progress to more formal financial practices (using marketable financial instruments and financial institutions). In this way, indirect finance will be strengthened and the prospects for better allocation of investment and supervision of credit, according to the national scale of priorities, will be improved.

We are led to the second point, namely, that it is desirable in promoting economic and financial development to integrate the informal and formal financial sectors. As we have seen in passing, and not withstanding the survival of a degree—high in some countries—of financial dualism, there are already a number of points of contact between the two sectors. For example, some moneylenders have access to funds from financial institutions; some banks actively seek to finance moneylenders and pawnbrokers; some Groups own banks; some final or retail borrowers may have access to both formal and informal sources of credit; many chains of credit run back from village shops to regional warehouses, to big merchant firms, to overseas capital markets. These linkages should be sustained; additionally, a much greater and freer flow of funds between the formal and the informal financial sectors should be promoted. As will be seen when the question of integration is taken up again in the final chapter, this policy would in many countries entail a considerable rise in interest rates within the formal financial sector. It is now time to examine that sector; the next two chapters deal first with financial institutions and then with the markets for negotiable securities in which financial institutions, firms, governments and individuals operate.

Further Reading

A general introduction to the issues raised in this chapter is provided by Wai (1957). Abundant and rich descriptive detail of informal financial practices in underdeveloped societies can be found in Swift (1961), Freedman (1961), Campbell and Chang (1962) and especially Gamba (1958). Ward (1960), in an article that has unfortunately not received due recognition in later literature, reports most interesting first-hand research and offers a satisfying explanation of the large numbers of informal lenders. Nisbet (1967) is another good field study. Rozental (1970a, pp. 50–77 and Chapter 7) provides a substantial account of all forms of informal finance in Thailand: his Chapter 7 is especially recommended for the detailed results of a sample survey of urban credit which brings out the very great importance of informal finance.

In addition to works already mentioned, the question of informal interest rates is discussed by Chandavarkar (1965,

1971), Bottomley (1963, 1964) and Usher (1967). The apparent disagreement between Bottomley and Chandavarkar is based on differing assumptions about the prevalence, rather than the existence, of true monopolists in the rural credit markets. Usher's substantial and detailed account and analysis of Thai interest rates provides an especially valuable case study which in many aspects is of wider relevance and interest.

My disposition towards a policy of maintaining traditional financial practices while simultaneously encouraging their integration with the formal financial sector is discussed, and endorsed, by Rozental (1967), Myint (1970) and a number of the other writers cited.

CHAPTER 7

Financial Institutions

In all countries, rich and poor, organized financial institutions of some sort have in fact developed; they have obvious advantages—monetization, specialization, the displacement of self-finance by direct and indirect finance—which contribute to the provision of large-scale investment sums and an improved allocation of capital funds, as we have seen in Chapter 3. In most countries there has been a spontaneous evolution of financial institutions, moving along the spectrum from simplicity to financial sophistication. Institutional finance generally begins with banks, moves to more institutional diversity and specialization, and leads eventually to markets for financial assets. In this model credit rationed by banks (and other institutions) gives way in the end to credit rationed by the price mechanism. The less common model (as exemplified by Mexico) is where institutional development is hurried along by some form of government intervention or promotion, with the government playing a more or less direct role in the allocation of credit. The establishment of a central bank may be either one of the final stones in a financial edifice that grew fairly naturally and slowly, or the foundation stone of a consciously designed and rapidly developed system.

Within the evolutionary style of development of financial institutions—beginning with just banks—there have been some very interesting differences of form and practice in different countries. As is well known, the British banks favoured narrow canons of lending, concentrating on short-term, self-liquidating credit, disbursed through overdrafts and the acceptance of trade bills.

> The industrialization of England had proceeded without any substantial utilization of banking for long-term investment purposes. The more gradual character of the industrialization process and the more considerable accumulation of capital, first from earnings in trade and modernized agriculture and later from industry itself, obviated the pressure for developing any special institutional devices for provision of long-term capital to industry. [Gerschenkron, 1965, p. 14.]

The very narrow British conception of the role of banks was possible only because there had already developed in Britain the money and bill markets, on one side of the banks, and the stock exchange and new issue system—for industrial financing—on the other side. In other words, and at any given level of risk, the British banks were able to specialize in supplying short-term, self-liquidating credit and could afford to stand off from what they regarded as 'unsuitable' forms of lending because of the existence of other avenues by which these credit needs could be met.

By contrast, the more rapid industrialization of continental Europe required, in short order, both entrepreneurial vigour and a massive supply of funds for industrial investment. In France, the Crédit Mobilier of the Pereire brothers provided the necessary financial form for the direct provision of finance to nascent industry, in the process displacing the more traditional continental bank activities of conducting foreign exchange transactions and floating government bond issues. Other industrial finance banks of the Crédit Mobilier type sprang up around the Continent. These were highly specialized institutions at the other extreme of specialization from the British banks. Beginning in Germany, specialization eventually gave way on the Continent to diversification, with the advent of 'universal' banks.

> The difference between banks of the crédit mobilier type and commercial banks in the advanced industrial country of the time (England) was absolute. Between the English bank essentially designed to serve as a source of short-term capital and a bank designed to finance

the long-run investment needs of the economy there was a complete gulf. The German banks, which may be taken as a paragon of the type of the universal bank, successfully combined the basic idea of the crédit mobilier with the short-term activities of commercial banks. [Gerschenkron, 1965, p. 13]

In the New World, the traditional British-type bank was incapable of providing long-term finance for industrial and agricultural development. The United States therefore began to develop their own unit (local) banks. Australia found the traditional British system quite unsuitable for its sparsely populated, and predominantly pastoral, economy. Short-term, self-liquidating bank loans could not meet Australia's needs, and there were no stock exchanges or non-bank institutions to provide long-term capital. Australia therefore developed two ways of financing pastoral investment. First, bank overdrafts began to be rolled over, if not carried on in virtual perpetuity. The short-term overdraft became in effect a long-term loan against the security of pastoral or agricultural land. Secondly, the companies that were engaged in export–import activities related to the pastoral industry developed a financial arm to go with their marketing arm, and raised sums in Britain specifically for the purpose of financing rural production. Japan, perhaps most interesting of all, began with the continental model which, incidentally, was characterized not only by the absence of a new issues market and stock exchange, but also by the lack of direct finance in the form of retained profits. (Subsequently, however, Japan actively developed the new issue and securities markets.)

In short, the advanced countries of the modern world went about the initial financing of their economic development, within a *laissez-faire* environment, by tapping one or other of three broad sources: undistributed/retained profits (self-finance); issues of shares and debentures (direct finance); and bank credit (indirect finance). (There was, of course, some overlap between the latter categories as when, for example, the banks directly acquired shares in industrial ventures.) The presently underdeveloped countries, naturally impatient for effective ways of financing investment in agriculture, industry and the tertiary sector simultaneously, must make as much use as possible of all three methods, undertaking whatever institutional establishment or adaptation that may be required, and must give serious consideration to a greater or lesser degree of government participation in the raising and allocation of credit. In practice, all this may mean bending the lending attitudes of existing financial institutions, establishing new, specialized financial institutions, and fostering the development of securities markets where shares and bonds may be issued and traded.

Commercial Banks

By far the most important—and in many developing countries until quite recently the only—financial institutions are the commercial banks. Virtually without exception, commercial banking in the less developed countries was begun by foreigners, usually taking the form of overseas colonial branches of banking concerns having their head offices in Europe, principally in Great Britain. The historical preeminence of British overseas banks is great and clear: for instance, over 80 per cent of the branches of foreign banks operating around the world in 1913 were of British origin. The initial dependence of the underdeveloped world on British overseas banks is hardly surprising in view of the fact that the British Empire/Commonwealth once embraced the largest part of the presently underdeveloped regions of the world. And what is true of the erstwhile British territories is largely true of banking arrangements in the former colonies of France, Belgium and Germany; French and German overseas banks expanded from the 1880s to World War I. In the period between the wars American overseas banks became prominent, primarily but not exclusively in Latin America and the Caribbean. This expansion was parallelled by a decline in the number and influence of German overseas banks as a consequence of the German loss of colonial territories in World I (Goldsmith, 1969, pp. 362–3).

Foreign banks have been of central importance in the financial development of less developed countries. Without their presence it is hard to see that monetization could have proceeded very far or very fast. The foreign banks have provided the depositing facility that has made possible the conduct of transactions by a transfer of bank deposits by cheque; the banks in many countries have also been directly responsible for the provision of physical currency (coins and bank notes, initially imported and subsequently issued locally against bullion or foreign exchange backing). It is not arguing too strongly to say that the banks first facilitated the use of coin, then established and developed public confidence in the use of bank notes, and finally led the public to regard bank deposits as a completely acceptable alternative to notes and coin.

The centrally important point that foreign banks provided the cornerstone on which monetization and wider financial development could be built needs particular stress, for a number of strong criticisms have been levelled at the *modus operandi* of the foreign banks. In referring now to these criticisms, it must not be forgotten that the foreign banks were the *sine qua non* of financial development, without which economic growth would have been tremendously handicapped. 'Metaphorically finance is a lubricant of the process of economic growth, and the banking system is the principal dispenser of finance' (Cameron *et al.*, 1967, p. 2).

The first and most powerful complaint against foreign banks is that they exported to metropolitan countries much of the funds that they collected in the underdeveloped world. This point is made with statistical support by Nevin (1961, pp. 50–1). We need to remember however, first, that the historic export surpluses of many developing territories made the stockpiling of overseas assets inevitable (Drake, 1972) and, second, that there has in the last decade or so been a considerable reversal of this behaviour. Foreign banks operating in underdeveloped countries have by and large brought back the funds hitherto sent abroad and have, moreover, been responsible for a net inflow of bank funds into developing countries (this point has been discussed in Chapter 5 above). To some extent, of course, the repatriation of bank assets has been a consequence of legislation and/or pressure introduced and applied by newly independent governments and their central banks; but it should not be overlooked that the foreign banks have in many cases found it profitable to increase their assets in the developing countries, sometimes even at a rate faster than that at which their local deposits have grown.

Except when recent local legislation has required otherwise, the foreign banks operated in underdeveloped countries as mere branch extensions of the international networks rather than as institutions that identified their operations in any one country with the economic development of that country. Consequently the volume and pattern of business in any country tended to be determined by Head Office and had 'no necessary connection with the demand for credit or the state of output and employment in the overseas territory' (Nevin, 1961, p. 46). Credit went mainly to commerce and expatriate export producers. Little lending to indigenous customers was demanded or sought, possibly because expatriate bank officials discriminated against native customers or seldom took the trouble to assess carefully the unfamiliar loan propositions that may have been put to them. A related feature was the application of home-country standards and methods of assessing credit applications (especially the emphasis on collateral security) and of home-country means of implementing those applications that were approved. This behaviour, and the obvious reasons for it, are discussed by Nevin (1961, pp. 45–9). He reminds us, however, that:

it would be inaccurate and unfair to omit reference to the immense benefits which these territories have secured through their possession of a commercial banking system which has established and retained extremely high standards so far as stability, integrity and safety are concerned. It is by no means obvious that if the international banks had never operated in these countries any really adequate local banking would have emerged instead; local banking in many of them has had an unhappy history of improvident operation and inefficient administration which has ultimately resulted in bank failures and has scarcely been conducive to confidence in banks and banking on the part of the local population. The expatriate banks, by contrast, can point to a longer history of reputable and completely dependable banking: consequently, the habit of banking has become established, and a tradition of integrity and efficiency has been built up which will serve these territories well in the years ahead. [Nevin, 1961, p. 52]

The British overseas banks lent principally by overdrafts rather than loans and for short rather than long terms. The self-liquidating, short-term overdraft, being a basic principle of British banking, was naturally carried into colonies. The banks' general adherence to this principle should not, however, be allowed to obscure the fact, that a significant number of nominally short-term overdrafts were repeatedly renewed to the point where they actually constituted a long-term line of credit for the borrower; this was especially the case in financing the capital works of expatriate agricultural enterprises.

A great part of bank credit was used to finance international trade via the short-term bill of exchange. By the time bills matured exporters would have received their sales revenue in London and importers would have sold their imports in the local market. It is perhaps not yet sufficiently appreciated that the early banks in the British colonies necessarily subsisted principally on bill of exchange finance and the purchase and sale of foreign currency because there was initially little opportunity in the colonial territories for making advances. (Hence the conventional usage of 'exchange banks' to describe the expatriate banks operating in the colonies. This term reflected the preoccupation of the banks with transactions involving foreign exchange.)

Indeed, this lack of opportunity for overdraft lending was one of the reasons why the expatriate banks sent deposits back home for investment in metropolitan money markets (there being, of course, no local money and securities markets suitable for liquid investments). The banks sometimes also sent home portions of their own capital, for want of suitable uses in the colony.

Not only were the expatriate banks hampered by a scarcity of local lending opportunities (given the adoption of conventional canons of creditworthiness), but they were also subject to keen competition among themselves for the available business in exchange and trade finance. For instance, as late as 1928 a bank chairman could say: 'It must also be recognised that the competition in Eastern Exchange banking grows wider and keener every year resulting in sharp competition for any passing business and in the acceptance of rates which show very meagre profits. Differences in exchange are now reckoned by sixty-fourths or even worse as compared with the fair and reasonable differences which prevailed in happier days' (Sir Montagu Turner of the Chartered Bank; quoted in Baster, 1929, p. 231). For many years funds perforce had to be employed in foreign exchange to yield any profit. Occasionally local managers displayed initiative and adventure and circumvented conventional lending standards by giving overdrafts to substantial traders in the local bazaars. This kind of engagement with the Chinese and Indian (especially *chettiar*) traders was common in Singapore. The funds of course trickled down to the borrowers' compatriots in small parcels of credit. In this way there was, from the earliest days of expatriate banking, some link between institutional finance and the informal credit market. `

The foreign banks located themselves in the ports and cities of the developing countries and refrained from spreading branches into the rural hinterland. After the turn of the century, and especially in the interwar years, local banks sprang up, usually copying the foreign model but being more willing to develop branch networks. (Some distinction should be made between the purely indigenous banks established by, and for the benefit of, indigenous residents and the local unit banks established by, for example, Chinese and Indians to cater principally for their ethnic communities. The business patterns of the latter were broadly similar to that of the British, European and American banks, which did not seek to do business directly with the native people.) The indigenous banks, however, did not find the going easy because they had to grapple with the unpromising, unreliable and relatively unprofitable business of lending to small-scale agriculturalists, traders and manufacturers.

Through their selection of assets (advances, loans, investments) the foreign banks 'exercised a far-reaching influence on commercial and industrial development, in particular on foreign trade' (Goldsmith, 1969, p. 366). The banks were certainly not oriented towards local development: they avoided lending to manufacturing industry if not to domestic activities altogether, and they did not provide any specialized forms of credit for innovative activities. Some change in this pattern of influence may be discerned in the period since World War II, which in some countries has featured a most marked expansion and growing importance of American overseas banks, the American banks having been rather more inclined to provide credit for manufacturing activity conducted within the developing territories (albeit often by foreign-owned manufacturing corporations).

In the last twenty years or so there has been in most underdeveloped countries a considerable shift of the focus of interest of the whole banking system away from international towards domestic lending. While to some extent this has been forced upon the foreign banks by newly independent governments and their new monetary authorities, it is nevertheless true that all banks, local and foreign, have come to perceive that worthwhile lending opportunities in developing countries are, if not abundant, much more common than the colonial bankers ever admitted. One wonders how far these better opportunities for banks in the developing countries result from development policies of independent governments—notably tariff protection and tax holidays—which have raised the apparent profitability of local manufacturing as compared with the free-trade policies of the colonial era. This fascinating question seems not yet to have been the subject of serious study.

With this general picture in mind we now discuss in more detail some features of the sources, and then the uses, of funds handled by commercial banking systems in developing countries. Tables 7.1–7.3 provide examples that broadly illustrate the ensuing discussion. Further detail and analysis can be found in any of several country case studies, some of which are mentioned in the 'Further Reading' section at the end of this chapter.

Bank funds are provided by shareholders and depositors. As we have seen above, over the last century foreign banks generally began with their own imported capital, collected deposits locally, then repatriated capital and undistributed profits, and even sent funds raised from depositors in underdeveloped territories to metropolitan investment markets. More recently, there has been a reverse flow of bank capital from the richer to the poorer countries and a substantial growth in local deposits, which have then been deployed locally. Fundamentally, the deposit expansion indicates that a high degree of public trust in banks has been developing, so that the public are now ready to hold bank money instead of currency.

A widespread feature of the growth of deposits has been a rise in the proportion of fixed (interest-bearing) deposits to demand (current account) deposits, reflecting a much faster rate of growth of the former: this has been noted for example in Malaysia, Singapore, Thailand and Uganda (see Drake, 1969a, pp. 122–7; Trescott, 1972; Gershenberg, 1972). The reasons for this behaviour are many and complex. To a great extent the shift in public preference from demand to interest-bearing deposits has been fostered by the banks

TABLE 7.1 *Malaysia—Sources and Uses of Commercial Bank Funds*

	As at end of		
	1960	1970	Sept. 1978
	(millions of Malaysian dollars)		
Sources of funds			
Domestic			
Capital and reserves	22	141	589
Deposits:			
Public sector	109	343	2,451
Private sector	838	3,057	11,254
Balances held for banks	58	422	498
Other	125	210	1,676
	1,152	4,173	16,468
Foreign			
Balances held for banks	73	252	1,565
Other	7	35	197
	80	287	1,762
Total	1,232	4,460	18,230
Uses of funds			
Domestic			
Cash	72	117	251
Statutory reserves	38	167	816
Balances with banks	68	453	719
Investments:			
Treasury bills	34	536	999
Government securities	57	297	1,901
Private securities	7	52	257
Loans, advances and trade bills	474	2,194	11,227
Fixed assets	32	147	323
Other	82	128	566
	864	4,091	17,059
Foreign			
Balances with banks	316	183	551
Trade bills	36	166	547
Investments	6	3	18
Other	10	17	55
	368	369	1,171
Total	1,232	4,460	18,230

Source: simplified from Bank Negara Malaysia (1979) pp. 146–7.

TABLE 7.2   *Thailand—Sources and Uses of Commercial Bank Funds*

	As at end of			
	1955	1960	1965	1967
		(millions of baht)		
Sources of funds				
Deposits				
Demand				
Banks	42.3	170.1	617.4	964.7
Government	79.9	223.8	656.6	722.3
Private residents	1,885.7	3,619.1	5,709.1	7,371.8
Non-residents	21.4	20.2	75.6	118.7
Time				
Banks	—	141.9	194.7	123.0
Government	71.9	197.3	442.4	794.8
Private residents	168.0	1,025.7	6,406.8	10,979.4
Non-residents	3.7	0.6	39.1	51.4
Other	—	160.7	188.4	256.5
Borrowings from				
Bank of Thailand	3.0	98.5	244.3	298.5
Banks in Thailand	56.0	202.2	241.4	154.4
Banks abroad	338.2	804.9	2,760.5	2,901.4
Other liabilities	821.1	821.4	893.2	1,529.3
Capital accounts	455.0	561.0	1,258.7	1,772.7
Total	3,946.2	8,047.4	19,728.1	28,038.9
Uses of funds				
Cash on hand	135.6	262.9	360.4	467.5
Balance with banks				
Bank of Thailand	309.6	480.6	942.2	1,247.2
Banks in Thailand	54.3	227.0	769.9	1,078.8
Banks abroad	170.9	283.8	679.0	777.3
Investments				
Treasury bills	53.5	23.5	197.0	514.7
Bonds	188.1	394.8	2,342.7	4,343.5
Others	22.7	40.8	201.1	255.3

TABLE 7.2 *cont.*

	As at end of			
	1955	1960	1965	1967
		(millions of baht)		
Loans and overdrafts	1,620.4	3,809.3	8,930.7	12,590.7
Bills				
Domestic	250.1	497.5	995.7	1,631.0
Import	271.0	735.6	971.0	1,083.8
Export	249.9	354.9	929.5	704.4
Trust receipts	—	—	968.6	1,252.2
Fixed assets	161.9	458.1	897.7	1,197.8
Other assets	458.2	478.6	542.6	894.7
Total	3,946.2	8,047.4	19,728.1	28,038.9

Source: Rozental (1970a), pp. 113–14.

themselves: in competing for funds they have not been slow to emphasize the interest-bearing attractions of fixed deposits, and there often appears to have been some competitive bidding between banks for these funds. Undoubtedly, too, the general public have come to appreciate better the opportunity costs attached to idle current accounts, as financial understanding deepens in the course of economic development and is spurred by the experience of inflation.

While growth of government deposits (including in some countries the repatriation of government funds from abroad) has been important, it is generally clear that the deposit expansion has come mainly from the private sector and principally from the indigenous populations. This is of course associated, *inter alia*, with the monetization we have so frequently stressed. The spread of bank branches undoubtedly promotes monetization and the two things have been clearly associated in a striking expansion of deposits in the 1960s and 1970s. As banking facilities become more widespread and accessible they lower the cost of monetary

TABLE 7.3 *Papua New Guinea—Sources and Uses of Commercial Bank Funds*

	As at end of	
	1976	1978
	(millions of kina)	
Sources of funds		
Demand deposits, not bearing interest:		
Government sector	22.7	38.2
Private sector	70.2	86.7
Demand deposits, bearing interest:		
Government sector	0.4	0.6
Private sector	46.9	63.9
Term deposits:		
Government sector	26.3	71.4
Private sector	63.4	47.0
Deposits denominated in foreign currencies	13.9	25.9
Balance due to banks abroad	12.5	31.4
Shareholders' funds	76.1	30.0
Other liabilities	6.7	8.0
Total	339.1	403.1
Uses of funds		
Approved liquid assets (including short-term government securities)	136.8	123.6
Other PNG government securities	11.6	11.8
Forward exchange deposits with central bank	3.0	30.6
Loans, advances and bills discounted:		
Denominated in kina	108.2	183.1
Denominated in foreign currencies	55.5	—
Other overseas assets	8.0	26.3
Other assets (bills, receivable, premises, etc.)	16.0	27.7
Total	339.1	403.1

Source: abridged from Bank of Papua New Guinea, *Quarterly Economic Bulletin* December 1978.

transactions and encourage the use of money. Bank expansion implies willingness of people to hold bank deposits as well as, or instead of, currency.

A considerable spread of bank networks, with branches reaching nowadays into relatively small towns, has occurred in many underdeveloped countries. To take just one example, Thailand had 24 bank offices in 1945, of which 16 were in the greater Bangkok area; by 1967 there were 535 bank offices, of which 353 were outside the metropolis (Trescott, 1972, p. 272). Similar examples can be found in many other countries. But there comes a point where a spread of bank branches, and hence perhaps further monetization of the economy, depends upon prior and substantial growth of rural incomes. As Maynard (1970, pp. 116, 119) has noticed, the banks will not go into areas where incomes are low, transport and communications poor, and lending opportunities limited. Access to remoter areas is costly, as are the administrative costs of handling small credit accounts; while small rural loans may be unprofitable, insecure and illiquid. However, the absence of banks retards monetization in remote areas. It may therefore be desirable, in the interests of financial development, to apply some pressure on the banks to extend their services into such areas. 'This pressure could take the form of direct government participation in the costs involved in advertising for promoting and collecting small savings; or by means of bribing the banks through offering them government deposit and account business. . .' (Maynard, 1970, p. 116).

An interesting note by Daly (1967), referring to Uruguay in 1958–64, demonstrates that rapid expansion of bank offices and growth of all classes of bank deposits can be profitable both to the banks and to the public, even in times of serious inflation and declining real income per head. The one proviso is that inflation does not destroy money as a medium of exchange, even though the inflation may erode it as a store of value.

Overriding all the discussion that now follows about the

uses of bank funds is an important shift in bank portfolios from external assets to local assets. This shift—noted above and in Chapter 5—has been associated principally, but by no means exclusively, with the foreign banks; it has been a once-and-for-all, seemingly irreversible, phenomenon, for banks in developing countries must nowadays expect to hold most of their assets in the countries from which their deposits originate.

Cash (in the sense of currency notes and coin held in bank tills and safes plus demand deposits with any local monetary authority) is a necessary but unprofitable bank asset. It is an item that may be expected to grow in the early stages of monetization as transactions conducted in currency displace subsistence production, barter transactions, etc., with the banks providing the mechanism for introducing and maintaining a supply of currency. In time, however, as people become accustomed to, and develop a preference for, the bank deposit form of money, the banks may reduce their own holdings of currency. The cash requirements of banks will fluctuate in accordance with the seasonal economic and social patterns of the community; for example, notwithstanding a high degree of acceptance of bank deposit money, there may be times such as Chinese New Year when the public in many South East Asian countries make considerable demands for conversion of deposits into currency (see Drake, 1969a, pp. 133–5 for illustration).

First among the banks' earning assets come short-term bills of exchange, which are usually associated with exports and imports. The bills by no means represent the banks' total involvement with the finance of international trade, for a large share of loans and advances commonly goes to producers of exportable commodities and distributors of imports, as would be expected given the open nature of most underdeveloped economies.

Loans and advances, the principal and most profitable of commercial bank assets, tend in developing countries to have been given in the main not merely to firms engaged in foreign trade but especially to large-scale, expatriate enterprises. These tendencies—already referred to and much discussed in the literature—are bound up with the traditional insistence of the commercial banks upon collateral security and their reluctance to undertake the costs and effort of assessing loan applications by unknown, small-scale, indigenous entrepreneurs. Such bank behaviour has been criticized strongly by Bhatia and Khatkhate (1975, especially pp. 136–7, 151–4) who, arguing that banks have been deterred from lending to indigenous entrepreneurs because of the relatively high risks facing those entrepreneurs and their inability to absorb losses, propose that banks and other financial institutions in developing countries should widen their horizons and set about attenuating the risks faced by indigenous entrepreneurs. As we shall shortly see, central banks may be able to contribute importantly to such a beneficial change in bank lending practices.

Banks also invest in negotiable securities, public and private. In the last two decades the banks have moved from holding almost all their negotiable investments in foreign securities to having the greater part in local securities, especially those issued by national governments. As will be discussed in the next chapter, private securities have not yet assumed any great importance in most developing countries. By contrast government securities have expanded rapidly and the banks have acquired large holdings of them. Much of the government security expansion has been due to governments selling bonds to finance development programmes, and the banks have been obliged (through legislation or moral suasion) to take up a portion of these bonds. In addition, the development of local central banks has given rise to the need for short-term securities of a type readily discountable at the central bank. In many countries this had led to a rapid expansion of Treasury bills on issue and an associated growth of short-term money and bills markets.

Further discussion of commercial banks needs to be in the

context of their relationships to the central bank, and at this point it is necessary to turn to the subject of central banking.

Central Banks

Central banks have already been mentioned and discussed to some extent in Chapter 5 (pp. 108–9 especially). In advanced countries, the central banks are concerned chiefly with the goals of internal stability—'fine tuning' the money supply or rate of interest in order to maintain the economy at full employment with reasonably stable prices—and balance-of-payments equilibrium. Bloomfield has suggested that stability (and, by implication, external balance) must also be the main objective of central banks in underdeveloped countries. He argues that financial instability will misallocate resources in the short run and inhibit growth in the long run. Stability is thus a necessary, though not a sufficient, condition for increasing saving and promoting the investment (from both home and abroad) that will produce growth (Bloomfield, 1956, pp. 244–7). Nevin (1961, Chapter 2) makes an equally strong case for the central bank to concentrate on development. However, there is no fundamental conflict between his views and those of Bloomfield. Nevin is suggesting not that stability be ignored but rather that the central bank in any developing country must not become so absorbed with the pursuit of stability that it overlooks the potential that it has to do something directly about development. This point is well taken, for the designers of new central banks have sometimes been so engrossed in providing ways of controlling the money supply, so as to achieve stability, that they have failed to consider the adoption of unorthodox money strategies and methods in order to promote economic development. The main drift of the following discussion is that central banks in the less developed countries must play a leading role in financial development: guiding the activities of foreign banks towards local needs; fostering the establishment of domestic banks and specialized financial institutions; supervising the operations of all financial institutions so that local confidence may be maintained and monetization and intermediation thus encouraged; promoting the development of money and securities markets and the spread of financial technology; and endeavouring to influence the money supply and manage the exchange rate so as to avoid inflation.

The traditional tools for monetary management consist of open market operations, reserve ratio variations, administrative (i.e. direct) controls over banks' rates of interest and the volume and direction of bank lending, and influence—or 'moral suasion'—over the commercial banks. It has already been shown in Chapter 5 that the nature and structure of most underdeveloped economies is such that a central bank is not, in its early years at least, likely to be able to exert much direct control over the volume of money or the rate of interest. In particular, it has been argued that a primary task for the central bank is to weaken the influence of external forces upon the generation of the local money supply. However, even if the external influences on the volume of money are moderated, there are several reasons why there is still not much scope for the exercise of the traditional central banking tools of open market operations and bank discount rate variations. First, the absence of a well-developed bond and securities market makes open market operations technically very difficult if not impossible. Secondly, a major reason why the local market for securities has not developed is the past practice of the commercial banks of holding reserves and investments in external securities. This same practice has also inhibited the use of bank rate policy, which is feasible only when commercial banks hold their first-line or 'sensitive' reserves in the form of securities that are discountable locally (the historical need to hold liquid reserves abroad is a further reason, along with exchange rate fixity and freedom of international capital movements, why the local institutional rate of interest has been often determined in foreign money markets). Thirdly, even if open market operations are feasible, their effects could be offset readily in any open economy when international banks are present; for those banks can easily shift funds to or from abroad, so long as they are left free to do so. The last point would also appear to undermine the use of reserve ratio requirement controls over foreign banks; and to this may be added the further consideration that, where banks are not especially worried about local liquidity, changes in their local reserves or legal variations of the reserve ratio may not cause them to change their lending policies. For all these reasons, it is important to bring commercial banking operations much more under the influence of the local central bank, along the lines discussed in Chapter 5.

The imposition by the central bank of some form of local assets ratio (i.e. a prescribed minimum percentage of local assets to deposits being required to be maintained by each commercial bank) is likely to be trebly beneficial. It would bring about a transfer of some foreign assets to the central bank (thus inhibiting the foreign payments freedom of the commercial banks and giving the central bank some foreign reserves of its own). Secondly, it would generate a demand for local liquid assets of a rediscountable nature: here the central bank must persuade government to provide an increasing supply of Treasury bills and other gilt-edged securities and must itself readily provide rediscounting facilities (a commendable Malaysian example is recounted by Drake, 1969a, pp. 214–16). Thirdly, and most important, the local assets ratio may have beneficial effects on the supply of domestic credit to the private sector and thus on domestic economic development. As Nevin has said, 'the imposition of a local assets ratio presents the banks with the alternative of either finding suitable outlets for their credit locally or holding a significant part of their resources in the form of idle balances within the territory' (Nevin, 1961, p. 66). This blunt choice is likely to cause the banks to re-examine their ideas about what constitute suitable loans and advances and to have striking effects upon the effort they put into discovering suitable local assets. There can be many variations on the local assets theme: an obvious one is the local *liquid* assets ratio which would raise particularly the banks' demand for Treasury bills.

Local assets ratios may also be desirable for financial institutions, such as insurance companies, pension funds, savings banks, etc., some of which historically have also exported domestic savings to metropolitan capital markets. Indeed, given competent staff, there seems no good reason why central banks should not assume greater general supervision of, and responsibility for, the soundness and good conduct of all financial institutions. Just as public trust in the banking system is necessary for monetization to proceed, so wider financial development will depend upon faith in financial institutions generally. The system of licensing, inspection, supervision, reporting and sanctions under which central banks guide and support commercial banks should be easily adaptable for use in respect of other financial institutions. A related benefit, of course, is that such procedures will serve to keep the central bank better informed about, and its staff much more familiar with, the day-to-day workings of the financial markets.

Of course, local asset prescriptions, and other forms of central bank intervention and supervision, may be applied injudiciously, or mismanaged, if the central bank staff are inexperienced, incompetent or dishonest. At the worst, local monetary authorities may allow foreign exchange commandeered from the commercial banks to be dissipated on ill-conceived government works or private consumption of imports; scarce administrative resources may be absorbed in the implementation of banking controls; and any incompetence of the officials may lead to such a degree of rationing and misallocation of credit that the commercial banking system may contract. However, the fear of such possibilities should not in general be used to prevent the establishment of central banks or to shackle their powers. The skills of economic and financial management may be scarce, but that is not to say that developing countries cannot be trusted to manage their monetary affairs. The able performances of many young central banks show that any general prejudice against them is unwarranted.

As banker to the national government, the central bank may also exert a beneficial influence. Not only will the central bank normally handle the government's foreign exchange transactions and manage the domestic public debt, but it will also be called upon to be financial adviser to the government. In this last role its advice will be the better the more closely it is in touch with and understands monetary and financial conditions in the private sector and in the rest of the world.

A potentially effective monetary weapon available to central banks is what has been termed 'moral suasion' or, colloquially, 'jawbone', which in developing countries amounts to persuading the commercial banks of the congruence between their own long-run interests and the development of the local economy. Although this policy cannot be discussed in explicit detail, and certainly has no quantitative dimensions, it is far from unimportant. Indeed, it may well be the most fundamental task that the central bank of a developing country has to perform in its early life. The establishment of a good relationship between the central and commercial banks, based on a mutual understanding of each other's aims and responsibilities, is vital to the development of an effective and efficient financial system. This point joins with the need for a central bank to look beyond the mere banking system and promote growth and diversification of the whole financial sector (see also Goldsmith in Krivine, 1967, pp. 381–2). An improvement in the financial framework greatly enhances the scope for monetary management; whereas without adequate financial development, local assets ratio and jawbone attempts at monetary control will founder for the want of a sufficient volume and range of local financial assets and institutions. The rest of this chapter considers the institutional forms that might desirably be promoted, while Chapter 8 goes on to deal with markets for financial assets.

As already noted, the diversification of financial institutions and other practices may be either evolutionary or forced. If the developing countries wait for financial development to occur at an evolutionary pace, they are likely to find that the wait is intolerably long. History shows that banks are slow to diversify, while more specialized borrowing and lending institutions follow rather than precede growth and change in the economy. For instance, in many countries financial specialization is confined to such obviously profitable avenues as life insurance, house mortgage loans, and the financing of motor vehicles and other durable consumer goods. All these opportunities are associated with the emergence of an urbanized middle class with growing incomes. Manufacturing industry, agriculture and small business are not so eagerly served by financial institutions. To satisfy their needs without creating credit rationing and constraints on economic growth it may be necessary to indulge in 'supply leading' financing, in which government plays a strong role, either directly by establishing its own financial institutions or indirectly by subsidizing private and semi-private institutions. (Little more than tedium is to be derived by elaborating arguments for the provision and promotion of financial institutions. These have already been touched on in Chapter 3 and have been much written about in other works. The reader who wants a pithy and vigorous example would do well to read Nevin, 1961, Chapter 4, entitled 'The Creation of Lending Institutions'.)

Before going on to discuss some of the difficulties which a policy of forced development of financial institutions may encounter, it may be appropriate here to say a few words about one aspect of evolved institutions that needs official attention. The point concerns the investment of funds collected rather automatically by those 'collecting' institutions which tend to flourish as the payroll of government is extended, commercial and administrative centres grow, and urbanization occurs. Associated with all of these things is usually the emergence of a white-collar class of employees whose incomes are more secure and grow faster than the national average. Commonly a considerable volume of savings, often contractual, is set aside from the incomes of these people to provide for retirement. The funds are held in savings bank accounts, or go to insurance companies or pension or provident funds (usually government-owned, in the case of pension funds for civil servants). These collecting agencies serve the dual purpose of amassing small unit savings into large totals and simultaneously habituating people to new financial methods. It is therefore very important that they command public confidence and run no risk of failure. Hence some form of government supervision of their activities and perhaps guarantee of their solvency may be desirable.

Whether because the funds go direct to government instrumentalities, or because insurance companies, banks, etc., may be obliged to hold a prescribed percentage of their assets in domestic government securities, the effect of this flow of contractual savings is to provide handsome subscriptions to government securities issues. It does not seem wise for financial enterprises (especially those virtually under government control) to invest so considerably in government securities. Industrial development and the capital market would be better served if the institutions that collected contractual domestic savings were required to put a portion of them at the disposal of private investors, either by subscribing to securities issued by private enterprise or by investment in financial institutions, for example development banks, which would lend long-term funds to private industry. The problems, of course, are that there is likely to be a limited supply of private issues (as will be discussed in the next chapter), while specialized lending agencies may not exist or may need stronger promotion, as we shall now see.

Specialized lending agencies which are established in anticipation of future need for their services are likely to be unprofitable on short-run, private, economic calculations; otherwise they would have evolved spontaneously in response to perceived opportunities for profitable activities. Forced institutional development relies for its justification on long-term, social cost-benefit calculations. If governments are to take a hand in the creation of financial institutions to serve neglected economic needs, it is important that the principles and priorities observed by these institutions be consistent with the objectives of any national development plan (Nevin, 1961, p. 71).

For convenience I propose to discuss these specialized institutions under four distinct headings: development banks, agricultural credit institutions, co-operative finance societies and institutions for the finance of small business. It should be borne in mind, however, that these headings are far from mutually exclusive: for instance, development banks sometimes engage in lending to agricultural producers and to small business, even though they may generally be concerned predominantly with large-scale manufacturing, mining and construction enterprises.

Development Banks

It follows from the recent discussion that development banks should be predominantly, if not wholly, financed by government (see also Furness, 1975, pp. 28–9). The need for government guarantee of private funds invested in these institutions implies a high degree of public responsibility, the more so to any extent that savings–collecting institutions may be encouraged or obliged to invest in securities issued by the development bank. The fact that development banks are designed to serve the national advantage in the long term cannot be emphasized too frequently. Over and above the narrow private profitability calculations of any proposed loan, the bank should have regard to such issues as the creation of new employment opportunities, the earning of foreign exchange, and the development of external economies accruing to other firms and individuals [which] are as important as the advantages that accrue directly to the borrower. The bank's resources may legitimately be used even for the implementation of policies that are not strictly economic, as for example in the support of indigenous entrepreneurs in order to improve their effective participation in certain sectors of the economy, even though this will involve less efficient productive use of the bank's resources than could be expected with other borrowers. [Fisk, 1975b, p. 2]

Development banks will be presented with proposals tha⁺ are unfamiliar, less amenable to cost–benefit calculatᵢons, and riskier than proposals ordinarily made to conventiɔnal commercial lending institutions. The costs of evaluating and administering development bank loans are ⁺herefore higher than those of conventional bank loans and advances; moreover, since a greater proportion of the proposals investigated by development banks do not in the end attract loans, the operating costs per unit of credit provided tend to be higher. Similarly, as well as supplying finance, the development banks must often extend technical and other advisory assistance to borrowing firms; this too raises the banks' costs of operation. For all these reasons it is apparent that a development bank must expect its operations to be subsidized by government—the alternative being that the bank could operate profitably only if it charged such extremely high rates of interest on its 'successful' loans as to limit severely the number of enterprises it could assist. It is therefore clear that government capital must be an important source of funds for a development bank. A development bank may also be able to raise overseas loans (official and/or private); it may sell bonds to, or raise loans from, the private sector; and it may hope to expand its activities by use of retained earnings.

The main business of most development banks is the making of long-term and medium-term loans to firms that could not otherwise obtain such finance. Loans are usually scheduled precisely, as to disbursement and repayment, and frequently involve large amounts; some development banks indeed have minimum loan values, beneath which they do not lend. Hire-purchase contract loans for the acquisition of industrial equipment are offered usually by development banks too. It is no accident that emphasis is given to providing finance for the industrial sector; long-term credit to this sector is the significantly neglected area in *laissez-faire* financial systems, while it is industrial development that is expected to bring the desired employment opportunities and technological advances to complement local programmes of education and generally to conform with the aspirations of development plans.

Under-capitalized applicants for loans present a common and often major problem for development banks. This has led some of the banks to assist firms in raising equity capital: sometimes advice about where and how to tap equity funds is sufficient; sometimes development banks undertake to underwrite new issues of shares; and sometimes development banks themselves become shareholders in industrial firms. Generally, it would be unwise for a development bank to assume a majority shareholding, and hence ownership responsibilities, in any enterprise, and it is a good rule to dispose of the shareholding, if possible, once the enterprise is well established. (This, of course, implies the existence of a securities market in which the shares can be unloaded.) Applicants for development bank loans are often also uninformed and inexperienced; hence the development bank will probably find it worthwhile, if not indeed necessary, to maintain an advisory or extension assistance service. The bank may also need to counsel applicant firms about the process of applying for a development bank loan. However, it is necessary to make sure that counselling and assistance in the preparation of a loan application does not too easily slide into guaranteeing a commitment of funds to the counselled applicant. Given the unconventional nature of development banking, the generally under-capitalized position of loan applicants and their inability to provide adequate collateral security, it is necessary for development bank loan assessments to be very thorough and to require much information from applicant firms; nevertheless, development banks would do well to avoid the difficulties created in Malaysia at one stage where the process of obtaining a development loan was so searching and difficult as to tax impossibly the abilities of all but the best managed local enterprises (see Drake, 1969a, pp. 163–4).

Finally, development bankers need to be as imaginative and innovative as is possible within the economic, political and social limitations of the particular economy. This point may perhaps be best driven home by brief reference to some of the activities of the Papua New Guinea (PNG) Development Bank (what follows draws heavily on the work of Anne De Bruin, 1977). The Papua New Guinea economy is a diverse mixture of high-technology copper mining, export-oriented agriculture (smallholder and plantation), urban-based light manufacturing and commerce, all superimposed upon a substantial primitive non-market economy. Education and technology are unevenly spread among the diverse tribes and races, and much of the country is barely accessible because of very rugged terrain. In this context, the development bank is called upon to assist industry, agriculture, commerce and infrastructure, and also to spread its efforts so as to assist in redressing regional and racial economic imbalances. The PNG Development Bank has adopted the 'we lend to the man' philosophy which obliges it to find ways around conventional bank insistence on borrower equity and security. 'Sweat equity', whereby the borrower contributes his own labour instead of cash to a project, is encouraged. As well as recognizing formally that technical advice and loan supervision are far more important ingredients in successful lending than formal security, the PNG Development Bank has pioneered the practices of lending to communal groups and to individual borrowers under a 'Clan Usage Agreement', whereby the leaders of the clan acknowledge to the Bank the right of the borrower to use communal land for his business activity (De Bruin, 1977, pp. 101–8).

Agricultural Finance

The volume of savings flowing to financial institutions from rural areas is small while the credit needs of peasant producers are great. This imbalance has rendered impractical the desires of many governments to marshal rural savings and lend them to rural producers. The alternatives of injecting into the rural area funds raised from urban dwellers, or from foreign loans, or by taxation have generally failed for the want of sufficient government recognition of the difficulties involved in supplying agricultural credit, and the consequent lack of resolution to 'tough out' the inevitably long period of initial unprofitability associated with credit provided for the modernization of traditional agriculture. The fundamental problem is that any financial institution or system which sets out to meet the needs of small-scale, rural producers, and which aims to be self-sufficient, requires (1) access to savings from outside the agricultural sector as a major source of funds, and (2) a 'hard' banking attitude towards rural loans, for 'soft' lending will only fritter away loanable funds without impressing upon the peasants the true value of capital or improving the productivity of their farming.

The proper approach to small-scale, agricultural credit is well illustrated in the following statement by a Treasury official:

> We are lending here to a large mass of people who are essentially, in a banking sense, not credit worthy. This is why government provides this credit; and in the very nature of the scheme financed I think we have to accept the fact that there is bound to be arrears. To adopt a purely legalistic approach to this scheme would merely lead to its winding up in one year at considerable loss and also to defeat [*sic*] the government's policy of trying to improve the position of the rural cultivators. [quoted in Drake, 1966, p. 81]

If a large-scale onslaught on the rural credit problem is desired, government must lead the way, for there are bound to be losses and only government should be expected to underwrite losses in the interests of rural betterment. A developing economy cannot afford failures among financial institutions, for such might destroy the confidence of many people in the money and credit system. However, not even government should play fairy godmother. Strict supervision of rural borrowers is needed wherever the credit comes from and however it is distributed.

In the rural economy there is an integral relationship between the provision of credit and the processing and marketing of produce. It is this relationship that is often exploited by middlemen. This same relationship suggests a way in which the government could more effectively assist the small rural producers. A government marketing authority could supply seasonal credit to agriculturalists, or to local buyers of produce, against the future (compulsory) delivery of produce. (The marketing authority would thus be either competing against informal village moneylenders or providing them with the opportunity to expand the scale of their activities.) The funds to finance the marketing authority could be obtained by the issue, under guarantee, of 'rural produce bills' (and, where long-term credit for capital formation is needed, 'rural development bonds'). With a guarantee that was virtually that of government, banks and other finance houses, including urban co-operative credit societies, might then be encouraged to hold such bills. The bills would be especially attractive if they were rediscountable at the central bank. Of course, the government, through the marketing authority, would have to assume responsibility for losses, occasioned by non-delivery of produce, etc. But under this arrangement government would only have to cover losses, not outlay its own capital to finance the scheme; and in the long run, if farm productivity increases and peasants come to place the meeting of commercial obligations high on their scale of duties, it may not be too much to expect the loss rate to diminish greatly. Any such scheme would require detailed and careful examination and evaluation to determine its feasibility in any actual situation. But the line of investigation seems promising, especially as there would be the associated advantages of providing additional local financial assets and perhaps linking informal to institutional credit.

In contrast to some other sectors, there is usually no reluctance to borrow or lack of the will to invest in the rural economy. The issue of rural credit bills or bonds would be a means of taking advantage of this willingness to borrow, at the same time providing a local outlet for the savings of other sectors. Moreover, since rural produce paper would be expected to yield a higher rate of interest than Treasury bills, and since a range of maturities could be designed to suit different products and methods of production, the variety as well as the supply of local paper would be augmented. However, the quality of the paper would have to be ensured, because bad bills or bonds would wreck the system; it must be repeated that it would be necessary that the paper be issued or guaranteed by government. Of course, the proposal might be regarded simply as the extension of government domestic debt with a portion ear-marked for a specific purpose. But this view overlooks the intangible advantages and political goodwill that should follow from the creation of a recognizably separate authority, with its finances divorced from general revenue and expenditure and with the challenging responsibility to achieve something worthwhile in the rural economy.

Nevertheless, rural underdevelopment is not merely a problem of insufficient finance. There would be no point in increasing the supply of rural credit without simultaneously tackling the related problems of low productivity and commercial and technical backwardness and, in many cases, the pressure of fast-growing populations on limited land. Innovations and reforms in the financial field are not enough.

Co-operative Societies

Many countries have consciously promoted co-operative societies, particularly with a view to making them vehicles for the promotion of economic and financial development in rural areas. It should be noticed, however, that the most successful co-operative societies have been urban based (a good example is reported by Drake, 1966). Urban societies have many advantages over their rural counterparts. Urban members are mostly white-collar workers of good educational background. On average, they have higher incomes, more income in cash form, and greater financial sophistication than their rural brethren. Members of urban societies who serve voluntarily and without payment on management committees of co-operatives are indeed capable of managing the societies. Above all, urban societies are often able to arrange with employers for the deduction of member's contributions from their wages and the direct payment of those contributions to the co-operative. By contrast, rural co-operative finance societies have no guarantee of a regular flow of contributions and, if reliant on their members, cannot generally count upon good management. Inevitably, rural co-operatives have come to depend upon funds provided by government; and these funds, when trickled down to members as loans, are sometimes treated as though they were gifts from government.

However, it should not be thought that all peasant farmers are invariably profligate and irresponsible with borrowed funds. There is good evidence that many peasant farmers who borrow from the co-operatives meet their obligations in full and on time, which in turn implies income levels noticeably above subsistence (see Drake, 1966, p. 80). The reasons why some deficiencies persist in rural areas are to be found in the hazardous nature of much small-scale agricultural production, the low productivity of many farmers, and ill-assessed, inadequately secured and unsupervised credit.

If a country judges it desirable to promote rural credit it must face up to the fact that small-scale rural credit institutions (such as agricultural co-operative societies) are likely to take a long time to become self-sustaining. Hence the government must either counternance disbursing loan funds of its own into the rural areas (through co-operative societies or as suggested in the previous section), with appropriate assessment and supervision of loans, or, while still providing funds, rely upon local moneylenders to select and supervise borrowers (in the manner suggested in Chapter 6). Indeed, it may be desirable to attack the problem along both lines.

Finance for Small Business

The term 'small business' is generally taken to mean non-agricultural enterprises under single, partner or family proprietorship and having only a handful of employees. Commonly, such non-corporate firms are struggling to hold on to or break into existing markets or are attempting to establish markets for new products; they are likely to be competing against foreign-owned firms or large local enterprises which enjoy some monopolistic advantages through owning exclusive franchises of well-known foreign products. And even when operating profitably, small businesses often lead a hand-to-mouth financial existence because of under-capitalization. Many such firms, however, are doubtfully or irregularly profitable and could not be regarded as desirable recipients of scarce institutional credit. The capital market does the economy a service when it will not lend to those who seem likely to dissipate savings on unsuccessful or low (social) priority ventures.

All this would seem to suggest that there is no case for extending to small businesses the sustenance and protection of finance on privileged terms. Such a view, however, is too narrow in the context of a developing economy. First, those firms that can be helped through infancy to unprotected economic survival will provide a desirable increase in the number of local entrepreneurs and employers. Secondly, the capital market may be unconsciously discriminating against the small firms because of lack of knowledge. Thirdly, the nurturing of local enterprise, initially in the form of small businesses, is likely to be an important social aim of any developing economy, the more so where it is desired to strengthen the economic standing of indigenous *vis-à-vis* immigrant ethnic groups and international firms.

The provision of special financial arrangements for small businesses is thus, for one reason or another, either an exercise in infant firm protection or a means of redressing capital market imperfections, and it is wise for it to be seen as such. A special financing authority, or a separate department of a development bank, is desirable to take care of the financial needs of small business, to the extent that it be judged wise to do so. The relevant agency cannot hope to be self-sufficient and should not try to raise funds from the public for the finance of small businesses (unless the repayment of such funds be government-guaranteed). Inevitably, the financing of small businesses requires a substantial government subsidy which should be apparent to the public and not concealed under the profitable other activities of a development bank or other large and diversified institution.

Loans to small businesses are very expensive to administer: the costs of investigation, servicing and collecting repayments are high, per dollar of loan, because the lending agency must deal with a large number of loan applications of small average value; counselling of applicant firms and the extension of technical advice will often also be required; and the incidence of default may be great.

The parallel with agricultural credit is thus almost exact; a development finance institution seeking to hold out to investors the promise of the use of funds on reasonably economic lines, and of being profitable at least in the long run, cannot hope to achieve this end if it is involved with the provision of credit to small business. Such business is simply incompatible with the operation of an institution on a break-even basis, let alone on a profitable one. [Nevin, 1961, p. 85]

It may indeed be preferable, as some countries have found, for the small business agency to concern itself exclusively with credit investigation, counselling, extension and follow-up activities related to the small firms, while leaving the actual provision of credit to the established lending institutions. The small business agency would assess the worth, viability and efficiency of the applicant small firms; if it decided that the firm should obtain credit the agency would then refer the application with its endorsement and guarantee to a suitable lending institution. To the extent that the bank or other institution provided credit on privileged terms to the small business, the government agency might reimburse the institution for the difference between its preferential charges and the ruling market rate of interest. In this way the government would be seen to finance the investigation, counselling and default element in small business lending while leaving the actual provision of capital funds to financial institutions. A variation on this scheme— perhaps necessary in countries where the skills of financial evaluation are very scarce—would be for initial credit appraisals to be made by the banks, etc., with government paying the fees for such services.

Most of today's underdeveloped countries started their institutional development simply with commercial banks, oriented towards international trade. There was no specialization of financial functions and certainly no market for securities. This simple—bank-only—institutional form nevertheless had distinct advantages over the informal moneylenders that preceded it. Eventually diversification within the financial system emerged: specialized savings, rural, mortgage, industrial and, most recently, development banks arrived on the scene, as also did pension funds, insurance companies and consumer credit financiers. Following institutional diversification, some countries have moved to a further stage when institutions have been joined by markets for the issue and exchange of financial assets. Nevertheless, there remain in many countries capital market imperfections and financial bottlenecks which may warrant a judicious degree of official action to improve knowledge and increase the supply of finance for particular purposes. Such intervention needs to be managed with the greatest care, as I shall discuss in the final chapter.

Further Reading

I have deliberately avoided details of financial institutions, and tried to deal concisely with broad issues of institutional development. There are available many books and articles dealing in detail with the institutional structures and problems of particular countries. Any recommended selection from that literature is bound to be idiosyncratic, and perhaps invidious to the authors of works neglected: nevertheless, in my view, some useful monographs are those by Sowelem (1967), Drake (1969a), Rozental (1970a), Jao (1974) and a commendable unpublished work by De Bruin (1977). A survey of banking systems in the British Commonwealth is contained in Crick (1965), while Emery (1971) covers financial institutions in South East Asia. On a broader plane, Nevin (1961) is a fine and stylish essay, still sound, wise and relevant nineteen years after it was first published. Gerschenkron's brilliant essay (1965) brings out the great historical role of banks in economic development. Cameron *et al.* (1967) expound the contributions of the banks in more comparative detail, while Goldsmith (1969, Chapter 8) gives a pithy summary of the development role of financial institutions. Central banking in developing countries is covered generally by Nevin (1961), De Kock (1954), Fousek (1957), Aschheim (1961), Ally (1975) and particularly in the studies of individual countries mentioned above. An essay by Ahrensdorf (1959) discusses central banking problems and policies in four less developed economies in a way that reflects several of the issues raised in this chapter and Chapter 5. Development banks are dealt with by Boskey (1959), Diamond (1957), and Basu (1965). The literature on agricultural credit, co-operative societies and small business finance is too specific and detailed to warrant mention here, but for many countries there are both official reports and private articles on these subjects. A brief essay by Cairncross (1962, Chapter 10) touches lightly and perceptively on many of the issues discussed in this chapter.

CHAPTER 8

Securities Markets

The term 'securities markets' is used to denote the markets for those financial instruments/claims/obligations that are commonly and readily transferable by sale—namely, the shares, debentures, etc., issued by companies as well as the bonds, bills, debentures and stock issued by government and public authorities. 'Securities' is used as the generic term for these various forms of financial instruments. The securities market is, therefore, a narrower concept than *capital market*, which embraces all forms of borrowing and lending, whether or not evidenced by the creation of a negotiable financial instrument. For further discussion of concepts and terminology see Drake and Mathews (1974, pp. 3–7), Wai and Patrick (1973, pp. 253–7), Wilson (1966).

The view has long prevailed among economists that, in less developed countries, securities markets would be difficult to create, costly (in both budgetary and opportunity senses) to establish and maintain, and of little economic benefit. The virtual neglect of securities markets in the literature of development economics reflects a general academic attitude that the subject is unimportant. Opinion in underdeveloped countries and international agencies has been similar to that of academics, save for the 'institution-building' attitude sometimes found among politicians and officials.

The small amount of relevant academic literature gives no enthusiastic endorsement to the promotion of securities markets. Policy conclusions are tentative and caution predominates. A recent and comprehensive article concludes:

192

Our study has drawn attention to the dangers of expecting capital markets (as we have defined them) to have a sizeable and rapidly increasing effect on the process of development in the less developed countries in the foreseeable future. This does not imply that policies to develop capital markets should not be used, but it should be recognized that their effects are limited. We support a positive and comprehensive but gradualist approach to capital market development by the government authorities. [Wai and Patrick, 1973, p. 301]

(Their use of the term 'capital markets' approximates 'securities markets' as used in this book.) While this is essentially the right approach, it could be advanced with more vigour and conviction. The inherent obstacles to securities market development seem to have been overplayed, and the prospects for beneficial community response to positive policies correspondingly understated, in the limited literature. In this chapter, therefore, an attempt is made to redress the balance, by taking a more optimistic attitude towards the prospects for, and the possible benefits of, securities market development in the poorer countries.

A market for securities provides potential liquidity to the owners of otherwise illiquid financial assets, without inconveniencing the enterprises that originally issued the shares, debentures, bonds, etc., in order to raise funds. Hence a securities market encourages financial development through fostering intermediation, and the liquidity that the market confers may enhance the rate of saving and investment. Next, the yield promised or anticipated on security ownership may be sufficiently great to attract a net saving of income that would otherwise have been consumed. Further, net saving may occur because of other attractive features of securities ownership, e.g. the possibility (though fraught with risk) of capital gain, or the protection of savings against inflation.

U Tun Wai and Patrick (1973, p. 257) incline to the generalization that the existence of a securities market 'has relatively little effect on the aggregate rate of private savings at the level of development of most less developed countries', because there are sufficiently close financial substitutes to satisfy most would-be owners of financial assets. Those disposed towards risk-taking may participate in direct business investments of their own, or of relatives or friends. Although those authors concede that the liquidity of publicly traded shares may attract 'to that level of risk those savers who would not be willing to accept the illiquidity of investment in their own or their friends' projects', they do not judge this attribute to be aggregatively important enough to influence the savings rate. They base their qualified generalization on 'scattered evidence' (Wai and Patrick, 1973, pp. 257–8) which is not directly cited. But there is alternative evidence (discussed directly below) which suggests that small savers *are* attracted by the opportunity to acquire corporate securities: in most cases probably because of the prospect of capital gain, although the liquidity and yield attributes of the securities cannot be disregarded (Drake, 1969b; Arowolo, 1971). It is, at the very least, arguable that a portion of the funds that have been subscribed to corporate shares and debentures in the developing countries would not otherwise have been saved and invested locally.

Any financial development that causes investment alternatives to be compared with one another is bound to produce allocational improvement over a system of segregated investment opportunities. Moreover, just as the availability of financial assets makes saving independent of any concomitant act of investment, so too does finance divorce investment acts from the ability of investors to save. But a securities market is not the only avenue of external finance for a firm, nor the only means by which prospective investment alternatives may be compared. The question at issue is whether a market improves the allocational machinery over and above the functioning of banks and other institutional lenders.

In contrast to financial institutions, the securities market does not intermediate and provides no institutional assessment of the competing claims for finance as is made, for example, by the loan officers of banks. (However, new issues of shares and debentures are often approved by sponsoring issue houses before being offered in the market place.) The disposition of investible funds via the securities market is made in accordance with the apparent profit prospects of the companies that compete for share and debenture issues. Unfortunately, relative profit rates (adjusted for risk) may not reflect relative efficiencies between firms because profit rates may be distorted by market imperfections arising from monopoly power, tariff protection, import quotas, credit rationing and so forth. In such circumstances the allocative effect of the securities market may even be harmful (Wai and Patrick, 1973, p. 258). If these imperfections did not exist, it might appear that the securities market would allocate investible funds neutrally, in strict accord with expected investment yields. In fact, however, the knowledge of individual saver–subscribers, acting *en masse*, is necessarily inadequate to make sharp marginal evaluations of the profit prospects of alternative investments. Accordingly, the marketability of new issue securities tends to be weighted in favour of large, well-known, long established and successful firms (often foreign controlled) and against newer, smaller, domestic enterprises. Moreover, organized securities markets rarely assist fund-raising by agricultural enterprises, tending rather to be the exclusive preserve of metropolitan industrial and commercial firms. But the disposition of bank and institutional credit may also be biased in exactly the same directions.

The allocative effect of the securities market is even more complex than the previous paragraph suggests. For example:

It can be argued that in less developed countries only the most creditworthy firms can sell their securities via a capital market, that these firms also have prime access to bank loans, and hence that such firms have greater freedom of choice between different sources of finance (in terms of availability of funds), for example, between bank loans and security issues. Development of capital markets provides no reallocation of resources to such firms. We have to examine instead where the buyers of securities obtain their funds, and how they would have used them alternatively; and how the lending bank

> derives its loanable funds, and to what use it would have put them alternatively. [Wai and Patrick, 1973, p. 259]

Without this information the allocative effects of the securities market cannot be identified.

In the light of the discussion to this stage, one cannot come to any firm conclusion as to whether or not a securities market would improve upon the allocational machinery provided by the financial institutions. The most that can be said is that, since the securities market constitutes an additional avenue of borrowing and lending, the capital market is wider than hitherto and should function more competitively.

Inasmuch as securities markets enlarge the financial sector—promoting additional and more sophisticated financing—they increase the opportunities for specialization, division of labour and reduction of costs in financial activities.

Securities markets need not be costly to operate. The issue of shares and debentures can be carried out with relatively small costs of advertising, postage and clerical wages; subsequent trading of securities requires little more than a meeting place, telephones and clerks. Further discussion of these costs will be deferred to the end of this chapter. Suffice it now to say that securities markets cannot be presumed either to be wasteful of administrative resources or to be more expensive than financial intermediaries in handling a given amount of finance.

Beyond the broad ways, already discussed above and in Chapter 3, in which securities markets and other financial developments may assist economic growth, are certain developmental benefits that may be derived more particularly from the existence of a securities market. First, the securities market provides a first-rate breeding ground for the skills and judgement needed for entrepreneurship, risk-bearing, portfolio selection and management. These capacities may develop in the proprietors and managers of firms 'going public'; in those who conduct stockbroking, underwriting and new issue activities; and in the managers of financial institutions and individuals who trade in stocks and bonds. All such individuals perforce must improve their knowledge of finance and their ability to evaluate risk and seize opportunities (see also Patrick, 1966, p. 176).

Second, active securities markets serve as an 'engine' of general financial development and may, in particular, accelerate the integration of informal or traditional financial systems with the institutional financial sector. Shares and bonds may directly displace traditional assets such as gold and stocks of produce or, indirectly, may provide portfolio assets for unit trusts, pension funds and similar financial institutions that raise savings from the traditional sector.

Third, the existence of a securities market enhances the scope, and provides institutional mechanisms, for the operation of monetary and financial policy. In the last few years, volatility of capital internationally, flexibility of exchange rates and new theoretical ideas (about the nature and purpose of monetary policy) have called discretionary monetary policies into question if not disrepute (especially for open underdeveloped economies). Nevertheless, it remains true that national central banks require influence over interest rates and the size and composition of the assets of an economy's financial institutions. A flourishing securities market is invaluable for the implementation of general official financial policy, which is less damaging to resource allocation than are selective controls.

In turning now to discuss factors limiting the development of securities markets, it is necessary first to distinguish between government and corporate securities. In most countries enough government securities seem to be available to provide the basis for a market in such paper (Wai and Patrick, 1973, p. 270), though some discussion will be devoted later to the problem of securing an appropriate supply–demand balance of government paper. But both the supply of, and the demand for, corporate securities is, by its nature, very limited in most underdeveloped economies.

On the supply side, there are basic economic and institutional reasons for the dearth of corporate securities. To begin with, underdeveloped economies are dominated by agriculture, which is usually organized on smallholder lines. Where corporate agricultural enterprises exist, they are usually foreign-controlled with their shares predominantly held abroad. Public utilities (i.e. non-corporate enterprises) commonly provide power, transport and communication services, while the industrial sector is small and weak.

The activities (industrial, commercial, extractive) that are in private hands and would be large enough to warrant the corporate form of business organization are commonly owned and controlled abroad. Foreign companies generally have little need or desire to raise capital locally, unless persuaded or obliged to do so by local authorities (see below, pp. 208–9. The remaining domestic corporate concerns are often not in need of further capital, or are unwilling or unable to raise funds by public subscriptions.

Family, or clan, companies are common in underdeveloped countries, and it has often been observed that such firms are reluctant to admit outside capital and risk dilution of control. (For example, Maniatis, 1971, pp. 660–2; Wai and Patrick, 1973, pp. 260–88; see also Leff, 1976, on Groups.) Indeed, where outside equity is admitted, 'unsavory policies detrimental to the interests of the minority (outsider) shareholding groups (with respect to dividend policy, stock manipulation, corporate disclosure, excessive compensation to executives who are family members) are not unknown' (Maniatis, 1971, p. 607). Such activities will discourage demand for equities issued by family-controlled firms. Some such firms have attained what they regard as optimum size and do not wish to expand their operations.

Maniatis draws attention to the further practice, common in Greece, of *premature diversification*, in which profits are siphoned out of industrial companies into non-industrial activities (family trusts, real estate, etc.) before the original company reaches full industrial maturity. Thus possible equity issues are frustrated not only because the industrial company's expansion is arrested, but also because the activities into which funds are diverted are not carried out by public companies.

Firms that are bent on expansion may finance it with retained profits and/or bank credit. Bank overdrafts, nominally short-term, are so continuous as to be long-term in effect. Good banking connections permit this system of finance to be perpetuated (indeed, interlocking ownership and direction between banks and other companies is very common in underdeveloped countries), and may lead to a dependence on bank finance which the banks may not wish to curtail. This pattern probably owes much to artificially low bank rates of interest. Cheap bank finance is much sought after and is rationed to favoured borrowers, who benefit at the expense of those who unsuccessfully seek bank credit and the bank depositors whose funds earn inadequate—if not negative—real rates of interest. (However, this state of affairs may not survive a liberal reform of interest rates; see below.)

These practices lead in general to low ratios of equity to debt in the capital structure of firms. Maniatis (1971, pp. 600–3) has argued, at some length, that this seemingly weak capital structure puts firms that desire to raise equity funds by new issues of shares into a 'vicious circle'. The firm's unsatisfactory equity:debt ratio makes the new issue appear too risky and unattractive for potential subscribers, but only new subscription capital could improve the equity : debt ratio. (Of course, ploughed-back profits could improve the equity : debt ratio, but this would normally require more time than Maniatis probably has in mind.) Although this argument may seem intuitively persuasive, it is unsupported by empirical evidence. It cannot therefore be asserted that firms with thin equity structures will invariably be unable to float share issues successfully. Much less can one generalize, from this view of under-capitalized firms, that any willing company will find it difficult to promote a successful issue of equity in an underdeveloped country: as we shall soon see, there is strong evidence to the contrary.

Fundamentally, the limited supply of private securities in underdeveloped countries is related to the small size and limited investment horizons of many local businesses. It will inevitably take time for such firms to reach the point of raising funds through public share and debenture issues, thus providing the necessary augmentation of the supply of private paper. Meanwhile, it might in some countries be desirable for development banks, etc., to raise funds by issuing shares and debentures publicly, or for governments to increase their own borrowing beyond the amounts needed to finance public sector investment, and re-lend to under-capitalized local firms.

It is therefore sometimes argued that the whole machinery of public companies, issuing shares and bonds which are traded on the stock exchange, is inappropriate to underdeveloped countries, where there is likely to be, for some time, a preponderance of firms that are too small to approach the public capital market and that depend upon self-finance or institutional finance for expansion. In these circumstances, a case can perhaps be made for long-term bank financing, in the traditional way of the continental banks which provide equity capital, often substantial, to firms. Moreover, it has recently been suggested that financial institutions—either public or private—might sell their own bonds abroad and employ the proceeds in making long-term loans to domestic enterprises (McKinnon, 1973, pp. 176–7). While there is something to be said for these approaches in conjunction with the development of a securities market, they seem to be inadequate substitutes for the machinery of share issues and trading. In the first place, in the absence of a securities market the investments (equity and debenture type) made by banks and other institutions will lack liquidity—with a consequential diminution of the flexibility and an increase in the costs of bank operations; second, total reliance on institutional finance would close off the important entrepreneurial avenue of direct appeal to the public; finally (as will be discussed later), it cannot be presumed that institutional lending will be conducted at lower real social cost than fund-raising via the securities market. And we shall see below that there are measures at hand that would encourage the issue of marketable securities.

There are a number of *a priori* reasons for expecting the demand for securities to be limited in an underdeveloped economy. The arguments, which are well put by Maniatis (1971, pp. 603–5), are as follows.

(i)   Individual savings accrue in the main to unsophisticated people, who are financially inexperienced and have conservative attitudes towards money. Such people are apathetic towards advanced forms of wealth-holding, and this threshold of insensitivity will be overcome only gradually and most likely through a fairly protracted learning process.

(ii) Share ownership by individuals tends to be confined to those with high incomes who may spread their risks through diverse portfolios (this risk-spreading is not possible for those with limited funds to invest and for whom transactions costs are high); there is not a sufficiently large class of well-to-do persons to sustain a corporate securities market in an underdeveloped country.

(iii) The generally underdeveloped financial system means that there is little or no institutional demand for securities.

(iv) Price uncertainty reinforces the traditional preference for money over financial assets which fluctuate in value.

(v)   Accurate information is scarce and the costs of obtaining it are inordinately high; market regulation is limited. Hence, investment in securities is extremely risky and in the nature of a racecourse gamble.

No widespread empirical evidence has yet been marshalled

in support of these arguments (nor does Maniatis document his assertions about limited demand for securities in Greece). While they seem intuitively sensible, there is enough contrary argument and fragmentary evidence to suggest that it would be wrong to regard the characteristics just described as universal constraints on securities demand.

Experience in Malaysia/Singapore casts a lot of doubt on arguments (i) and (ii). In the course of a stock market boom in those territories between September 1961 and June 1964, twenty-four industrial and commercial companies were offered in public subscriptions considerably more than the $M128m which in total they had sought for new issues of shares and debentures. (For a detailed account and analysis see Drake, 1969b. A similar experience occurred again in 1973–4 but I have not been able to obtain comparable figures.) It is plain beyond all doubt that the subscriptions for these securities came mainly from local sources. Most applications were in the names of locally domiciled Chinese; these were chiefly individual subscribers, although some were apparently buying on behalf of syndicates. From data about the geographical distribution of applications, it is evident that interest in securities investment was concentrated in the wealthier urban centres (Singapore, Kuala Lumpur and Petaling Jaya, Ipoh, Penang). But it is also clear that the subscribers were by no means confined to the high-income class. Very many subscriptions were for small blocks of shares, and the occupational range of subscribers descended through the clerical lower-middle class to domestic servants, gardeners and labourers. Even after allowance is made for massive speculative behaviour in the Malayan boom, a wide distribution of 'steady' share ownership remained (e.g., Malayan Tobacco's share register maintained 38,000 different names three months after the initial post-issue speculative trading had died down).

Similar, though not so striking, evidence of public interest in acquiring industrial securities comes from Nigeria. In the period 1959–66 (prior to the economic disruption caused by the civil war in 1967–8) £N14·5m was subscribed to twenty new issues made by fifteen companies; of the total sum, £N5·5m (38·1 per cent) was raised in ordinary shares. (Arowolo, 1971, p. 456. At the relevant time £1 Nigerian exchanged at $US2·40.) Participation by Nigerians in the share issues was at an encouraging level and was well maintained throughout the period: five issues each attracted over 1,000 Nigerians (the highest recorded number of local subscribers being 2,150 for the £1 ordinary shares issued by Nigerian Cement Co. Ltd), while Nigerian individuals took up between 38 and 72 per cent of the value of subscriptions in six issues.

In the light of such evidence, one must have reservations about believing that the attraction of securities ownership is confined to a very narrow, high-income section of the population, the rest of which may become interested only through 'a fairly protracted learning process'.

The proposition (iii), that there is little demand by financial institutions for securities, relies on the conventional view, based on earlier observations, that there is but a small number and range of financial institutions in most underdeveloped countries. Nowadays this view hardly accords with the facts, as a number of recent studies attest (Sowelem, 1967; Drake, 1969a; Rozental, 1970a; Emery, 1971). Because of the rapid financial development that has occurred in many less developed countries since the mid-1960s, one may reasonably expect that financial institutions will provide a growing source of demand for securities, both corporate and government, of a wide range of maturities, Policy measures by which institutional demand for securities may be augmented will be discussed later. It is here apposite to observe that the emergence and growth of institutions such as pension funds, insurance companies and unit trusts (which would be greatly encouraged by a free market interest rate policy) provided the means whereby small amounts of individual saving may be gathered together into sums large enough for the institutions to channel into securities purchases. This form of financial intermediation also provides for the spread of risks which is otherwise impossible within the individual small portfolio.

The observation (iv), that price uncertainty leads savers to prefer money over financial assets which fluctuate in value, does not necessarily hold when a country is experiencing inflation and/or exchange rate uncertainty. Irrespective of fluctuations, if the trend of share prices is upward, equity investment may be preferred to holding money which is losing real value. Wai and Patrick (1973, p. 280) suggest, however, that inflation may increase uncertainty to such an extent that the attractiveness of equity investment is reduced.

Finally, the scarcity of accurate information about corporate behaviour and prospects leads to 'lack of confidence [which] is probably the most important inhibition to capital market development' (Wai and Patrick, 1973, p. 285). This is a real and severe problem which has certainly not been exaggerated; indeed, apart from Wai and Patrick, few writers have made enough of this difficulty, which will be discussed more fully later in this chapter.

This is not the place to recount in detail the structure and performance of securities markets in individual countries. (For detailed accounts, refer to the cited articles by Arowolo, Drake, Maniatis, Wai and Patrick, Porter, and Ness.) In the next few paragraphs we attempt to distil some general observations about market patterns and behaviour in less developed countries, drawing particularly on data provided by Wai and Patrick (1973, especially pp. 265–8, 306–17).

The most notable characteristic of less developed country securities markets is the great, and often increasing, importance of government as both issuer/seller and buyer of securities. So far as new issues are concerned, government securities accounted for 60–80 per cent of total new issues of securities in 1965–70 in thirteen countries surveyed by U Tun Wai and Patrick. Moreover, the government share of new issues was the greater, the lower the ratio of total securities issues to GNP; conversely in countries where the ratio of new issues to GNP was high, 'private issues are predominant and are purchased mostly by business corporations and individuals' (Wai and Patrick, 1973, p. 267). In general, the supply of government securities is now sufficient to meet current domestic demand for them. However, exceptions have been observed in particular circumstances, e.g., the occasional shortages of Treasury bills in Malaysia and Singapore (Drake, 1969a, Chapters 12, 13).

Government is also the major buyer of securities (often of its own debt), either directly or through its sinking funds, pension funds or agencies, such as public corporations and government banks. Central banks are powerful buyers, often, apparently, in order to shore up the market in government paper. Of private sector buyers, commercial banks are the most important (frequently to meet the requirements of official liquidity standards), followed by other financial institutions, businesses and, lastly, individuals.

Private sector issuers are manufacturing and commercial companies and, to a lesser extent, financial enterprises (though commercial banks seldom issue new securities). The finance sector is, as one would expect, more active in trading paper than issuing it. On the whole, however, private securities are very limited in supply: further, many new securities are issued by private placement so that the volume of truly public issues made by companies is small (Wai and Patrick, 1973, pp. 270, 273, 312–13). Malaysia/Singapore, however, provides an exception to the last statement.

In the century before 1914 a major element in the growth of the London stock exchange was the issue and subsequent trading of the securities of railway, tramway, canal, dock, gas, electricity and water companies, operating in Britain and in the colonies (Morgan, 1965, pp. 136–8). In the less developed countries of today such activities invariably belong in the government sector, where they are not financed by shareholders and rarely by the issue of debentures or bonds.

The turnover of securities is typically low in underdeveloped countries. In the main, new issues are bought for holding rather than trading. U Tun Wai and Patrick found that only in China (Taiwan), Malaysia/Singapore and Mexico was the ratio of securities turnover to GNP at all substantial. Occasional and intermittent sharp accelerations of turnover have been observed in connection with speculation. Instances of substantial share speculation (possibly including manipulation of the share market) are not uncommon and have occurred in Malaysia/Singapore, Korea, Brazil, Colombia, China (Taiwan) and Hong Kong (Wai and Patrick, 1973, pp. 271–2, 280, 286–8; Drake, 1969b).

The narrow and fragmented markets just described are very susceptible to discontinuities in supply and demand—and also to manipulations—which produce wide price fluctuations. These conditions may make equity securities unattractive to investors. Maniatis (1971, p. 599) even goes so far as to argue that generally increasing the yields on equities would not lead to an increase in the demand for them so long as sharp price fluctuations, and the consequent risk, persist. On the other hand, one cannot expect any sustained augmentation of equity supply and demand, sufficient to iron out discontinuities, to occur unless and until the general yield of equities relative to other assets is increased. It seems, indeed, that an increase in yields is a necessary—though not sufficient—condition for improved functioning of the equities market.

To sum up this section, the securities markets of underdeveloped countries are characterized by a limited number, volume and variety of stocks traded; and by a narrow range of participants, with government often dominant. Turnover activity is low, except when speculation erupts. The value of corporate new issues floated publicly is not significant in relation to GNP or real investment. Government issues are much more substantial but are taken up largely by captive buyers. We turn now to a consideration of policy measures which might increase the size, range, activity and usefulness of securities markets.

It is surely obvious that the securities market in an under-developed country should be viewed and assessed in relation to the country's limited economic and financial development. Consequently, any specific measures for fostering the growth of the securities market should be introduced as part of a general programme for economic and financial develop-ment. This view is well argued by U Tun Wai and Patrick, who refer also to necessary legal and political improvements, and there is no need for detailed repetition here. Suffice it to single out for emphasis the importance of curbing inflation and freeing interest rates, if securities markets are to germinate and flourish (Wai and Patrick, 1973, pp. 280–4, 301; Shaw, 1973, Chapter 5; McKinnon, 1973, Chapter 7).

Inflation unquestionably has deleterious effects on the real value and the yield of bonds, debentures, etc., whose capital values are expressed in fixed money amounts and whose yields are fixed as a given rate of interest. This has led some economists to commend the practice of *indexation* (i.e., basing the principal and income of such securities on some appropriate price index) and to advocate its adop-tion in some countries (Wai and Patrick, 1973, pp. 282–3; Ness, 1974, p. 456). However, a major practical problem is how far (within the wide range of nominal value assets) to extend the practice of indexation. The indexation of some financial assets would be expected to depress further the capital values and drive up the yields of instruments that were not indexed. It follows that indexation may lead to a change in the composition of demand for various financial assets. The effect of inflation upon equity securities (which have neither capital value nor yield expressed in fixed money terms) is uncertain: it must be presumed that they would be attractive as a 'hedge', but, on the other hand, inflation might undermine the operating profitability of the firms whose shares provide equity securities for investors.

Expert opinion is united against government interference with the pattern of interest rates and allocation of investible funds that would be determined by the free play of market forces. The fullest arguments have been put persuasively by McKinnon (1973) and Shaw (1973); see also Wai and Patrick (1973), Porter (1966), Ness (1974). Such views have been noticed several times throughout this book and the threads will be gathered together in the final chapter. There is little doubt that the development of securities markets is stifled by interest rate ceilings and would be encouraged by a more liberal policy about interest rates. (Porter, 1973, shows how quickly a bill market in Colombia grew in response to realistically high interest rates.) For instance, higher interest charges on bank loans would encourage company borrowers to seek equity finance instead. Any net increase in the attractiveness of equities for individual savers would depend upon the added availability and marketability of equity assets outweighing the lure of increased interest obtainable on deposits in banks and other financial institutions. This seems probable and, in any event, the demand of financial institutions (other than commercial banks) for equities would seem likely to increase in step with any rise in their deposits, as the institutions would be looking for high yielding assets, with prospects of capital gain also.

Specific measures to promote the supply of marketable securities are concentrated on the concessions that may encourage companies to issue shares and debentures. This tactic has been tried in various European countries (OECD, 1967) and used with great success in Brazil (Ness, 1974, p. 461). Stronger measures would be to oblige firms above a certain size to offer shares publicly and to restrict the granting of bank credit to under-capitalized firms, in order to force them to seek equity funds through public issues of shares. But such drastic measures would be difficult to administer, and they clearly conflict with the economic philosophy of the free capital market (Wai and Patrick, 1973, p. 289; Maniatis, 1971, p. 615).

More realistically, consideration should be given to the policy of requiring foreign corporations to issue some local equity, or encouraging them to do so by penalizing overseas borrowing. Such action would certainly be in tune with nationalistic sentiments.

> The rise of economic nationalism in many countries already raises uncertainties as to the continued foreign ownership of many of these companies. The pressures for increased local participation in such companies is not confined to securing the appointment of a few local people as senior personnel who are usually without much responsibility in policy decisions. The offer of shares and securities [*sic*] on a voluntary basis to local subscribers might provide a safety valve and reduce the risk of nationalization. [Arowolo, 1971, p. 464]

The Malaysia/Singapore experience suggests that there is likely to be very strong local demand for securities issued by first-class international firms (Drake, 1969b, p. 81).

Although foreign firms may be under considerable pressure to issue shares and debentures in the underdeveloped host country, they will not need to do so as long as they continue to have ready access to cheap local bank loans or international capital markets, and/or to generate high profits which provide the wherewithal for self-financed expansion. For example, the General Motors–Holden company has flourished in Australia for many years, its growth having been financed principally by retained profits (Penrose, 1956). General Motors–Holden has not issued any equity in Australia (other than the preference shares issued in 1931 to acquire the Holden Company), despite frequent and vociferous demands that it should do so. (The company's associate General Motors Acceptance Corporation has raised large sums by debenture issues in Australia, chiefly to finance credit sales of the motor vehicles, etc., manufactured by the main company.) Moreover, one must have reservations about recommending a policy which, by perhaps restricting capital inflow, might serve also to reduce the total amount of investment resources available to an economy. An alternative strategy, which, while restraining foreign direct investment, might sustain the total inflow of international capital by encouraging portfolio investment, is outlined by McKinnon (1973, pp. 176–7).

Arowolo makes two further proposals in respect of local enterprises. First, he suggests that statutory corporations engaged in essentially 'industrial' activities could offer their securities—either directly or through subsidiaries—to the public (incidentally permitting the public to 'have a more direct say in the management of such enterprises'). Secondly, he argues that, when joint ventures are undertaken between government and private interests, 'the base of equity ownership could be substantially broadened if the government would divest itself of part of the ownership of such ventures as they become successful' (Arowolo, 1971, p. 463).

The demand for securities is much more amenable to official influence than is their supply. It may be promoted, first, by tax concessions in favour of shareholders. Ness's account of the Brazilian experience provides a rich and detailed illustration of the efficacy with which fiscal incentives may foster the growth of the share market. In brief, the Brazilian incentives included: (1) provisions for shareholders to deduct substantial proportions of the purchase cost of shares from taxable income; (2) provisions for part personal income tax exemption of dividends, and for concessional rates of withholding tax for shareholders in those 'open capital' companies that undertook to achieve a wide dispersion of equity; and (3) provisions for individuals and corporations to discharge a proportion of their tax liabilities by subscribing to special mutual funds ('the 157 funds'), withdrawals from which could not begin for at least two years. The 157 funds, in turn, were required to invest in company securities, particularly new issues. The generous tax-relief provisions not only swelled the 157 funds but seem also to have encouraged the growth of mutual funds generally. The Brazilian fiscal incentives quickly produced striking increases in the volume of share issues, the number of firms issuing, stock exchange turnover and share prices (Ness, 1974, p. 460).

Secondly, indexation of the principal and income of nominal value securities, as previously discussed, will enhance the demand for such securities. Thirdly, distinct from giving protection against inflation, government may guarantee the redemption value and dividend rates of certain securities in order to alleviate risk. Fourthly, the demand for securities may be greatly augmented by the imposition of portfolio rules upon banks and other financial institutions. A related measure would be to restrict capital outflow or to prohibit/limit the transfer abroad of funds accruing to financial institutions (e.g. premiums on life insurance). If finance houses are required to hold a proportion of their assets in the form of local securities—government or private —a demand for such securities is readily generated, as has been demonstrated, for example, in Malaysia, Kenya and Nigeria (Drake, 1969a, pp. 180, 186, 213; Arowolo, 1971, pp. 439, 455, 457). Next, the demand for securities will be stronger the greater is their liquidity, which will be improved by the willingness of a central bank to rediscount private paper, as well as that of government, and to accept securities as collateral for loans to commercial banks. In their turn, the commercial banks will enhance the liquidity of securities if, within reasonable margins, they will accept them as collateral for overdrafts.

Finally, official supervision of trading in the securities markets is imperative if shares and bonds are to become attractive assets. Otherwise, the public may justifiably feel too exposed to the risk of market manipulation and other abuses, and may decline to invest. (See Drake, 1974, pp. 528–30, for a description of common forms of market abuse.)

The objectives of official regulation and supervision should be: to provide for the full disclosure and wide dissemination of accurate information about the companies whose stocks and bonds are traded; to prevent the various forms of market rigging; to protect the interests of minority share-holders; and to encourage the development of specialized financial services and techniques. For these purposes, adequate legislation for disclosure and shareholder protection as well as some sort of supervisory body are necessary. The latter, however, need not, and should not, be too sophisticated or expensive. Wai and Patrick (1973, p. 286) warn of the 'danger of regulatory overkill . . . which may actually inhibit capital market development'. It is better to promote disclosure of information and interests, which not only engenders confidence among investors but—by creating a climate of opinion favourable to 'clean' trading—may actually diminish the need for close supervision of transactions.

Honest and capable stockbrokers are necessary if trading is to be clean and efficient, but it cannot be taken for granted that brokers will measure up to the required standards. Dissatisfaction with brokers' behaviour has been expressed in many countries—advanced as well as underdeveloped—and has led to a variety of reform proposals. (Several of these, and the rationale and role of brokers, are discussed by Drake and Mathews, 1974, and Drake, 1974. See also Wai and Patrick, 1973, pp. 286–8.) The essence of the problem is that a conflict of interest often arises between the obligations of a broker as an agent—executing share purchases and sales, for commission, on behalf of clients—and the personal economic freedom, and attractions, for the broker to trade on his own account, to underwrite new issues, to act as company promoter or director, etc. While it would be possible legally to restrict brokers to the agency role, it might not be wise to do so in underdeveloped countries where the volume of transactions is not large and where financial skills are scarce. The public and the economy might be better served by brokers who also sustain other financial activities, develop their knowledge and skill accordingly, and ultimately contribute to the spread of financial techniques. For instance, two essential activities in any securities market are the floating and underwriting of new issues and the 'jobbing' of existing securities (Drake and Mathews, 1974, pp. 14–15). In embryonic markets, at least, brokers are best placed to perform these functions. However, there are no clearcut and universally desirable boundaries for broker activities, nor is it an easy matter to ensure that brokers always conform to the appropriate activities and canons of conduct in any country. It is essential, therefore, that the roles and responsibilities of brokers be formulated after public discussion, be well publicized subsequently, and be capably supervised.

The conscious promotion of a securities market would have costs. In the first place, a government might spend money directly on what could be described as 'securities markets infrastructure', e.g. buildings, communication facilities, market supervision, staff training, etc.; but these expenditures are not likely to be very large, especially as private enterprise is usually more than willing to undertake the operations, as distinct from the supervision, of the market. Arowolo recounts the occasion in Kenya in 1954 when brokers resisted the idea that government be invited to establish and finance a stock exchange, preferring instead to form a stockbrokers' association which subsequently was incorporated as the Nairobi Stock Exchange (Arowolo, 1971, p. 441). Similarly, the trading of shares and bonds, albeit in a small way, developed spontaneously in a number of underdeveloped countries as long as one hundred years ago.

A much more important consideration is that the government budget would suffer a fall in revenue as a result of allowing any of the tax concessions outlined earlier. The opportunity cost of subsidizing the development of securities markets in this manner is presumed to be high by Wai and Patrick (1973, p. 290), although they concede that 'it is difficult to reach a judgement in this matter, as only society can decide whether the trade-off was worthwhile' (1973, p. 298).

In the light of the manifold demands made for urgent government assistance for agriculture, industry, education, health, etc., few governments in underdeveloped countries are likely to give high priority to any substantial inducement to participants in the securities market. This is not just a matter of assistance to the latter having an apparently high opportunity cost. Even if an administration judged that a given amount of assistance to the buyers and sellers of securities would be preferable to, say, a subsidy for industry of the same order, it might be reluctant to act accordingly. This is because the incidence of the benefits from government incentives for the issue and purchase of securities seems sure to conflict with the objective of a more equal distribution of income, at least in the short run (Wai and Patrick, 1973, pp. 291, 298). Over the longer period, however, a more general participation by the population in financial activity and a more widespread dispersion of share ownership (perhaps fostered by reserving some shares in new issues for local workers or domestic nationals) may be expected to contribute to a more even and acceptable distribution of income (Lloyd, 1977, pp. 5, 8–10). Wai and Patrick (1973, p. 298) note that the Brazilian stock market boom 'may have dispersed ownership somewhat from the highest 5 per cent; it has attracted the so-called middle class (say, the next 15 per cent of the income distribution)'; much the same could be said for Malaysia/Singapore. Moreover, in the absence of a securities market, dependence on bank loans may sustain and exacerbate a maldistribution of income for so long as bank credit is available only to a priviledged and relatively limited clientele.

The social costs (opportunity and distributional) of government assistance to those who participate in the securities market should be viewed in relation to the costs of government intervention elsewhere in economy (to begin with, the administrative and compliance costs of interest rate controls and other forms of capital market repression). When compared, for instance, with the massive, and often fruitless, government assistance given by tariff protection and subsidy to agriculture and manufacturing industry in so many less developed countries (to say nothing of the consequent price and output distortions in the product markets), the costs of promoting a securities market may not look so great. In an intervention-ridden world, it is scarcely appropriate to judge a proposed further intervention by the canons of theoretical welfare economics. The provision of a measure of government encouragement for the securities market, which is cheap relative to government subsidization of other activities, may well be a good gamble on generating savings and enterprise in the longer run.

There remain the resource costs incurred directly in the operation of the securities market. These need not be great, despite Shaw's vehement assertion—unsupported by any evidence—of the contrary opinion (Shaw, 1973, p. 145). Marble halls, computers, electronic price boards, etc., are not necessary for the conduct of securities trading, especially in small countries. Securities trading has been going on in Singapore, for example, since the late nineteenth century, but not until 1960 did the brokers adopt even a trading room. The Nairobi Stock Exchange has operated, in effect, as a regional exchange serving Kenya, Tanzania and Uganda, yet the method of dealing in securities there is quite simple and does not involve expensive paraphernalia (Arowolo, 1971, p. 442). A market requires only communication between traders and the accurate recording of transactions. This boils down to a meeting place, telecommunication links between the main cities of a country and with the outside world, and a few good clerks. Financial institutions which require permanent buildings, furniture, equipment and a large staff would seem to be more expensive to operate than simple facilities for issuing, buying and selling securities and recording and publishing their prices.

While not providing a key to rapid economic growth, a securities market makes too useful a contribution to be neglected. And as securities markets take root in developing economies, some of the basic retarding features of the backward economy—notably the monopolistic powers of various financiers—may be reduced. If governments eschew authoritarian financial policies and instead cultivate the conditions in which financing can flourish naturally, then securities markets will emerge spontaneously to perform a significant and useful role. There are indeed obstacles, inherent in the nature of poor and backward societies, to the germination and quick growth of securities markets. But it has been argued above that the constraints are not as binding as they appear at first sight and may have been magnified by other writers.

In the right circumstances, it may be justifiable to go a stage further and introduce measures to promote securities markets. More research is needed about market structure, performance and potential in individual countries. The limited empirical work so far conducted gives some grounds for thinking that the development of securities markets may be more feasible and beneficial than has generally been believed. Appropriate supply and demand inducements are available, have proved effective where tried, and do not seem to be prohibitive in cost. On the other hand, it would be foolish to attempt to impose a securities market upon an economy in which complementary economic and financial developments were not occurring. Securities markets will bear promotion only as part of a consistent package of economic policy. It seems most important to awaken official awareness of the benefits of financial development generally and of the need to eliminate economic and financial dualism.

Further Reading

As must be apparent, the small number of academic articles on the specific subject of this chapter have all been cited and are generally worth reading in full. Somewhat more general discussions of capital market development can be found in Wilson (1966, 1968) and Lloyd (1976, 1977). Lloyd, while perhaps rather more pessimistic in outlook, shares my general disposition towards official encouragement of securities markets development and emphasizes the distinction between 'right' and 'wrong' forms of government intervention. His 1977 paper is particularly recommended.

CHAPTER 9

Approach to Policy

Several themes have emerged, some repeatedly, in the preceding chapters. It is time to bring the main themes together in a coherent way and to draw out, if possible, a consistent set of monetary and financial strategies for developing countries. The long-run nature of such strategies must never be forgotten. Monetization and financial development and their beneficial interaction with economic growth do not occur overnight. Consequently, great emphasis and attention must be given to getting the foundations of any monetary and financial system in order. On good foundations can be built a financial structure that will permit, eventually, shorter-term monetary variations designed to steer or stabilize the economy.

In advanced countries money and credit are viewed, in short-term macroeconomic perspective, as variables to be controlled in the interests of internal and external balance. Indeed, in such economies money is discussed virtually exclusively in terms of its use in macroeconomic stabilization; little if any attention is given to the role of money and credit in financial development, presumably because the critical stage of financial 'take-off' is long past and a well developed financial structure already exists. By contrast, in less developed countries the deficiencies in financial structure constrain economic development. Primary attention in those countries should therefore be given to the promotion of financial development in order to improve economic efficiency. In other words, a suitable and well-functioning

217

financial system is a communal producer good of very great importance and, more specifically, is a necessary condition of sustained economic growth.

The first objective of financial policy is to promote monetization at the fastest rate consistent with reasonable stability of prices. Monetization permits and promotes division of labour and specialization—in production and between saving and investment—which generates increases in real output/income. The makers of economic policy should therefore study closely the motives for which people adopt general purpose money. In this respect it seems that wide and readily available opportunities to effect purchases of goods and services with money are very important. The special attraction of money as a highly liquid store of value—much more liquid than traditional value stores—also deserves great attention and emphasis in encouraging fuller monetization of many less developed economies.

Since monetization implies that the demand for real money grows faster than real output, it becomes a requirement of policy that the authorities permit the supply of money also to grow at a rate appropriately faster than real output grows. Excessive monetary growth, however, gives rise to the risk of inflation which has a most damaging 'backlash' effect on monetization and financial development, over and above the more commonly recognized adverse effects of inflation upon the level and distribution of real output/income. Reasonable price stability is centrally important in developing economies in order to engender and sustain confidence in money and in financial assets denominated in money. People cannot be expected to adopt money in preference to traditional mediums of exchange and stores of value when that money is obviously deteriorating in real purchasing power. In any economy that relies to any significant extent upon non-monetary forms of exchange and stores of value, inflation will therefore inhibit monetization and financial development. Not only will specialization, saving and resource allocation in the domestic economy thus be sub-optimal, but inflation will also prevent the nation from benefiting as fully from international trade and investment as it would if prices were stable. 'Hard' money is thus desirable because of both domestic and international economic considerations. One way of ensuring hard money is for a country to adopt a monetary system that requires a high and rigid external assets backing for local money, as under the currency board system. Such systems automatically prevent domestic credit expansion from occurring at a rate so far in excess of the growth rate of real output as to permit price inflation to originate locally.

In order to acquire more money under currency board type systems, the country as a whole must give up (net) goods, services and property rights to foreigners. In other words, the stock of money becomes dependent upon the balance of international payments. This state of affairs, however, may not make for economic satisfaction because, first, an undesirable deflationary bias may be imparted to the economy whenever real output expands without a corresponding balance of payments surplus and, secondly, the rigid exchange rate that this type of monetary system implies leaves the nation with no means of insulating itself against 'imported' inflation arising in the rest of the world.

On the whole, it seems desirable for a nation to adopt a discretionary rather than an automatic system of supplying itself with money; but nice judgement is needed in so exercising discretionary powers of currency creation and exchange rate variation as to steer away from the undesirable features of a rigid currency system without plunging into the possibly greater abyss of inflationary domestic credit expansion. It is important that the monetary authorities correctly gauge the pace of monetization and of the growth of real output and provide additional money up to, but not beyond, the level demanded by these developments.

Financial policy is more than mere monetary policy, and the span of official interest needs to be much wider than monetary management. The authorities in any country aiming at economic growth have responsibilities to promote financial development generally and to ensure that channels exist whereby demands for credit may be met and, if judged 'worthwhile' according to given economic and social criteria, satisfied. In terms of such criteria, for instance, it is not unreasonable to say that credit lines available to small-scale producers (rural and urban) who wish to expand their production levels are usually woefully inadequate. A high-priority task for the authorities in any economy is to identify deficiencies or obstructions in the channels of finance. Flow-of-funds social accounting provides a framework within which the authorities may assemble and analyse the financial pattern of any economy. While, of course, in developing economies where informal finance is so pervasive it will be especially difficult to chart financial flows in fine detail, the flow-of-funds framework does provide a coherent and consistent view of financial interrelationships and should prevent officials from slipping into partial, piecemeal and inconsistent policy measures. Even the broadest and most rudimentary flow-of-funds estimates can throw inter-sectoral financial relationships into sharp relief and expose financial surplus and deficit areas which may call for the building of intermediation bridges between them.

The pattern of financial flows in any underdeveloped country is likely to suggest—as has been mentioned so often in this book—a need for greater integration between institutional and informal finance. In this regard, it seems sensible to begin by recognizing the importance of the services provided by informal financiers and to strengthen any points of contact between such financiers and modern financial institutions.

We have noticed a number of links between these two financial sectors, such as bank lending to pawnbrokers/moneylenders and credit chains running from banks and mercantile firms eventually down to village shopkeepers. These connections, though they may not at any moment be the means of providing a considerable volume of outstand-

ing debt, constitute financial machinery of no mean importance (see Wai, 1957, pp. 94–8 for further evidence). There
seems to be plenty of scope both for strengthening these
linkages and promoting new forms of integration between
informal and institutional finance. First, as has been mentioned in Chapter 6 above, and following Myint's argument
(1970, pp. 138–42), it is desirable to facilitate the access
of moneylenders, and would-be moneylenders, to institutional finance. The consequent increased competition among
moneylenders as well as the augmented supply of total funds
to the informal sector could be expected to improve the
availability, and lower the cost, of credit to small-scale producers. Competitive pressures might induce moneylenders
not only to accept interest charges on funds obtained from
financial institutions or government, but also to offer attractive rates of interest to villagers for informal deposits, thus
at last linking the rates paid for their funds to the rates
earned by their lending activities. Additionally, the promotion of securities issues in general, and the use of rural
bonds in particular, may tap other sectors for savings to
be lent to small rural producers, through, or in competition
with, the moneylenders. Secondly, it is necessary for collecting agencies to go into the outlying areas so that rural
savers may have the opportunity to acquire financial assets
as an alternative to traditional stores of value. For this
purpose it is essential that those financial institutions that
invade the rural areas offer deposit rates of interest that
are so attractive to savers as to overcome the appeal of
traditional assets. Normally this implies raising institutional
deposit interest rates quite considerably.

Ronald McKinnon has been a vigorous advocate of 'free'
rates of interest, by which he means the removal of any
legal or oligopolistic ceilings upon interest rates in general
and bank deposit interest rates in particular. In McKinnon's
view, positive real rates of interest have an important stimulating influence on the demand for money. It seems to
follow from this that banks should offer positive real rates

of interest (possibly requiring very high nominal rates) in order to promote financial development and capital formation. To the extent that such deposit rates of interest attract additional bank deposits, the banks, in order to maintain profitability, would in turn need to search for borrowers prepared to pay high loan rates of interest, probably small-scale producers and traders, or moneylenders. Significantly, this seems to have been what happened in Indonesia (a country accorded commendation by McKinnon) in the late 1960s and early 1970s when there was a great influx of deposits into banks in response to high interest rates:

> the consensus among observers seems to be that real output in Indonesia did not decline and probably rose during this period of sharp deflation with increased real deposit and lending rates. The allocation of resources seems to have been significantly improved, and monetization has been extended. Indonesian deposit holders appear to be highly sensitive to real rates of return.... [McKinnon, 1973, p. 113]

From the viewpoint of our interest in integration between the informal and formal finance markets, it would be interesting to know the extent to which the funds that provided these extra bank deposits would have remained in hoards or in the informal market but for the rise in bank deposit rates.

In the absence of free–and high nominal–rates of interest in the formal financial sector, financial dualism is likely to exist, characterized by cheap but rationed credit in the formal sector in contrast to expensive credit in the informal sector. As Myint has shown so elegantly (1970, pp. 136–9), artificially cheap institutional credit has the effect of distorting the allocation of resources between the modern and the traditional sectors of the economy, as well as inhibiting the integration of the informal and formal finance markets. The same view has been well put by Myrdal (1968, pp. 2087–95), who notes especially the extent, causes and effects of remarkably low institutional rates of interest in India and Pakistan, and by Chandavarkar (1971, p. 72). See also

McKinnon (1973, Chapter 3) for a particularly good account of the economic distortions that are associated with the 'intervention syndrome' and repressed financial markets.

McKinnon sees 'free' interest rates not merely as the key to integration of the diverse components of the domestic credit market (with the consequent economic gains which follow from financial development), but also as the centre-piece of a general programme of economic liberalization, which he argues would reduce fragmentation and propel an economy along the path of economic development. In McKinnon's words, 'high rates of interest for both lenders and borrowers induce the dynamism that one wants in development, calling forth new net saving and diverting investment from inferior uses so as to encourage technical improvement' (1973, p. 15). Freer (and, in the formal finance sector, higher) interest rates would promote the integration of formal and informal finance markets, encourage enterprises and activities other than those that flourish under 'financial repression' and change the factor proportions in production.

> There would be changes in the relative prices of goods and services, the absolute change depending, in each case, on the extent to which capital was used in the production process, and changes also in the demand for factors of production. As a higher level of interest rates is more in harmony with the great scarcity of capital in the South Asian economies, these adjustments would generally lead to a more rational allocation of resources. More specifically, a higher level of interest charges would tend to induce greater economy in the use of capital in construction and in production processes, a desideratum in all the countries of the region. If very capital-intensive public investment projects were reappraised in terms of a higher interest level, many of them would appear inadvisable (even taking into consideration external economies and other benefits not reflected in their cost/return accounts). In the case of projects that would still be carried out, the costs of the services or goods that constituted their end products would rise. [Myrdal, 1968, pp. 2092–3]

Artificially low rates of interest prevail currently in the formal financial sectors of most poor countries; these rates are often maintained by banking cartels, through the use of quantitative credit rationing and discrimination in dealing with loan applicants. By contrast, the true scarcity of capital is reflected in the high interest rates charged in the informal financial sector. To the extent that integration of the informal and formal finance sectors occurs, rates of interest would be expected to fall in the former as well as rise in the latter.

Along with the abolition of interest rate ceilings and quantitative credit rationing, McKinnon calls for: the removal of tariff protection and import controls; a restructuring of taxation, in particular shifting away from taxes on foreign trade (exports as well as imports) towards an expenditure or value-added tax base; withdrawal of official intervention in the commodity markets; the removal of exchange controls; and at least some degree of exchange rate flexibility. All this might seem to be adding up to an ultra-neoclassical policy, were it not for McKinnon's specific abandonment of the neoclassical approach, on the fundamental ground of its mistaken treatment of 'capital' as a homogeneous factor of production with uniform productivity (McKinnon, 1973, pp. 8–9). However, neoclassical or not, McKinnon's generally persuasive analysis seems to me to have one important weakness, namely, undue faith in the efficacy of free capital markets. In key passages McKinnon, having previously drawn attention to the great disparities of rates of return on existing and prospective investments in underdeveloped countries, says:

> The capital market in a 'developed' economy successfully monitors the efficiency with which the existing capital stock is deployed by pushing returns on physical and financial assets towards equality, thereby significantly increasing the average return. . . .

[and]

> Thus it is hypothesized that unification of the capital market, which sharply increases rates of return to domestic savers by widening exploitable investment opportunities is essential for eliminating other forms of fragmentation. [McKinnon, 1973, p. 9]

Certainly, freedom in the capital market is necessary for overcoming fragmentation, but one doubts that this freedom is a sufficient condition for obtaining that result *or even for unifying/integrating the domestic capital market.* My scepticism is based upon the very uneven spread of information and understanding, to say nothing of great differences in economic attitudes and abilities, that persists in developing countries. This comment refers not only to the obvious case of peasant producers who fail to perceive new opportunities arising from changes in economic conditions but, much more importantly in the present context, to financial institutions that are unresponsive or incompletely responsive to changes in financial conditions. In McKinnon's leading example—a rise in institutional deposit rates designed to increase sharply the rates of return to domestic savers and, in due course, oblige institutions to search for new ways of utilizing the additional funds so raised—there loom two large problems. First, the institutions may prefer to act collectively as a cartel and refrain from raising deposit rates of interest. Secondly, the managers and officials of financial institutions may—consciously or unconsciously—discriminate in their lending against small-scale producers, peasant farmers, certain ethnic groups, females, the uneducated, and so forth. Imperfections in the capital markets do exist, and are based on patterns of behaviour that are deep-seated and self-perpetuating, if often unrecognized.

In a justifiably famous essay, George Stigler has made untenable any facile resort to the term 'imperfections in the capital market' as a substitute for inquiry and analysis. Stigler recognizes clearly that knowledge is often incomplete and ill-distributed, but he argues that the existence of such 'imperfections' is normally the simple consequence of the costs of overcoming them being too large in relation to the expected benefits. 'There is no "imperfection" in a market possessing incomplete knowledge if it would not be remunerative to acquire (produce) complete knowledge: information costs are the costs of transportation from ignorance to omniscience, and seldom can a trader afford to take the entire trip' (Stigler, 1968, p. 119). Optimum information for any person would require him to inquire only up to the point where his expected marginal benefit from the search for information would be equal to its marginal cost.

Like McKinnon, Stigler believes in the efficacy of the market, but one cannot be sure that the market might not sometimes need to be 'helped over a stile'. It seems unwise to be complacent about the ultimate beneficence of free market forces in the face of, for example, the ingrained discriminatory habits of so many financiers together with the fact that many have inadequate knowledge about the costs and benefits of acquiring additional information.

Institutional discrimination by financiers is but one of a host of 'imperfections', in both the credit and goods markets in underdeveloped countries, which do not seem to disappear or even diminish—and indeed may be exacerbated—under *laissez-faire* conditions. Far from all men starting economic life from roughly the same line, there are enormous disparities in inherited wealth and opportunity which are commonly compounded by the educational and social privileges usually accorded to the children of the rich and the well-born. The child of any rural tenant farmer begins with almost insuperable handicaps. Regardless of how intelligent and energetic he may be, he has no land, few if any other tangible assets, little liquid capital and scant education. Further, underdeveloped economies are riddled with ill-integrated ethnic, religious and social groups—some privileged, others not. Those who belong to the underprivileged groups have this further disadvantage added to the difficulties of any poor start in life.

Anyone starting with these handicaps will find that his initial access to sources of credit is inevitably limited to moneylenders, pawnbrokers and shopkeepers. In the unlikely event that he has the wit and know-how to seek credit from a financial institution, his application would not normally be looked on favourably because he would have no collateral security to offer. It is extremely improbable that most institutional loan officers would take the trouble to assess carefully the applicant's business prospects with a view to providing unsecured credit for promising ideas.

In these conditions, so common in poor countries, it would be naive to expect that the economy in general and the credit market in particular will function best without any form of government restrictions or intervention. In fact, intervention is practised in most countries on a grand scale; indeed, in many countries intervention is increasing as nationalistic governments move to improve the economic knowledge, opportunities and power of nationals against foreigners, and of indigenes against ethnic groups of foreign descent. Hence, as Lloyd (1977) has argued so well, what is needed by policy-makers is the ability to distinguish between 'right' and 'wrong' forms of intervention.

In the financial sphere, intervention by way of the establishment or clearing of channels for the finance of industry and agriculture, particularly for small businesses, seems desirable and justifiable. The creation of development banks and other specialized lending institutions is only one aspect of official 'interventionist' policy. The authorities must also be prepared to promote a better dissemination of economic knowledge, work towards the eradication of any inappropriate and possibly discriminatory lending criteria used by banks and other finance houses, and police honest, informed trading in the securities market.

In all this there is a crucial role to be played by the central bank. As the monetary authority with, desirably, at least some degree of independence from government, the central bank must first of all tread the fine line of discouraging intervention in general while promoting carefully calculated particular interventions in the finance market designed to overcome imperfections arising from inadequate knowledge, entrenched privilege or prejudice. The bank must then take care that those specific interventions deemed desirable are co-ordinated and not conflicting.

The central bank must further aim to regulate the money supply: not merely to iron out short-run, cyclical fluctuations in economic activity, but also to achieve optimal monetary growth in pace with long-run monetization and financial development; to avoid inflation; and to preserve domestic and international confidence in the value of money. In less developed countries novel if not unorthodox central banking tools may need to be forged for these purposes. It is the central bank also which will have to take any decisions on exchange rate adjustment, and supervise the general conduct of banks, other financial institutions and the capital market. The devolution of all these tasks upon the central bank would surely place it in an unrivalled position to co-ordinate all domestic and international monetary and financial policies. Moreover, given the severe shortage of financial and economic expertise that many underdeveloped countries suffer, it makes good sense to employ these scarce resources as centrally and fully as possible.

One should not, however, overlook the fact that many small underdeveloped countries may need very little in the way of monetary/financial management and would be unwise to commit capital and recurrent expenditures to the maintenance of superfluous monetary officialdom. Many small economies may be best served by attaching themselves to the currency of a large economy and eschewing any attempt to develop more than simple domestic capital markets. With increasing world economic integration, and great advances in telecommunications and in computer-based and electronic recording over the last decade, it may eventually become desirable, for reasons of comparative advantage and specialization, for major finance markets to be confined to a few key cities on the different continents. Even so, there will always remain, in every country, some scope for purely domestic financial intermediation. In a lively essay, Charles Kindleberger has touched on this aspect, and many others, of integration between domestic and international finance (Kindleberger, 1976; see also Patrick, 1976). The central point is that 'there are economies of scale in the larger market, owing to greater specialization in instruments and techniques, and the spread of risks through the insurance principle. At the same time, there is an important diseconomy of scale: the lack in the large financial center of local knowledge' (Kindleberger, 1976, p. 134).

It is important that the components of the domestic capital market be well-knit together and, where appropriate, integrated with the international capital market. The dismantling of financial restrictions, most notably the freeing of interest rates, is rightly regarded as the key element in complementary policies which will be conducive to monetization and wider financial development, preserving the internal and external value of money, integrating separate finance markets and achieving the best allocation of investible funds. Nevertheless, it is well to remember that the finance markets may not always respond to the mere removal of restrictions. Positive promotion may at times be necessary.

Bibliography

Abdi, Ali (1976) Banking in Uganda since Independence: Comment. *Economic Development and Cultural Change* January 1976.

Adekunle, J. O. (1968) The demand for money: Evidence from developed and less developed countries. *International Monetary Fund Staff Papers* July 1968.

Ahrensdorf, Joachim (1959) Central bank policies and inflation: A case study of four less developed economies, 1949–57. *International Monetary Fund Staff Papers* October 1959.

Ally, Asgar (1975) The potential for autonomous monetary policy in small developing countries. In P. Selwyn (ed.) *Development Policy in Small Countries*. London: Croom Helm.

Amatayakul, R. and Pandit, S. A. (1961) Financial institutions in Thailand. *International Monetary Fund Staff Papers* December 1961.

Analyst' (1953) Currency and banking in Jamaica. *Social and Economic Studies* August 1953.

Arndt, H. W. (1971) The future of New Guinea's monetary system. *Economic Record* March 1971.

Arowolo, Edward A. (1971) The development of capital markets in Africa, with particular reference to Kenya and Nigeria. *International Monetary Fund Staff Papers* July 1971.

Aschheim, J. (1959) Open-market operations versus reserve-requirement variations. *Economic Journal* December 1959.

Awad, M. H. (1971) The supply of risk bearers in underdeveloped countries. *Economic Development and Cultural Change* April 1971.

Ayre, P. C. I. (ed.) (1977) *Finance in Developing Countries*. London: Frank Cass.

Bain, A. D. (1973) Surveys in applied economics: Flow of funds analysis. *Economic Journal* December 1973.

Bank Negara Malaysia (1979) *Money and Banking in Malaysia*. Kuala Lumpur: Bank Negara Malaysia (Economic Research and Statistics Department).

Baster, A. S. J. (1929) *The Imperial Banks*. London: P. S. King & Son.

Basu, S. K. (1965) *Theory and Practice of Development Banking: A Study in the Asian Context*. Bombay: Asia Publishing House.

Baumol, W. J. (1952) The transactions demand for cash: An inventory theoretic approach. *Quarterly Journal of Economics* November 1952.

Bennett, R. L. (1963) *The Financial Sector and Economic Development: The Mexican Case.* Baltimore, Md.: Johns Hopkins University Press.

Bhatia, R. J. and Khatkhate, D. R. (1975) Financial intermediation, savings mobilization, and entrepreneurial development: The African experience. *International Monetary Fund Staff Papers* March 1975.

Birnbaum, E. (1957) The cost of a foreign exchange standard or of the use of a foreign currency as the circulating medium. *International Monetary Fund Staff Papers* February 1957.

Bloomfield, A. I. (1956) Monetary policy in underdeveloped countries. In C. J. Freidrich and S. E. Harris (eds.) *Public Policy* Vol. VII. Cambridge, Mass.: Harvard University Press; abridged version reprinted in L. S. Ritter (ed.) *Money and Economic Activity.* Boston: Houghton Mifflin, 1961; alternative version in *Journal of Finance* May 1957.

Bloomfield, A. I. and Jensen, J. P. (1951) *Banking Reform in South Korea.* New York: Federal Reserve Bank of New York.

Blyth, C. A. (1969) Primitive South Pacific economies: Their consumption pattern and propensity to save out of cash income. *Economic Record* September 1969.

Bohannan, Paul (1967) The impact of money on an African subsistence economy. In G. Dalton (ed.) *Tribal and Peasant Economies. Readings in Economic Anthropology.* New York: National History Press.

Bolnick, Bruce R. (1975) Interpreting Polak: Monetary analysis in 'dependent' economies. *Journal of Development Studies* July 1975.

Bonné, Alfred (1957) *Studies in Economic Development: With Special Reference to Conditions in the Underdeveloped Areas of Western Asia and India.* London: Routledge & Kegan Paul.

Boskey, S. (1959) *Problems and Practices of Development Banks.* Baltimore, Md.: Johns Hopkins University Press for IBRD.

Bottomley, Anthony (1963) The premium for risk as a determinant of interest rates in underdeveloped rural areas. *Quarterly Journal of Economics* November 1963.

Bottomley, Anthony (1964) Monopoly profit as a determinant of interest rates in underdeveloped rural areas. *Oxford Economic Papers* November 1964.

Bottomley, Anthony (1965) Keynesian monetary theory and the developing countries. *Indian Economic Journal* April–June 1965.

Brunner, Karl and Meltzer, Allan H. (1971) The uses of money: Money in the theory of an exchange economy. *American Economic Review* December 1971.

Cairncross, A. K. (1962) *Factors in Economic Development.* London: Allen and Unwin.

Cameron, Rondo, *et al.* (1967) *Banking in the Early Stages of Industrialization.* New York: Oxford University Press.

Campbell, C. D. and Chang Shick Ann (1962) Kyes and Mujins—Financial intermediaries in South Korea. *Economic Development and Cultural Change* October 1962.

Chandavarkar, A. G. (1961) The nature and effects of gold hoarding in under-developed countries. *Oxford Economic Papers* June 1961.

Chandavarkar, A. G. (1965) The premium for risk as a determinant of interest rates in underdeveloped rural areas: Comment. *Quarterly Journal of Economics* May 1965.

Chandavarkar, A. G. (1971) Some aspects of interest rate policies in less developed economies: The experience of selected Asian countries. *International Monetary Fund Staff Papers* March 1971.

Child, Frank C. (1976) Comment. In R. I. McKinnon (ed.) *Money and Finance in Economic Growth and Development.* New York: Marcel Dekker.

Copeland, M. A. (1952) *A Study of Moneyflows in the United States.* New York: National Bureau of Economic Research.

Corden, W. M. (1972) *Monetary Integration.* Princeton, N.J.: Princeton University Press.

Crick, W. F. (1965) *Commonwealth Banking Systems.* Oxford: Clarendon Press.

Crockett, A. D. and Nsouli, S. M. (1977) Exchange rate policies for developing countries. *Journal of Development Studies* January 1977; reprinted in Ayre (1977).

Dalton, G. (1967) Primitive Money. In G. Dalton (ed.) *Tribal and Peasant Economies: Readings in Economic Anthropology.* New York: National History Press.

Daly, Herman E. (1967) A note on the pathological growth of the Uruguayan banking sector. *Economic Development and Cultural Change* October 1967.

Davies, W. E. and Drake, P. J. (1964) Flow-of-funds social accounting: A Malayan example. *Malayan Economic Review* October 1964.

De Bruin, Anne M. (1977) *The Financial Sector and Indigenous Entrepreneurial Development in Papua New Guinea.* Unpublished M.Econ. dissertation, University of New England.

De Kock, M. H. (1954) *Central Banking* (3rd edn). London: Staples Press.

Diamond, W. (1957) *Development Banks.* Baltimore, Md.: Johns Hopkins University Press for Economic Development Institute.

Dorrance, G. S. (1965) The instruments of monetary policy in countries without highly developed capital markets. *International Monetary Fund Staff Papers* July 1965.

Dorrance, G. S. (1970) A framework for the determination of central banking policy. *International Monetary Fund Staff Papers* July 1970.

Drake, P. J. (1966) Financial aspects of the co-operative movement in Malaya. *Malayan Economic Review* April 1966.

Drake, P. J. (1969a) *Financial Development in Malaya and Singapore*. Canberra: Australian National University Press.

Drake, P. J. (1969b) The new issue boom in Malaya and Singapore, 1961–64. *Economic Development and Cultural Change* October 1969; reprinted in David Lim (ed.) *Readings on Malaysian Economic Development*. Kuala Lumpur: Oxford University Press, 1975.

Drake, P. J. (1972) Natural resources versus foreign borrowing in economic development. *Economic Journal* September 1972.

Drake, P. J. (1974) Performance, responsibility and control in the Australian securities markets. In R. R. Hirst and R. H. Wallace (eds) *The Australian Capital Market*. Melbourne: Cheshire.

Drake, P. J. and Mathews, R. L. (1974) The securities markets. In R. R. Hirst and R. H. Wallace (eds) *The Australian Capital Market*. Melbourne: Cheshire.

Duesenberry, J. S. (1963) The portfolio approach to the demand for money and other assets. *Review of Economics and Statistics* February 1963.

Einzig, Paul (1949) *Primitive Money* London: Eyre & Spottiswoode.

Emery, R. F. (1971) *The Financial Institutions of South East Asia*. New York: Praeger.

Fama, E. F. (1978) *Foundations of Finance*. Oxford: Blackwell.

Fisk, E. K. (1964) Planning in a primitive economy: From pure subsistence to the production of a market surplus. *Economic Record* June 1964.

Fisk, E. K. (1971) The significance of non-monetary economic activity for development planning. Mimeo, Australian National University.

Fisk, E. K. (1975a) The response of nonmonetary production units to contact with the exchange economy. In L. G. Reynolds (ed.) *Agriculture in Development Theory*. New Haven, Conn.: Yale University Press.

Fisk, E. K. (1975b) The justification and assessment of small loans by development banking institutions. *Malayan Economic Review* April 1975.

Fousek, P. G. (1957) *Foreign Central Banking: The Instruments of Monetary Control*. New York: Federal Reserve Bank of New York.

Freedman, M. (1961) The handling of money: A note on the background of the economic sophistication of overseas Chinese. In T. H. Silcock (ed.) *Readings in Malayan Economics*. Singapore: Eastern Universities Press; reprinted from *Man* Vol. 59, 1959.

Fry, Maxwell J. (1978) Money and capital or financial deepening in economic development? *Journal of Money, Credit and Banking* November 1978.

Furness, E. E. (1975) *Money and Credit in Developing Africa*. London: Heinemann.

Galbis, Vicente (1977) Financial intermediation and economic growth in less-developed countries: A theoretical approach. *Journal of Development Studies* January 1977; reprinted in Ayre (1977).

Gamba, Charles (1958) Poverty and some socio-economic aspects of hoarding, saving and borrowing in Malaya. *Malayan Economic Review* October 1958.

Geertz, Clifford (1962) The rotating credit association: A 'middle rung' in development. *Economic Development and Cultural Change* April 1962.

Gerschenkron, Alexander (1965) *Economic Backwardness in Historical Perspective: A Book of Essays.* New York: Praeger.

Gershenberg, Irving (1972) Banking in Uganda since Independence. *Economic Development and Cultural Change* April 1972.

Gershenberg, Irving (1976) Banking in Uganda since Independence: Reply. *Economic Development and Cultural Change* January 1976.

Gilbert, J. C. (1953) The demand for money: The development of an economic concept. *Journal of Political Economy* April 1953.

Goldsmith, R. W. (1965) *The Flow of Capital Funds in the Postwar Economy.* New York: National Bureau of Economic Research.

Goldsmith, R. W. (1969) *Financial Structure and Development.* New Haven, Conn.: Yale University Press.

Goldsmith, R. W. (1975) Some reflections on the past, present and future of financial institutions. In P. Frantzen (ed.) *Current Problems of Financial Intermediaries.* Rotterdam: Rotterdam University Press.

Grierson, Philip (1977) *The Origins of Money.* London: Athlone Press.

Grove, David L. and Exter, John (1948) The Philippine Central Bank Act. *Federal Reserve Bulletin* August 1948.

Grubel, H. G. (1977) *International Economics.* Homewood, Ill.: Irwin.

Gunasekera, H. A. de S. (1962) *From Dependent Currency to Central Banking in Ceylon: An Analysis of Monetary Experience 1825–1957.* London: Bell.

Gurley, J. G. and Shaw, E. S. (1955) Financial aspects of economic development. *American Economic Review* September 1955.

Gurley, J. G. and Shaw, E. S. (1967) Financial structure and development. *Economic Development and Cultural Change* April 1967.

Harberger, A. C. (1972) Reflections on the monetary system of Panama. In D. Wall (ed.) *Chicago Essays in Economic Development.* Chicago: University of Chicago Press.

Harris, L. (1969) Professor Hicks and the foundations of monetary economics. *Economica* May 1969.

Hazelwood, Arthur (1954) The economics of colonial monetary arrangements. *Social and Economic Studies* December 1954.

Hicks, E., *et al.* (1957) Monetary analyses. *International Monetary Fund Staff Papers* February 1957.

Hicks, J. R. (1967) *Critical Essays in Monetary Theory.* Oxford: Clarendon Press.

Hicks, J. R. (1969) *A Theory of Economic History.* Oxford: Clarendon Press.

Hooley, Richard W. (1963) *Saving in The Philippines*. Quezon City: Institute of Economic Development and Research, University of the Philippines.

Hunter, J. M. (1967) Investment in land: Inflationary and development debilitating? *Journal of Developing Areas* January 1967.

IMF (African Department) (1963) The CFA franc system. *International Monetary Fund Staff Papers* November 1963.

Jao, Y. C. (1974) *Banking and Currency in Hong Kong: A Study of Postwar Financial Development*. London: Macmillan.

Jao, Y. C. (1976) Financial deepening and economic growth: A cross-section analysis. *Malayan Economic Review* April 1976.

Johnson, H. G. (1972) The Panamanian monetary system. *Monetary Economics*. London: Allen & Unwin; reprinted from *Euromoney* January 1972.

Johnson, Harry G. (1976) Panama as a regional financial center: A preliminary analysis of development contribution. *Economic Development and Cultural Change* January 1976.

Jucker-Fleetwood, Erin E. (1964) *Money and Finance in Africa*. London: Allen & Unwin.

Khatkhate, Deena R. Analytic basis of the working of monetary policy in less developed countries. *International Monetary Fund Staff Papers* November 1972.

Kindleberger, C. P. (1976) International financial intermediation for developing countries. In R. I. McKinnon (ed.) *Money and Finance in Economic Growth and Development*. New York: Marcel Dekker.

King, F. H. H. (1957) *Money in British East Asia*. London: HMSO.

King, F. H. H. (1958) Notes on Malayan monetary problems. *Malayan Economic Review* April 1958; reprinted with revisions in P. J. Drake (ed.) *Money and Banking in Malaya and Singapore*. Singapore: Malaysia Publications, 1966.

Krivine, David (ed.) (1967) *Fiscal and Monetary Problems in Developing States: Proceedings of the Third Rehovoth Conference*. New York: Praeger.

Laidler, D. E. W. (1977) *The Demand for Money: Theories and Evidence* (2nd edn). New York: Dun-Donnelly.

Leff, Nathaniel H. (1976) Capital markets in the less developed countries: The Group principle. In R. I. McKinnon (ed.) *Money and Finance in Economic Growth and Development*. New York: Marcel Dekker.

Letiche, J. M. (1974) Dependent monetary systems and economic development: The case of sterling East Africa. In W. Sellekaerts (ed.) *Economic Development and Planning: Essays in Honour of Jan Tinbergen*. London: Macmillan.

Levenson, A. M. and Randall, Laura (1966) Money, barter and equivalencies. *Journal of Development Studies* April 1966.

Lewis, Sir Arthur (W. A. Lewis) (1979) The less developed countries and stable exchange rates. *Third World Quarterly* January 1979.

Lloyd, Bruce (1976) The role of capital markets in developing countries. *Moorgate and Wall Street* Spring 1976.

Lloyd, Bruce (1977) The efficiency of financial institutions and markets. *Investment Analyst* May 1977.

Maniatis, George C. (1971) Reliability of the equities market to finance industrial development in Greece. *Economic Development and Cultural Change* July 1971.

Maynard, G. (1970) The economic irrelevance of monetary independence: The case of Liberia. *Journal of Development Studies* January 1970.

McKinnon, R. I. (1963) Optimum currency areas. *American Economic Review* September 1963; reprinted in R. N. Cooper (ed.) *International Finance*. Harmondsworth: Penguin, 1969.

McKinnon, R. I. (1973) *Money and Capital in Economic Development*. Washington, D.C.: Brookings Institution.

McKinnon, R. I. (ed.) (1976) *Money and Finance in Economic Growth and Development*. New York: Marcel Dekker.

Melitz, J. (1974) *Primitive and Modern Money: An Interdisciplinary Approach*. Reading, Mass.: Addison-Wesley.

Menger, K. (1892) On the origin of money. *Economic Journal* June 1892.

Morgan, Victor E. (1965) *A History of Money*. Harmondsworth: Penguin.

Mundell, R. A. (1961) A theory of optimum currency areas. *American Economic Review* September 1961.

Myint, H. (1954) An interpretation of economic backwardness. *Oxford Economic Papers* June 1954.

Myint, H. (1965) *The Economics of the Developing Countries* (2nd edn). London: Hutchinson.

Myint, H. (1970) Dualism and the internal integration of the underdeveloped economies. *Banca Nazionale del Lavoro Quarterly Review* June 1970.

Myrdal, Gunnar (1968) *Asian Drama: An Inquiry into the Poverty of Nations*. Harmondsworth: Penguin.

Ness, Walter L. Jr. (1974) Financial markets innovation as a development strategy: Initial results from the Brazilian experience. *Economic Development and Cultural Change* April 1974.

Nevin, Edward (1961) *Capital Funds in Underdeveloped Countries*. London: Macmillan.

Newlyn, W. T. (1968) An African monetary perspective. In C. R. Whittlesey and J. S. G. Wilson (eds) *Essays in Money and Banking in Honour of R. S. Sayers*. Oxford: Clarendon Press.

Newlyn, W. T. (1969) Monetary analysis and policy in financially dependent economies. In I. G. Stewart (ed.) *Economic Development and Structural Change*. Edinburgh: Edinburgh University Press.

Newlyn, W. T. (1971) *Theory of Money* (2nd edn). Oxford: Clarendon Press.

Newlyn, W. T. (1977) The inflation tax in developing countries. *Journal of Development Studies* January 1977; reprinted in Ayre (1977).

Newlyn, W. T. and Rowan, D. C. (1954) *Money and Banking in British Colonial Africa: A Study of the Monetary and Banking Systems of Eight British African Territories.* Oxford: Clarendon Press.

Nisbet, Charles (1967) Interest rates and imperfect competition in the informal credit market of rural Chile. *Economic Development and Cultural Change* October 1967.

OECD (1967) *Capital Markets Study: General Report*: Paris: OECD Committee for Invisible Transactions.

Olakanpo, J. O. W. (1961) Monetary management in dependent economies. *Economica* November 1961.

Panikar, P. G. K. (1961) Rural savings in India. *Economic Development and Cultural Change* October 1961.

Patrick, H. T. (1966) Financial development and economic growth in underdeveloped countries. *Economic Development and Cultural Change* January 1966.

Patrick, Hugh T. (1972) Financial development and economic growth in underdeveloped countries: Reply. *Economic Development and Cultural Change* January 1972.

Patrick, Hugh T. (1976) Comment. In R. I. McKinnon (ed.) *Money and Finance in Economic Growth and Development.* New York: Marcel Dekker.

Peera, Nurali (n.d.) The colonial monetary system and export-led growth. Unpublished manuscript, University of Salford.

Penrose, Edith (1956) Foreign investment and the growth of the firm. *Economic Journal* June 1956.

Polak, J. J. (1957) Monetary analysis of income formation and payments problems. *International Monetary Fund Staff Papers* November 1957.

Polak, J. J. and Argy, Victor (1971) Credit policy and the balance of payments. *International Monetary Fund Staff Papers* March 1971.

Polak, J. J. and Boissoneault, Lorette (1960) Monetary analysis of income and imports in its statistical application. *International Monetary Fund Staff Papers* April 1960.

Polanyi, K. (1968) The semantics of money-uses. In G. Dalton (ed.) *Essays of Karl Polanyi.* New York: Doubleday.

Porter, R. C. (1966) The promotion of the 'banking habit' and economic development. *Journal of Development Studies* July 1966.

Porter, R. C. (1973) The birth of a bill market. *Journal of Development Studies* April 1973.

Powelson, J. P. (1960) *National Income and Flow of Funds Analysis.* New York: McGraw Hill.

Richardson, G. B. (1965) Ideal and reality in the choice of techniques. *Oxford Economic Papers* July 1965.

Ritter, L. S. (1963) An exposition of the structure of flow of funds accounts. *Journal of Finance* May 1963.

Robertson, Dennis (1965) *Lectures on Economic Principles*. London: Fontana.

Rosen, G. (1958) Capital markets and the industrialization of underdeveloped economies. *Indian Economic Journal* October 1958.

Rozental, A. A. (1967) Unorganized financial markets and developmental strategy. *Journal of Developing Areas* July 1967.

Rozental, A. A. (1970a) *Finance and Development in Thailand*. New York: Praeger.

Rozental, A. A. (1970b) A note on the sources and uses of funds in Thai agriculture. *Economic Development and Cultural Change* April 1970.

Sametz, Arnold W. (ed.) (1972) *Financial Development and Economic Growth: The Economic Consequences of Underdeveloped Capital Markets*. New York: New York University Press.

Shaw, E. S. (1973) *Financial Deepening in Economic Development*. New York: Oxford University Press.

Simpson, J. V. (1967) Development finance: A comment on 'contractor finance' in Sierra Leone. *Journal of Development Studies* January 1967.

Smith, Adam (1910) *The Wealth of Nations* with an introduction by Professor E. R. A. Seligman. London: Dent.

Sowelem, R. A. (1967) *Towards Financial Independence in a Developing Economy*. London: Allen & Unwin.

Stammer, D. W. (1970) Money in the territory of Papua New Guinea. Mimeo, Australian National University.

Stammer, D. W. (1972) Financial development and economic growth in underdeveloped countries: Comment. *Economic Development and Cultural Change* January 1972.

Stigler, G. J. (1968) Imperfections in the capital market. *The Organization of Industry*. Homewood, Ill.: Irwin; reprinted from *Journal of Political Economy* June 1967.

Swift, M. G. (1961) The accumulation of capital in a peasant economy. In T. H. Silcock (ed.) *Readings in Malayan Economics*. Singapore: Eastern Universities Press; reprinted from *Economic Development and Cultural Change* July 1957.

Thirlwall, A. P. (1974) *Inflation, Saving and Growth in Developing Economies*. London: Macmillan.

Treadgold, M. L. (1969) *Economic Growth and the Price Level in the Philippines*. Unpublished PhD thesis, Australian National University.

Trescott, Paul B. (1972) Demand for money and other liquid assets in Thailand, 1946–67. *Economic Development and Cultural Change* January 1972.

Usher, Dan (1967) Thai interest rates. *Journal of Development Studies* April 1967.

Wai, U Tun (1956) Interest rates in the organized money markets of underdeveloped countries. *International Monetary Fund Staff Papers* August 1956.

Wai, U Tun (1957) Interest rates outside the organized money markets of underdeveloped countries. *International Monetary Fund Staff Papers* November 1957.

Wai, U Tun (1972) *Financial Intermediaries and National Savings in Developing Countries*. New York: Praeger.

Wai, U Tun and Patrick, Hugh T. (1973) Stock and bond issues and capital markets in less developed countries. *International Monetary Fund Staff Papers* July 1973.

Wallich, H. C. (1950) *Monetary Problems of an Export Economy—the Cuban Experience, 1914–1947*. Cambridge, Mass.: Harvard University Press.

Ward, Barbara (1960) Cash or credit crops? An examination of some implications of peasant commercial production with special reference to the multiplicity of traders and middlemen. *Economic Development and Cultural Change* January 1960.

Wilson, J. S. G. (1966) Some aspects of the development of capital markets. *Banca Nazionale del Lavoro Quarterly Review*, December 1966.

Wilson, J. S. G. (1968) The art of developing a capital market. In C. R. Whittlesey and J. S. G. Wilson (eds) *Essays in Money and Banking in Honour of R. S. Sayers*. Oxford: Clarendon Press.

Wilson, P. A. (1957) Money in Malaya. *Malayan Economic Review* October 1957; reprinted with revisions in P. J. Drake (ed.) *Money and Banking in Malaya and Singapore*. Singapore: Malaysia Publications, 1966.

Author Index

Subject Index

244 *Subject Index*

money loan associations, 128, 134–42
money supply, *see* money, volume of
moneylenders, 129, 131–54, 184, 187, 220–2, 226
moral suasion, 173, 176
mortgages, 28, 141, 177

Nairobi Stock Exchange, 213, 215
national income accounts, 8, 12, 14
nationalism, economic, 209, 227
new issues market, 11, 156–7, 212
New Zealand, 101
Nigeria, 202, 211
Norway, 30

open economies, 82–3, 89, 91, 105, 107
    109–10, 116, 119, 197
overdrafts, 10, 156–7, 161, 199, 211

Pakistan, 42, 222
Panama, 101, 103
Papua New Guinea, 83, 100–1, 182
Papua New Guinea Development Bank, 182
pawnbrokers, 19, 137, 140–2, 153, 220, 226
pawnshops, 125–6, 141
Penang, 202
pension funds, 177–8, 203, 205
Pereire brothers, 156
Petaling Jaya, 202
Philippines, 24, 36, 68, 93

regulation, of finance markets, 211
resource allocation, 5, 33, 35, 37, 42, 55, 110,
    194–6, 218, 222–3, 229
retirement funds, 29
return, rate(s) of, 62–5, 77–9, 129, 149, 193,
    195, 206–7, 224
rice, 149
rural credit, *see* agricultural finance

savings, 8, 12–15, 20, 22, 32–7, 54, 55, 122–4,
    128, 193, 218–23
  contractual, 36, 177–8
Scotland, 31
securities, 10–11, 171, 192, *see also* financial
    assets

corporate, 197–206
government, 171–5, 178, 185, 197, 204–5
securities markets, 10, 158, 173, 181, 192–216
shopkeepers, 129, 131–3, 137, 140–2, 148,
    220, 226
silver, 4, 11, 80, 124–8
Singapore, 106, 138, 140, 162, 164, 202, 205,
    206, 209, 214, 215
small business finance, 187–9
Soviet Union, 30
Special Drawings Rights (SDR), 4–5, 104,
    117–18
specialization, 29, 51, 55, 70, 177–9, 196,
    218, 229
speculation, 206
stockbrokers, 212–13, 215
stock exchange, 10–11, 156–7, 200, 205,
    213–15
subsistence unit, 56–7, 72–9
'supply-leading' financial development, 40–2,
    177
Swaziland, 101
'sweat equity', 182

Tanzania, 121, 215
Thailand, 68–9, 128–9, 137, 149, 153, 164,
    169
Tontine, 134, 138
trade credit, 10, 132, 149
Treasury bills, 171, 174–5, 185, 205
Turner, Sir M., 162

Uganda, 121, 164, 215
unit trusts, 203
United Kingdom, 4, 28, 30, 158–63
United States of America, 4, 30, 33, 157
Uruguay, 169

Venezuela, 30
velocity of circulation, 68, 92, 95, 98–101
Vietnam, 140

yield, *see* rate of return
Yugoslavia, 30

Zaibatsu, 42